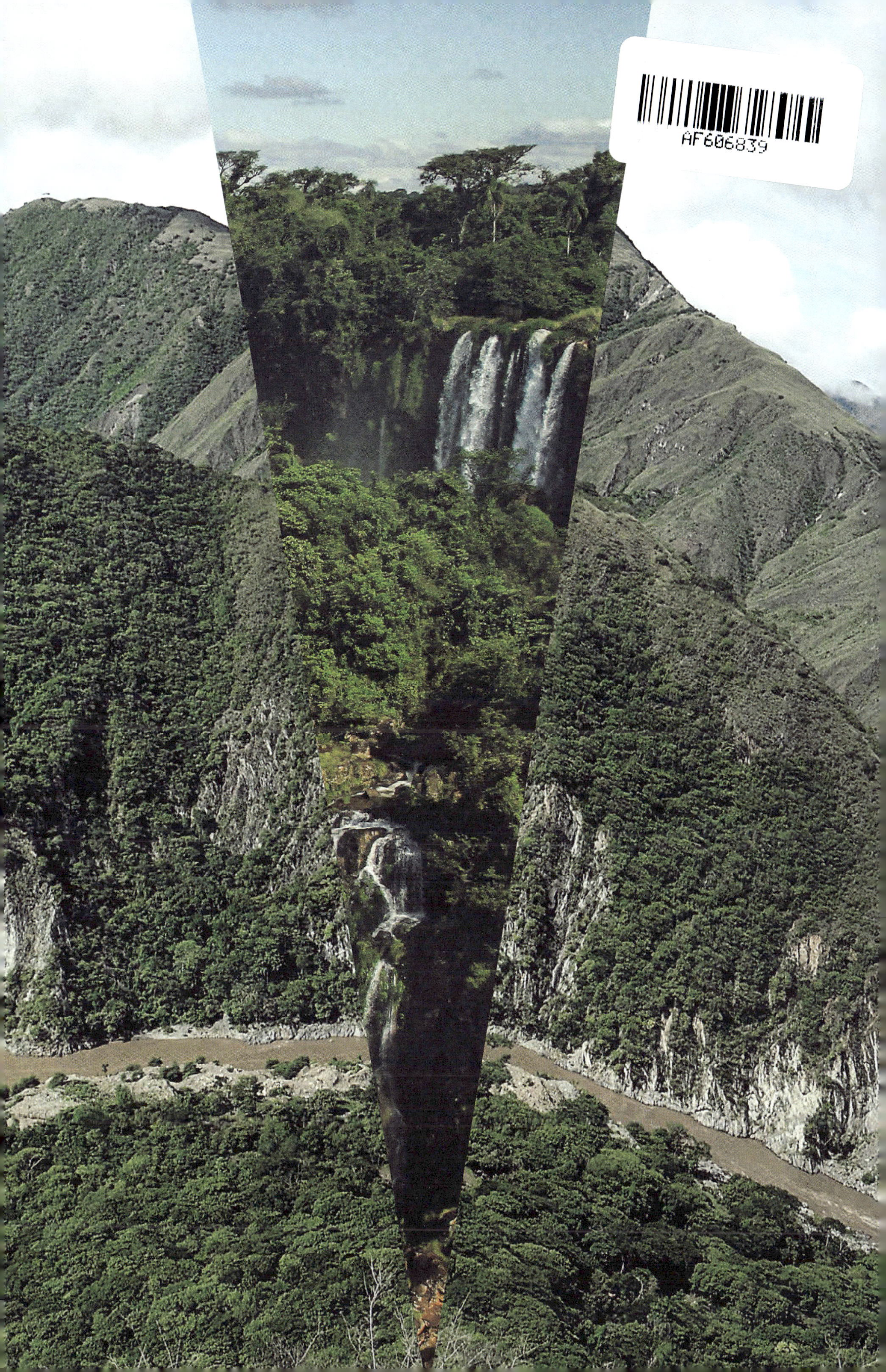
AF606839

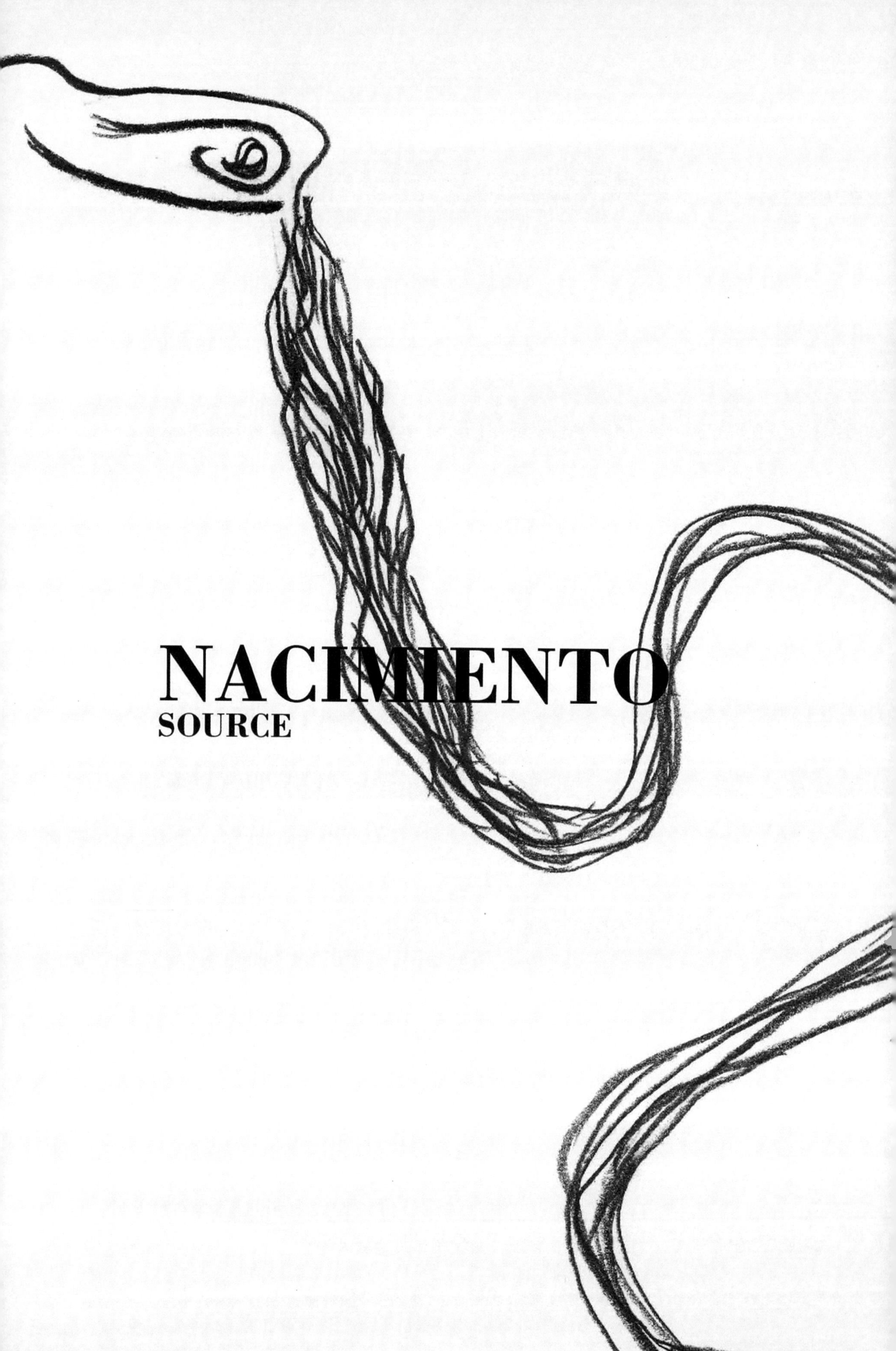

NACIMIENTO

SOURCE

UN CUERPO DE AGUA

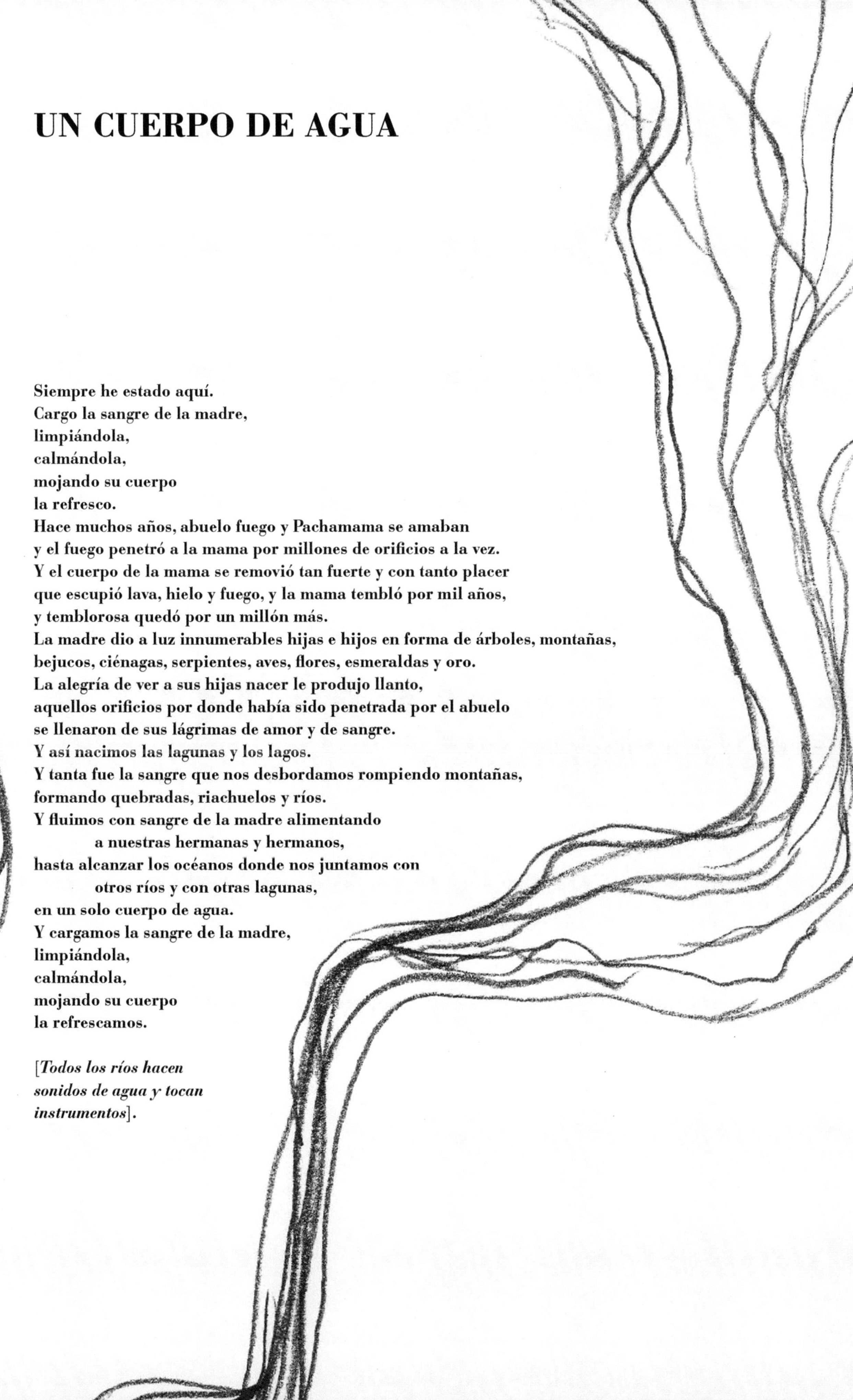

Siempre he estado aquí.
Cargo la sangre de la madre,
limpiándola,
calmándola,
mojando su cuerpo
la refresco.
Hace muchos años, abuelo fuego y Pachamama se amaban
y el fuego penetró a la mama por millones de orificios a la vez.
Y el cuerpo de la mama se removió tan fuerte y con tanto placer
que escupió lava, hielo y fuego, y la mama tembló por mil años,
y temblorosa quedó por un millón más.
La madre dio a luz innumerables hijas e hijos en forma de árboles, montañas,
bejucos, ciénagas, serpientes, aves, flores, esmeraldas y oro.
La alegría de ver a sus hijas nacer le produjo llanto,
aquellos orificios por donde había sido penetrada por el abuelo
se llenaron de sus lágrimas de amor y de sangre.
Y así nacimos las lagunas y los lagos.
Y tanta fue la sangre que nos desbordamos rompiendo montañas,
formando quebradas, riachuelos y ríos.
Y fluimos con sangre de la madre alimentando
a nuestras hermanas y hermanos,
hasta alcanzar los océanos donde nos juntamos con
otros ríos y con otras lagunas,
en un solo cuerpo de agua.
Y cargamos la sangre de la madre,
limpiándola,
calmándola,
mojando su cuerpo
la refrescamos.

[***Todos los ríos hacen sonidos de agua y tocan instrumentos***].

CURSO ALTO

UPPER COURSE

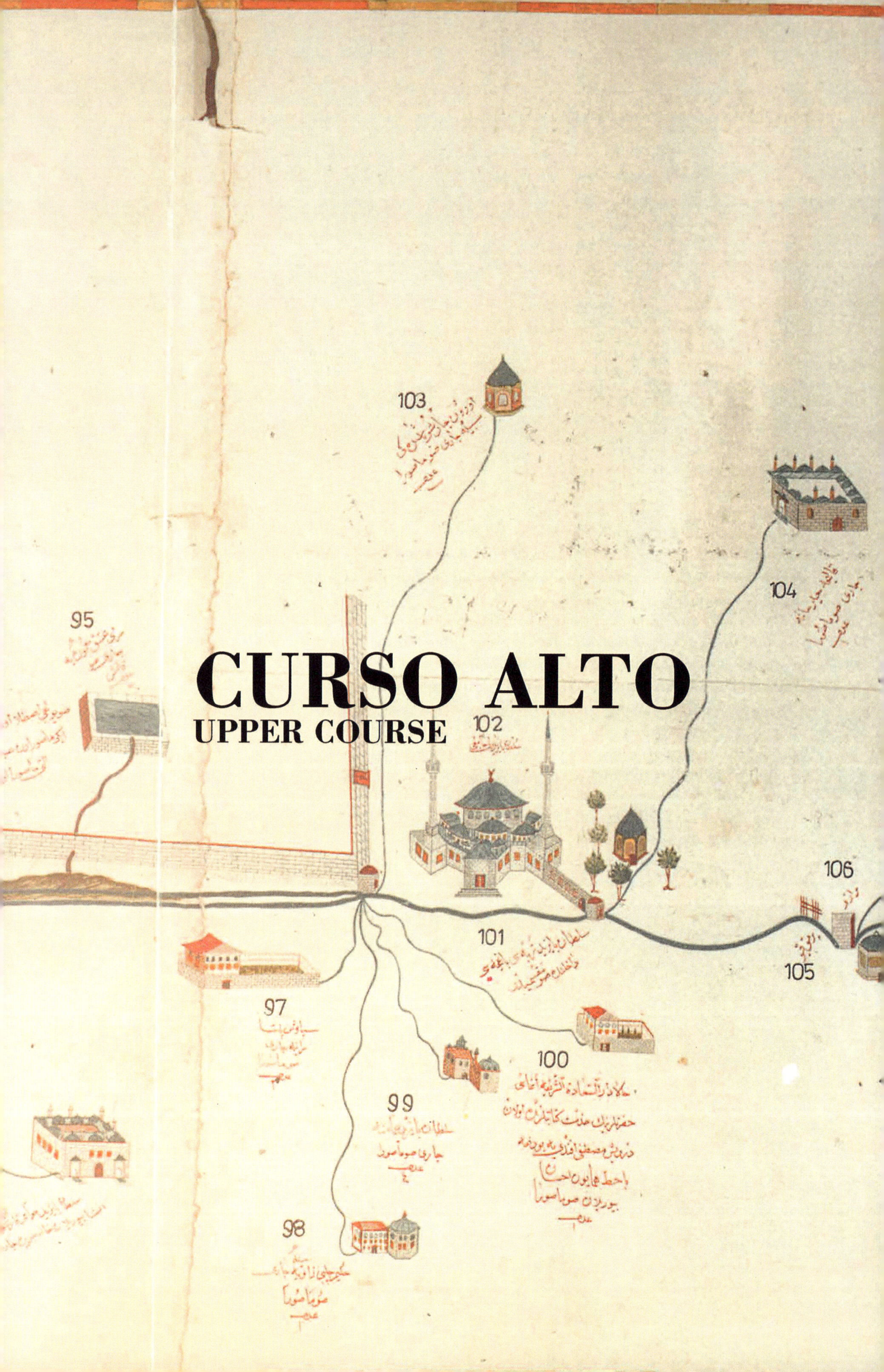

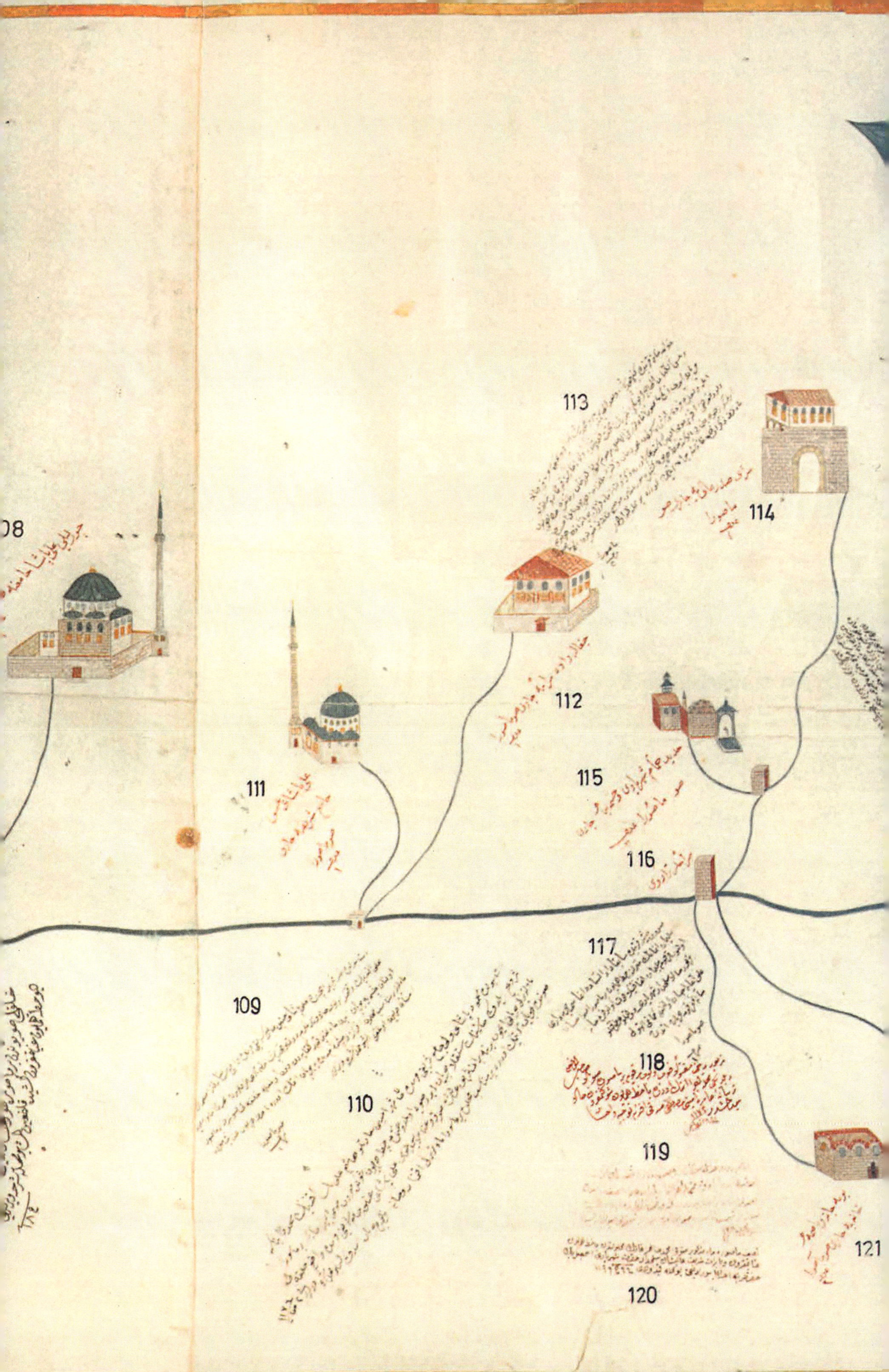
113
08
114
112
111
115
116
117
109
118
110
119
121
120

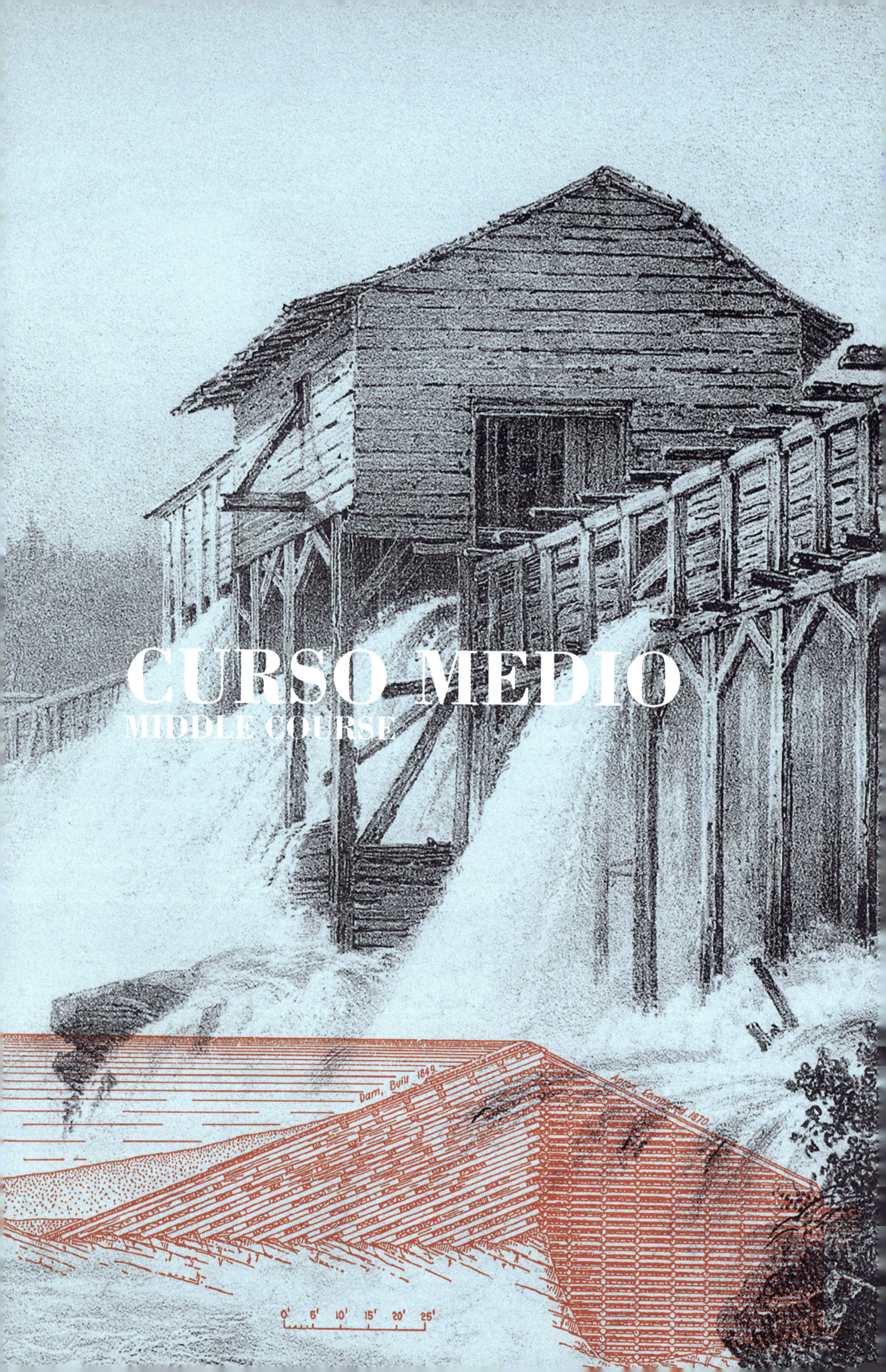
CURSO MEDIO
MIDDLE COURSE
Dam, Built 1849
Apron, Completed 1870
0' 5' 10' 15' 20' 25'

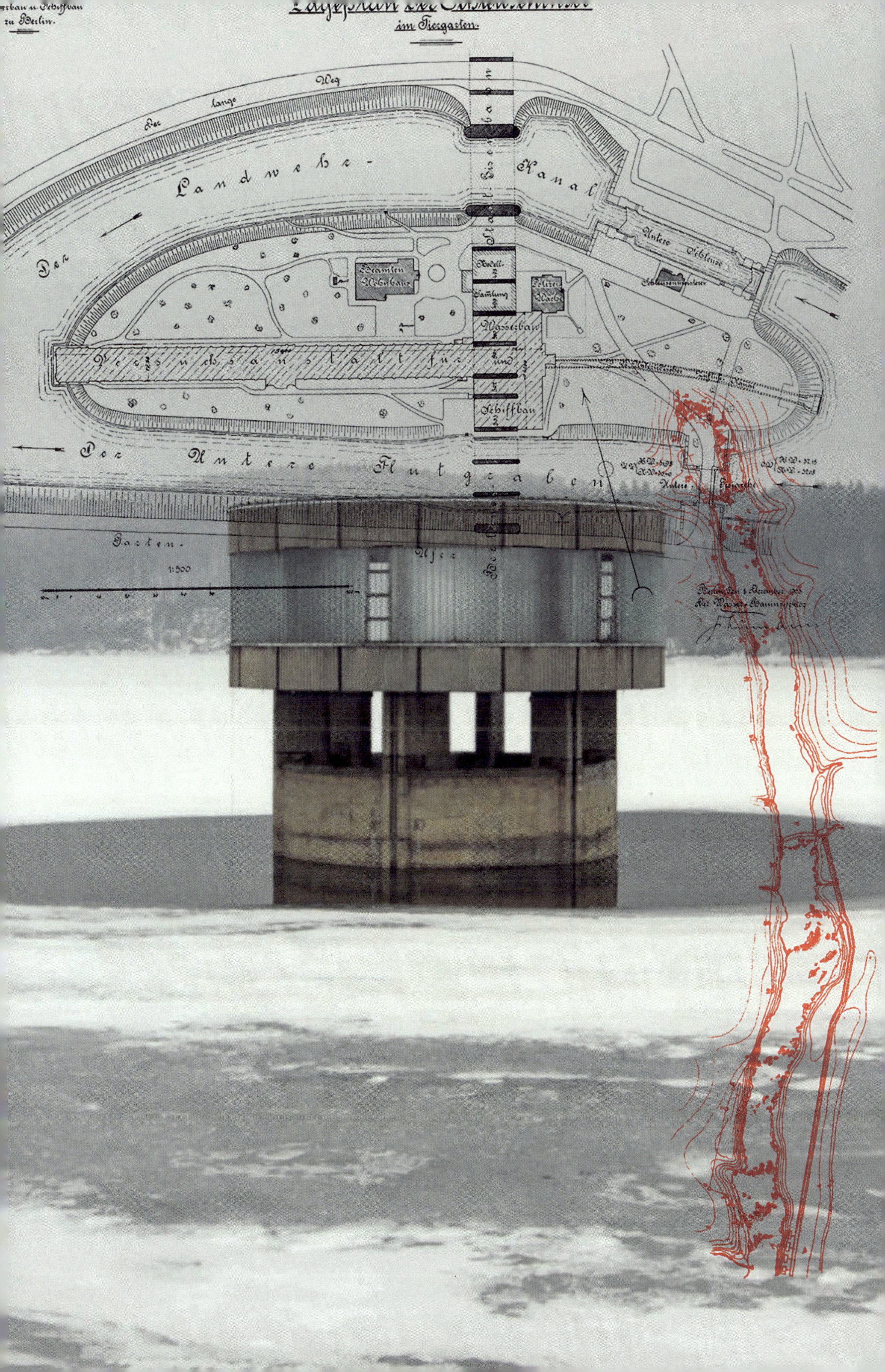

im Tiergarten
Der lange Weg
Landwehr-Kanal
Untere Schleuse
Beamten Wohnhaus
Modell-Sammlung
Polizei Wache
Versuchsanstalt für Wasserbau und Schiffbau
Der Untere Flutgraben
Garten-Ufer
1:500

CURSO BAJO
LOWER COURSE

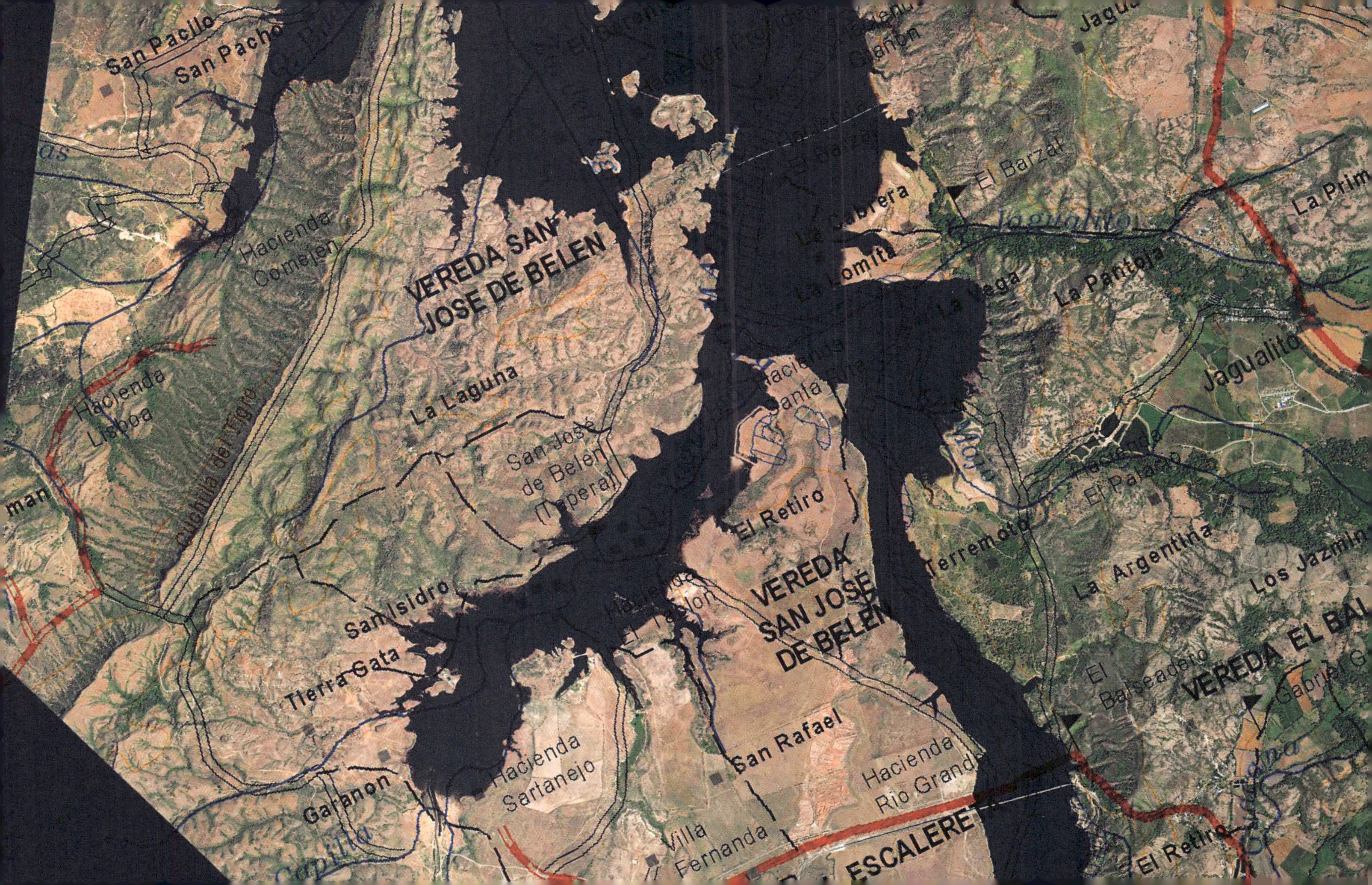
San Pacho
San Pacho
Hacienda Comejen
VEREDA SAN JOSE DE BELEN
Hacienda Lisboa
Cuchilla del Tigre
La Laguna
San José de Belen (Tapera)
San Isidro
Tierra Gata
Garanon
Hacienda Sartanejo
Villa Fernanda
San Rafael
Hacienda Rio Grande
ESCALERE
El Retiro
VEREDA SAN JOSE DE BELEN
El Barzal
La Cabrera
La Lomita
La Vega
La Pantoja
Jagualito
Terremoto
La Argentina
Los Jazmin
El Balseadero
VEREDA EL BA
El Retiro
La Prim

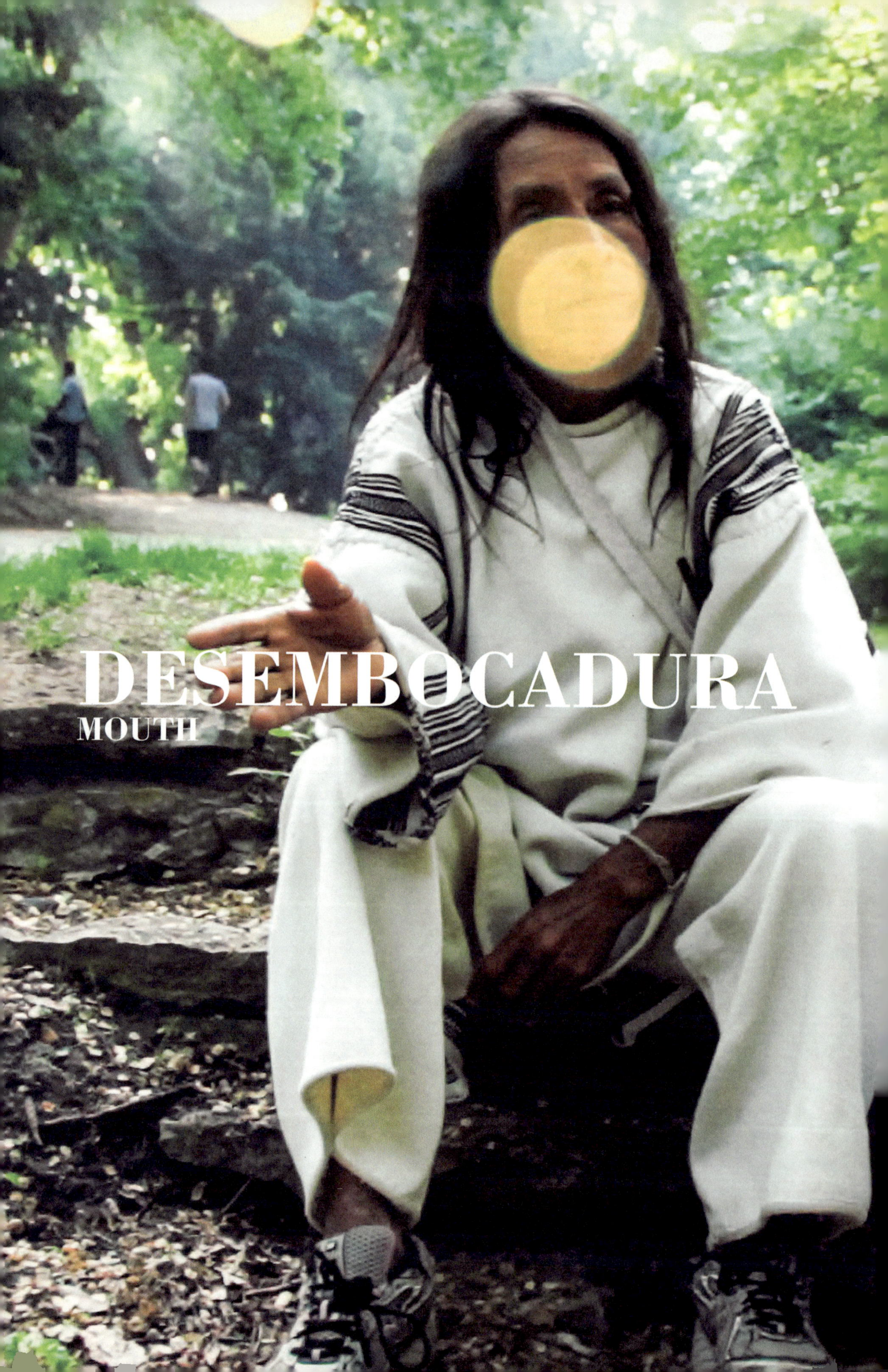

DESEMBOCADURA

MOUTH

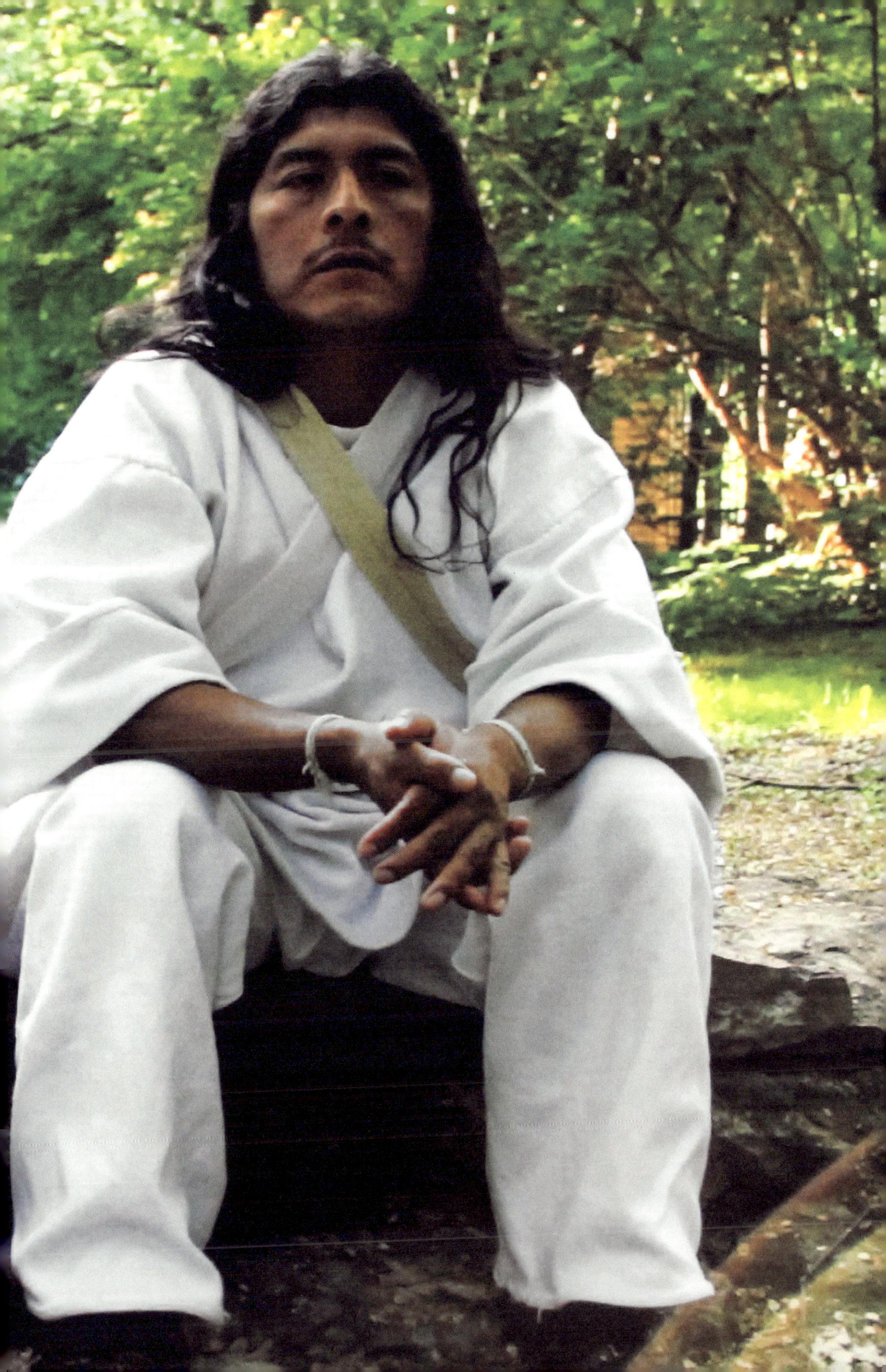

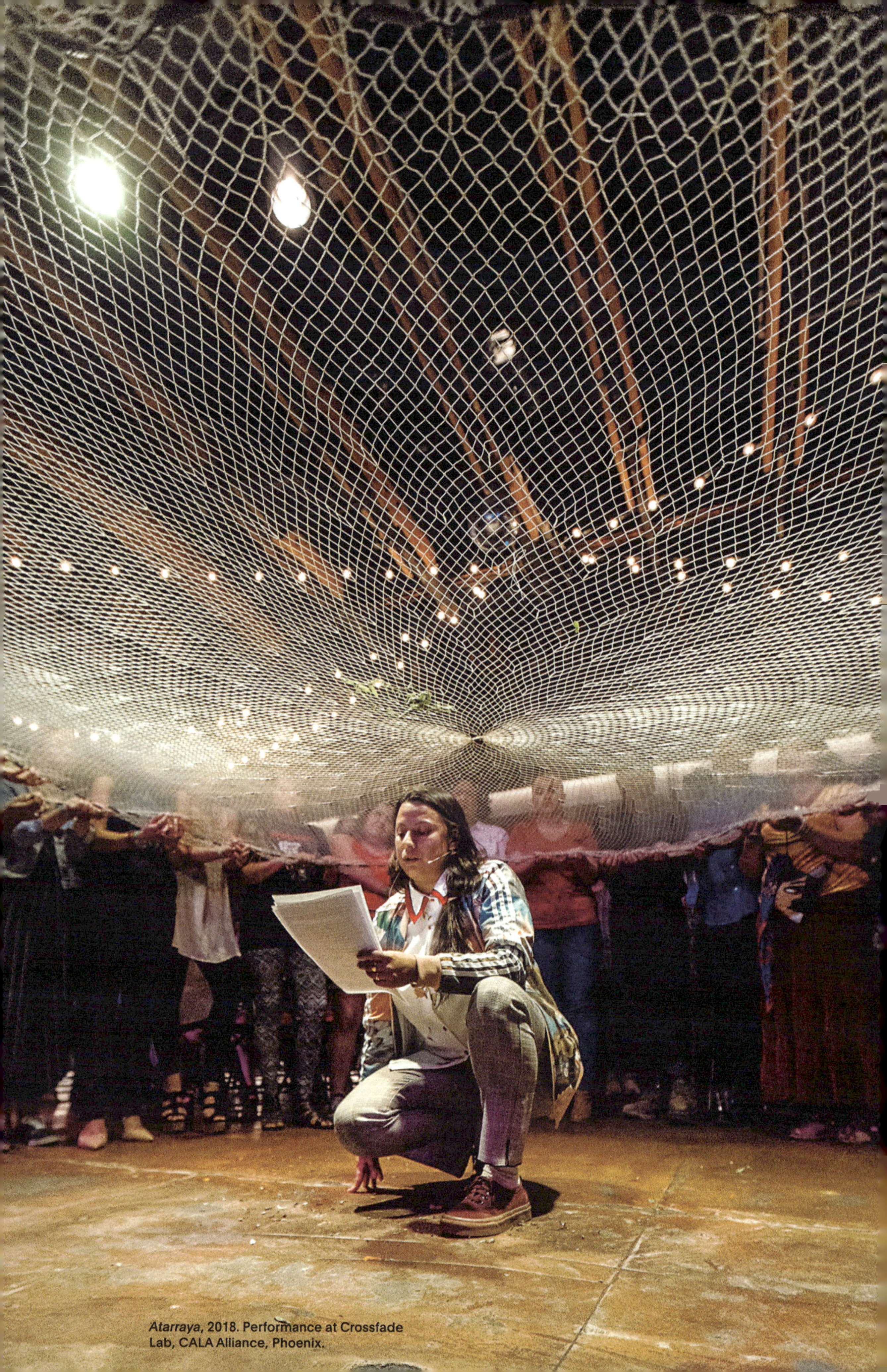

Atarraya, 2018. Performance at Crossfade Lab, CALA Alliance, Phoenix.

CAROLINA CAYCEDO

From the Bottom of the River

Carla Acevedo-Yates

Museum of
Contemporary Art
Chicago

DelMonico Books • D.A.P.
New York

Ascendant Artist Series

The Museum of Contemporary Art Chicago's Ascendant Artist exhibitions present the work and ideas of lesser-known contemporary artists to our museum-going public. In 2018, we redesigned the Ascendant Artist publication series to focus on the unique factors that have led artists to this moment—the influences that drive their practice, the working methods that shape their artworks, and the evolving themes and subject matter of the works themselves—revealing the threads of their development and suggesting the promise of their future directions. These catalogues offer an accessible and affordable introduction to tomorrow's most relevant artists.

A series of spreads from the artist's *Serpent River Book* introduce this volume. The artist-book, a seventy-two page accordion fold, combines archival images, maps, poems, satellite photos, and the artist's own images and texts. Following an instance of Caycedo's unique landscape collage are a series of spreads that visually embody the stages of a river.

Foreword

The multiform and complex work of Carolina Caycedo defies categorization. What might first seem like a beautiful hanging net sculpture is actually the end result of an intensive process of social, historical, and spiritual consideration. To fully regard any given piece by the acclaimed artist is to take in the histories, objects, gestures, and beliefs that are woven into its making. Exploring a variety of media and spanning several years of creative output, this Ascendant Artist exhibition introduces Chicago to Caycedo's dynamic and intricate practice. I commend Carla Acevedo-Yates, Marilyn and Larry Fields Curator, for bringing the work of this relevant artist to our audiences at the MCA.

This catalogue is the first major publication on Carolina Caycedo, and the three contributions contained herein provide compelling access and insight into her multidimensional world. Carla Acevedo-Yates submits a new way of considering the artist's practice. Pilar Tompkins Rivas, Chief Curator and Deputy Director, Curatorial and Collections, The Lucas Museum of Narrative Art, closely examines the role *Geochoreographies* play in the development of her work. And David Hernández Palmar, photographer, videographer, program organizer, and journalist, narrates a more personal journey through the heart of one of Caycedo's *Geochoreographies*.

Carolina Caycedo: From the Bottom of the River exists at the forefront of the MCA's mission to champion revelatory art and to create space for the exchange of ideas and cultures. Of course, putting together such an exhibition requires the unwavering support of many thoughtful and beneficent partners. Lead support was provided by the Harris Family Foundation, in memory of Bette and Neison Harris: Caryn and King Harris, Katherine Harris, Toni and Ron Paul, Pam Szokol, Linda and Bill Friend, and Stephanie and John Harris; the Margot and W. George Greig Ascendant Artist Fund; R. H. Defares; Zell Family Foundation; Julie and Larry Bernstein; Cari and Michael Sacks; and Anonymous. Major support was provided by Estrellita and Daniel Brodsky; and Charlotte Cramer Wagner and Herbert S. Wagner III of the Wagner Foundation. And generous support was provided by Anonymous; Commonwealth and Council; Marisa Murillo; and David Walega. I would also like to thank all of our lenders, listed on page 139, for entrusting us with these irreplaceable artworks.

Some of the more indelible images in Caycedo's ouevre come from the *atarrayas* ("cast nets"). As much as they exist as tools, artworks, and vessels, they also remind us of the essential relationship between body and river, self and earth. Bringing us to an awareness of that connection is one of the many reasons we have to thank Carolina Caycedo. Another reason is for allowing us the honor to share her brilliance. For that, and so much more, we express our gratitude.

Madeleine Grynsztejn
Pritzker Director
Museum of Contemporary Art Chicago

Acknowledgments

My deep admiration for Carolina Caycedo and her work comes from a very personal place. My mother Abby spent most of her childhood in Gigante, a small agricultural town in the department of Huila in Colombia. In 1963, at a time when violence was increasing in Huila, her family fled to Puerto Rico. I accompanied my mother to Gigante in 2014 for the first time since her family's departure. It was an emotional visit, and once there, we were saddened to see the social and ecological damage caused by the oil extraction and damming practices of transnational corporations. I soon learned that Carolina Caycedo, an artist who used to be based in Puerto Rico and whose work I had been following for years, was working on a research project in the region, engaging with local communities and activist groups all the while developing a compassionate way of working that she has termed spiritual fieldwork. Carolina's practice is both a testament to the regenerative possibilities that lie in other knowledge structures as well as an exemplification of how the process of art making offers meaningful ways to connect with others beyond the art object.

Fortunately, my appreciation for Caycedo's work was matched by Pritzker Director Madeleine Grynsztejn, James W. Alsdorf Chief Curator Michael Darling, and Manilow Senior Curator Naomi Beckwith, whose enthusiasm and support were evident from the exhibition's conception. I thank them for their guidance and encouragement. Similarly, I owe a great deal to Curatorial Assistant Iris Colburn, whose work behind the scenes and thoughtful contributions made much of this possible.

Carolina Caycedo is such a singular individual, and the rigor of her practice is matched only by her care and compassion. The same could be said for the galleries with whom she works: Instituto de Visión in Bogotá and Commonwealth and Council in Los Angeles, two stalwarts in the field. I've had the great pleasure of working with the teams at both galleries, and it should be noted that their efforts benefited the exhibition in untold ways. In particular, I'd like to acknowledge Omayra Alvarado, Beatriz López, and Young Chung for their unwavering support.

Communicating the depths of Caycedo's work is no easy task, which makes the contributions that follow all the more laudable. The close studies delivered by Pilar Tompkins Rivas and David Hernández Palmar on the profound subjects of Caycedo's practice are nothing short of revelatory, and I'm grateful for their attention, care, and expertise. Likewise, it takes a strong and steady vision to translate the beauty of her art into a lively and captivating book. For that, I would like to thank the Publications team at the MCA. Director of Content Strategy Kelsey Campbell-Dollaghan helmed the proverbial ship while Editor Tyler Laminack assisted in the development and maintenance of the manuscript. The thoughtful design was crafted by Pouya Ahmadi, whose care and creativity are quite evident throughout. The images themselves were secured by our ever-resourceful rights and images team—Manager of Rights and Images Bonnie Rosenberg, Rights and Images Assistant Elyssa Lange, and Photographer Nathan Keay—while the distribution and printing were handled by none other than our brilliant partners at DelMonico • D.A.P., led by Publisher Mary DelMonico. Lastly, I would like to thank former Associate Director of Interpretation and Visitor Research Rosie May, Editor Leah Froats, and Content Strategy Assistant Nora James for their energetic and careful consideration of the exhibition didactics.

Communication and belonging are at the heart of this project, and I'm grateful to have colleagues who exhibit those same values in their work. This includes Deputy Director Lisa Key, Senior Director of Finance Anne-Marie Eischen, and Senior Director of Development Gwen Perry Davis, who maintained the exhibition's fiscal stability alongside Assistant to the Deputy Director Rebecca Holbrook-Erhart, Director of Individual Giving and Major Gifts Nina Yung, Director of Institutional Giving Kristen Taylor, Director of Stewardship Claire Serpi, and Gift Officer Rachel Hite. Messaging and outreach were organized by Director of Strategic Communications Lauren Smallwood, Director of Media Relations Karla Loring, Associate Director of Communications Michelle Silverblatt, Media Relations Manager Katy O'Malley, Social Media Manager Abraham Ritchie, Marketing Manager Melissa Roels, Copywriter Anne Walaszek, and Web Developer Alexander Shoup. Senior Designer Christine Zavesky and Production Designers Greta McGuire and Paul Knipper brought the exhibition to life with their thoughtful designs. The transfer and installation of these works fell to our hardworking Collections and Exhibitions team, including Director of Collections and Exhibitions Management Angie Morrow, Senior Registrar for Collections Amy Louvier, Registrar for Loans and Exhibitions Leah Singsank, Chief of Exhibition Production Brad Martin, Exhibition Production Manager Erica Erdmann, Lead Preparator Colette Lehman, Manager of Technical Production Dennis O'Shea, and Lead Technician Jameson Zaerr. And Interim Director of Learning Billy McGuinness shepherded our incredible learning and education initiatives. A full staff list is included on page 142, and I thank each of them.

Through this exhibition and through the publication of this book, we are joined in Carolina's ongoing project to engage the intricate and eternal networks that not only connect us to the earth, but also to one another. Caycedo guides us through the long tributaries and waterways of our existence, and around the barriers and excavations of our destruction, all in the hopes of reaching the source from which her art emanates, a place characterized by rootedness, relatedness, and feeling. My hope is that we do our best to follow her there, to see what our world could be.

Carla Acevedo-Yates
Marilyn and Larry Fields Curator
Museum of Contemporary Art Chicago

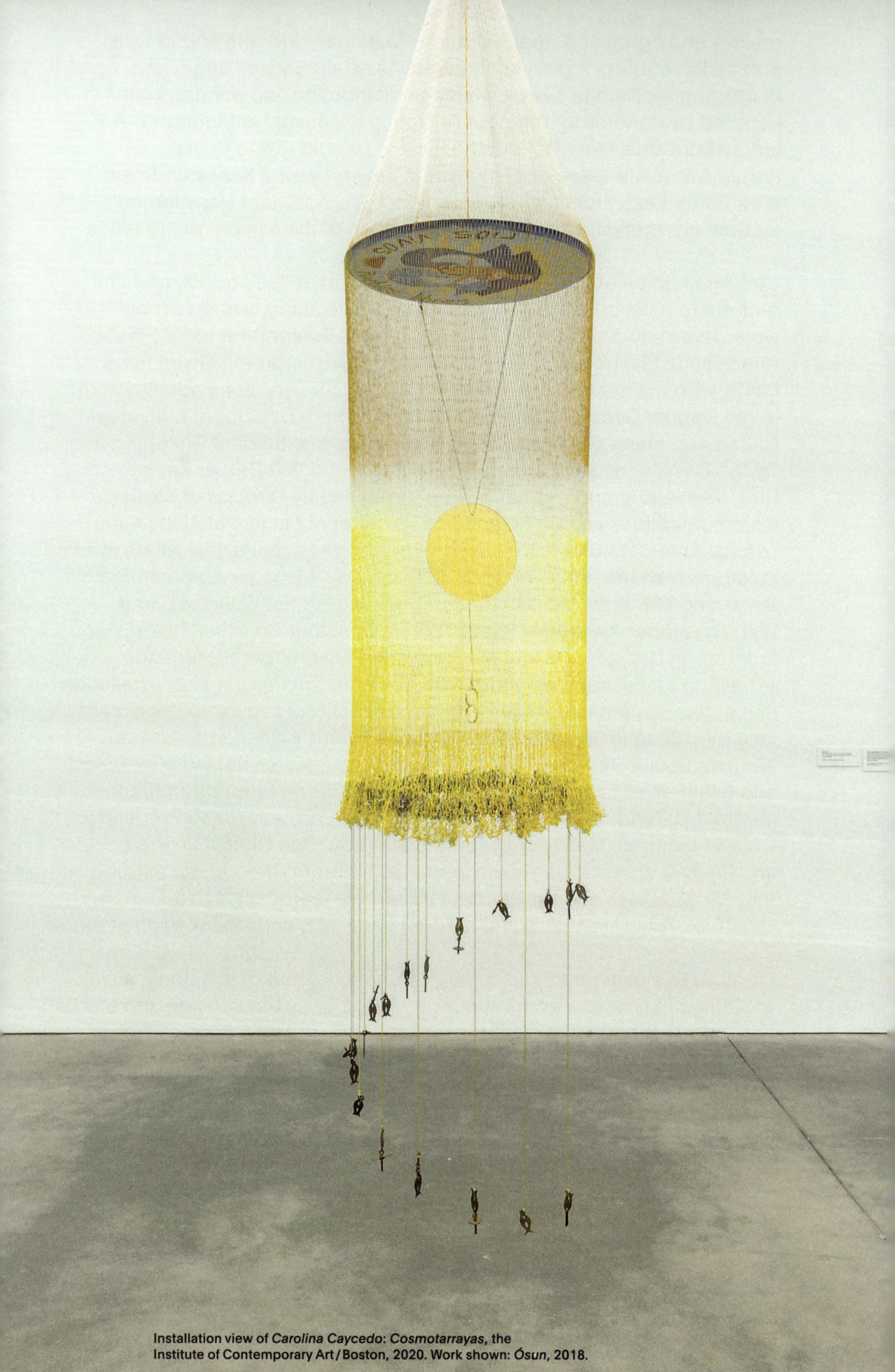

Installation view of *Carolina Caycedo: Cosmotarrayas*, the Institute of Contemporary Art / Boston, 2020. Work shown: *Ósun*, 2018.

A Note from the Curator

The web of objects, actions, and people that make up Caycedo's intricate practice comprises a galaxy of interrelation. Across media, time, and place, she has woven a tapestry, or rather *net*, of belonging, and all who are held in it, or have been witness to it, can understand its transformative power. Within a world delimited by artificial borders, barriers, and dams, Caycedo has constructed access points to a more meaningful and fruitful worldview, where connection, spirit, and permeability hold sway.

Organizing such a fluid and revolving body of work within the pages of a catalogue requires a more non-traditional approach. For this reason, rather than arranging by chronology or likeness, the works presented in this volume are positioned in a way that best conveys their conceptual and material relationship to one another and the essays that precede them. Net sculptures appear alongside water portraits, which abut artist books and performance works. They stretch across these pages in a confluence of color and material, showing the fluidity and openness of her practice across both time and space.

We hope that organizing the catalogue in this way offers a vision of that larger net bringing her work, participants, and ideas together. And we hope that by engaging with the catalogue in this way, readers will be able to feel like they're a part of the net as well, connected to the people, both past and present, and the territories, both alive and damaged, that are a part of it, too.

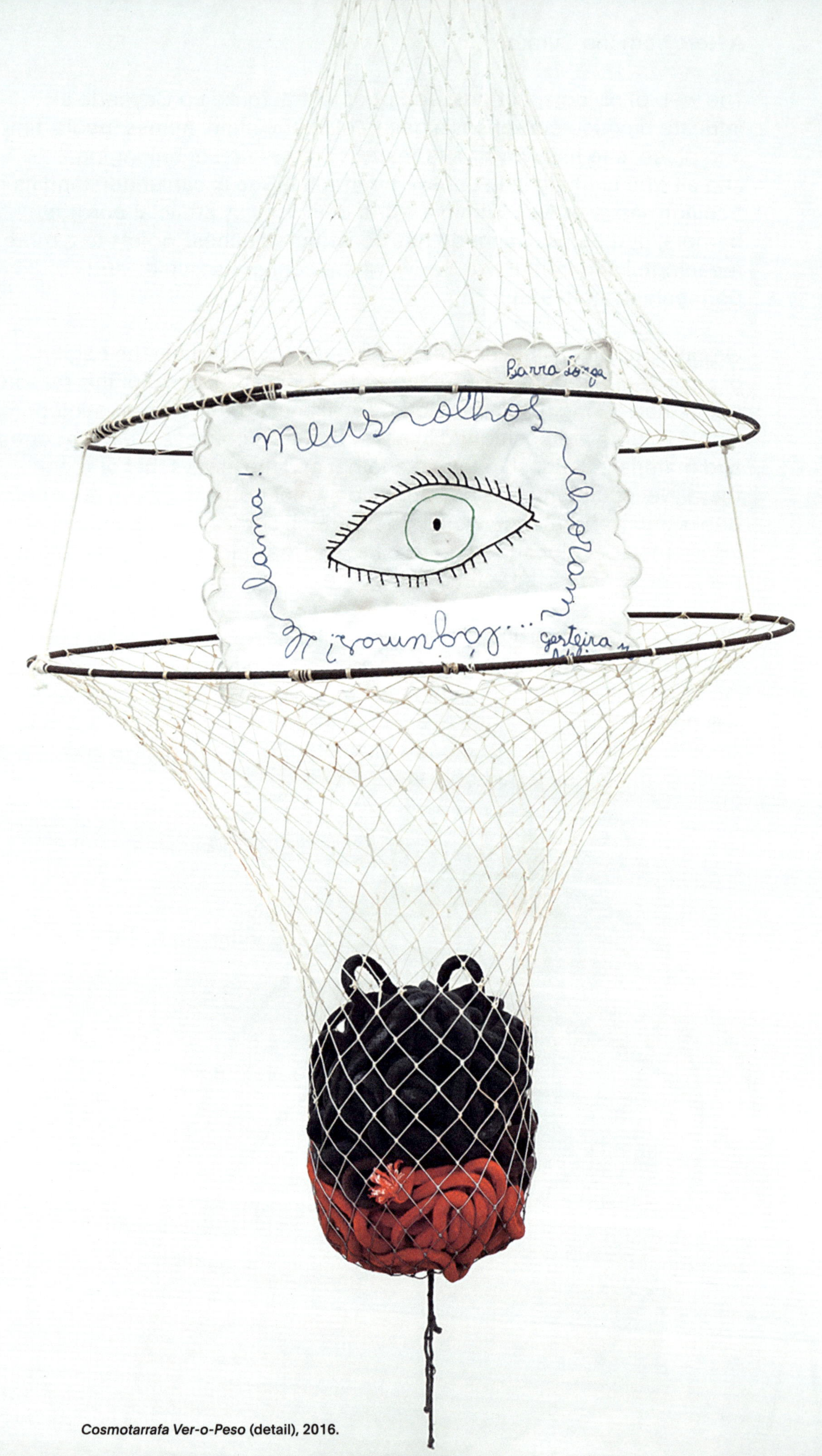

Cosmotarrafa Ver-o-Peso (detail), 2016.

Embodied Spiritual Fieldwork: Dismantling Western Perspectives Through Affective Exchanges

Trabajo de campo espiritual desde el cuerpo: Desmantelando las perspectivas occidentales por medio de intercambios afectivos

Carla Acevedo-Yates

Inspired by riverine communities in Colombia and their ways of doing and knowing, Colombian sociologist Orlando Fals Borda coined the term *sentipensante*, which translates to "feel-thinker," to describe a person that knows both through the heart and the mind. This concept is part of a larger research methodology developed during the 1970s that Fals Borda described as "participatory action research" (PAR): a way of conducting fieldwork that moves away from Western methods of observation and data collection to focus on participatory forms that are grounded in the knowledge of peasant and Indigenous communities. This method, a sociology from below, is a significant departure from object-based approaches in that it employs activist strategies and permits more subjective forms of understanding.[1] For Fals Borda, a body that feels is a thinking body and, therefore, a continuous, constant, and accessible source of knowledge.

Artist Carolina Caycedo both feels and thinks as part of her artistic methodology and draws from a wide range of sources and lineages to make her multidisciplinary work, including extensive research in "the front lines of environmental justice" and fieldwork in communities where she gathers experiences, sensations, and materials (fig. 1).[2] Contrary to conventional field research methods, where a person observes from a scientific and ethnographic distance, Caycedo conducts "spiritual fieldwork," implicating her own body and those of others, human and non-human alike, in affective exchanges. Caycedo defines spiritual fieldwork as:

> A process of developing relationships with the human and non-human entities of a particular place (or field). By adding the spiritual to these methodologies, I insist on my own and others' subjectivities, on not keeping an objective distance with my case study, but actually getting implicated in it, without losing the rigor of what it means to be in the field doing research work. It also acknowledges that fieldwork not only changes and molds your thoughts about a particular subject...but it has the capacity to mold your spirit and build solidarity between academic or creative individuals and communities.[3]

During this process, Caycedo does not exclude conventional research methodologies such as archival research, in-person interviews, or careful observation. Rather, she includes the rigor of these approaches alongside the construction of a thinking and feeling geography comprised of people, places, and non-human entities. It is also a process whereby artworks are made through collaborations and committed relations of care, an approach that challenges the rational and scientific perspectives associated with Western ways of thinking.

From an art historical perspective, her work references and is informed by the avant-garde movements that emerged throughout the nineteenth and twentieth centuries. Much like the work of those artists, Caycedo's oeuvre expands our understanding of what art is and what it is capable of doing.[4] Her spiritual methods and processes, however, are more closely aligned with Fals Borda's *sentipensante* and Charles Sepulveda's tradition as theory—"a tribal specific Acjachemen and Tongva understanding of lands and waters in contradiction to the Western dynamic of submission," where nature is not separate or distinct from human beings.[5] Tracing the development of Caycedo's artistic process and methodology through

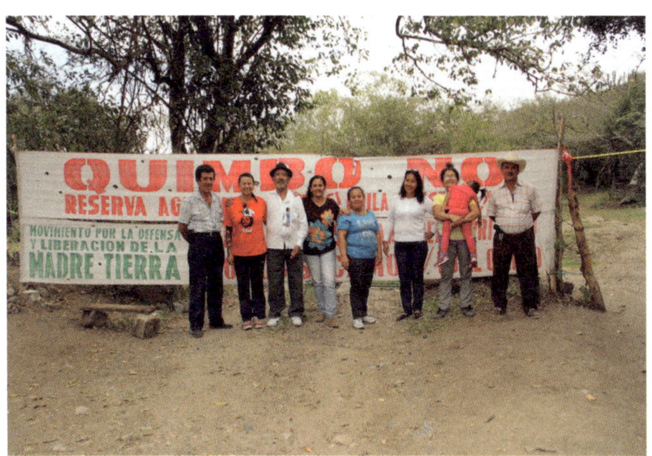

1 Carolina Caycedo with community members of El Jagualito, blocking the entrance to a construction site of El Quimbo dam, 2014.

specific works, starting with bartering projects such as *daytoday* and culminating in the artist's long-term project *Be Dammed* (2012–), not only allows for ways to analyze how her work has evolved over time, constantly moving from individual to more collective forms of affective exchange, but also highlights the more experimental and radical aspects of her artistic project, one that lends itself to increased social consciousness and new modes of seeing from non-human perspectives.

BARTERING: EXCHANGES AND EXPERIENCES OUTSIDE WESTERN LOGIC

Caycedo's work is shaped by her experience as a transcultural subject, whose numerous displacements and relationships with both people and places are important source materials for her art.[6] As such, and as an artist informed by everyday exchanges as well as more formal collaborations, Caycedo is constantly negotiating the imbrication of the private and the public sphere, the intimate and the social, thereby blurring the distinctions between artwork and life. Early projects, for instance, focused on social relations and consisted of bartering as a way to establish affective economies of exchange. In *Museo de la Calle* (Street Museum; 1998), Caycedo, as part of the artist collective Colectivo Cambalache, employed a small recycling cart named *El Veloz* with an "exchangeable collection" to barter on the street as a form of field research in the marginalized neighborhood of Cartucho in Bogotá, Colombia (fig. 2).[7] The collective describes the project as "a swap and informal redistribution project to promote cultural recycling and unlimited non-monetary exchange of goods and services."[8] As they exchanged objects with local residents, a shared knowledge emerged around the specific site of their transaction, as though they were conducting an urban archeology of the residents' daily lives.[9] Disinterested in the discrete object of

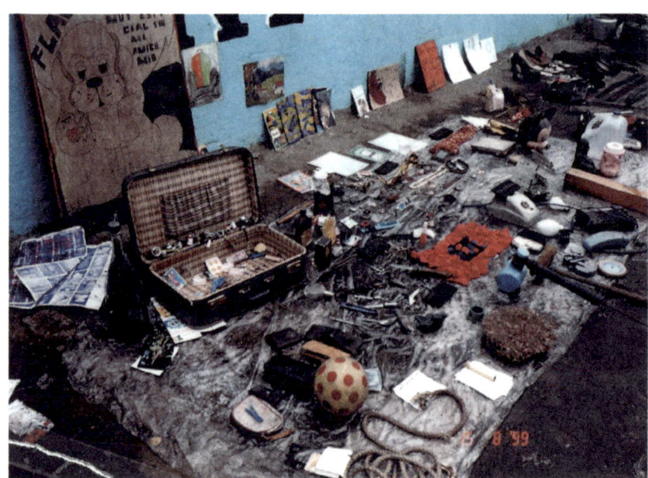

2 Object collection from Carolina Caycedo's (with Cambalache Collective) *Museo de la Calle* (Street Museum), 1998.

contemporary art, *Museo de la Calle* demonstrated Caycedo's commitment to creating networks of exchange outside capital accumulation and extraction. In 2002, Caycedo further developed this concept, transforming the act of bartering into a lasting venture in self-sustenance.

Known as *daytoday* (2002–09), the project allowed her to maintain a personal livelihood outside the formal economy of global capitalism. For approximately seven years, Caycedo exchanged her knowledge, talents, and skills for items that she needed to live her life, though the intention was not solely to highlight the viability of an alternative and non-monetary economy. She also gained an understanding about a place and its people. The project started in Vienna, Austria, where she was invited by the institution Secession to do a public art project. Here, instead of exchanging objects, Caycedo relied on her own personal skill-set (including salsa dancing, cutting hair, cooking, drawing portraits, and "reading a book loudly," among other skills) to negotiate for things that she wanted or needed, such as wine, soap, and a place to take a shower. To highlight the various possibilities of exchange, two different lists were published online and distributed through flyers ("CAROLINA GIVES" and "YOU GIVE"; fig. 3). The exchanges themselves took place either online or in her temporary, mobile "headquarters," a brown 1964 Ford van she drove all throughout Vienna. Existing outside capital structures of consumption and accumulation, the project not only relied on ideas of mutual trust, intimacy, and sharing, but also asked participants to reconsider notions of value in relation to objects, goods, services, and experiences.[10]

During its seven year run, *daytoday* further evolved and was realized in different cities and institutions across the world. Describing the project while in residency at g727 in Los Angeles in 2009, as the project was coming to a close, Caycedo offered the following:

> I understood that what I have been doing in this city so far is weaving together a tapestry of experiences and persons. And I don't mean weaving a new tapestry all together, but more like weaving a new color, a new thread into an already rich and multi-layered fabric of community networks, non-profit organizations, conscious individuals, creative collectives, anarchist city dwellers, and revolutionary thinkers, that share.[11]

Writing about *daytoday*, Caycedo explains that she "want(s) to think about it as a way of disobedience and escaping control by being in constant movement."[12] In varied forms, the concepts of movement and flow have long existed throughout Caycedo's personal life and artistic practice. In her bartering projects, her movements across cities, countries, and continents reflect her lived experiences as an immigrant and Mestiza woman in Europe and the United States. These projects ultimately express the fact that despite stoppages and obstacles, people and rivers are sovereign entities with the right to self-determination. With an attention to this notion and a care for the existing fabric of social relations, one can begin to trace a working method that would eventually inform a much larger artistic project, which has developed across time, media, and geography, and comprises an ever-widening array of social and environmental networks.

BE DAMMED (REPRESA/REPRESIÓN)

After ending the bartering projects, Caycedo shifted toward more collective forms of exchange that included both human and non-human entities. Her ways of working have also taken on an increasingly spiritual dimension, marked by a renewed interest in the river that framed her adolescence and the continued expansion of her network of participants, collaborators, and contributors (fig. 4). While pursuing her MFA in Los Angeles, Caycedo read an article written by activist Jonathan Luna describing the controversies and injustices surrounding the construction of El Quimbo Dam, the first hydroelectric dam by a transnational corporation in Colombia. The construction of the dam destroyed local ecosystems and displaced communities whose livelihoods depend on farming and artisanal fishing. In the article, Luna described how the Magdalena River, the main waterway in Colombia and the most important life force for the surrounding fertile valleys, rebelled against the transnational corporation Emgesa by rising from its banks and eroding the dike that was preventing its natural flow. Caycedo was particularly impacted by the fact that the Magdalena River had actively refused to be diverted.

The realization for local communities, and for Caycedo, was that the river itself has social as well as political agency. For most Indigenous cultures in the Americas, the rivers and waterways that connect diverse biospheres

CAROLINA GIVES	YOU GIVE
SPANISH LESSONS	FOOD (COOKED OR RAW)
ENGLISH LESSONS	BOOKS
SALSA DANCE CLASSES	HOUSE PLANTS
VIDEO EDITING LESSONS	BABY DIAPERS
SWIMMING LESSONS	MINI DV CASSETES
HAIR CUTTING	AUDIO MINIDISCS
COOK A MEAL (I MAKE SUSHI!)	PRINTER
CLEAN HOUSE OR WORK PLACE	SCANNER
MAKE A PORTRAIT	SURFBOARD
FILM A PARTY OR EVENT	WINE
VIDEO EDITING	MP3 PLAYER
PHOTOGRAPH RETOUCHING	USB PEN
IMAGE SCANNING AND DATA ARCHIVING	MEMORY STICK
INTERNET RESEARCH	SWIMMING POOL TICKETS OR SUBSCRIPTION
FOLLOW SOMEONE	SD MEMORY CARD FOR CANON DIGITAL CAMERA
PRODUCTION ASSISTANCE	2 AIRPLANE TICKETS TO PUERTO RICO OR COLOMBIA
GO TO THE BANK AND PAY BILLS	MASSAGE
BRING THE NEWSPAPER IN THE MORNING	SEWING MACHINE
GIVE ADVICE FROM MY POINT OF VIEW	MOVIE TICKETS
TELL MY SECRETS	TURNTABLE
EXPLAIN HOW TO USE THE WORLD WIDE WEB	MUSIC MIXER
TYPE A DOCUMENT	ARTWORK
POSE FOR AN ARTWORK	TATTOO
PAINT ROOM, ETC	VHS AND DVD MOVIES
TRY AND EXPLAIN COLOMBIA'S POLITICAL SITUATION	AIR HUMIDIFIER
TALK ABOUT ART	A PLACE TO LIVE
PERSONAL ASSISTANCE	CAR VACUUM
FLYER AND POSTER DESIGN	OVEN COOKWARE
SING A SONG	LAMP
BABY-CHILDREN SITTING	DR MARTEEN BOOTS
FRESH AND HOMEMADE BABY FOOD	PAIR OF SNEAKERS
READ A BOOK LOUDLY	ASTRAL CHART
GROCERIE SHOPPING	RECORDS
TAKE PETS FOR A WALK	INFANT TOYS AND CLOTHES (10 MONTHS PLUS)
TRANSPORT PEOPLE TO THE AIRPORT, DOCTOR, ETC..	INTERNATIONAL TELEPHONE CARD
PICK UP AND DELIVERY OF PACKAGES	
ESCORT TO A DINNER, PARTY, ETC..	
TIPS ABOUT LONDON, PUERTO RICO AND COLOMBIA	DON'T BRING MONEY
PAY A VISIT	
WHATEVER PERSONAL BELONINGS I HAVE WITH ME	THIS REALLY WORKS!!!
ANTIQUE BIG SUITCASE	
INFANT CLOTHES AND ARTICLES (1-9 MONTHS)	
MUSIC MP3 FILES (LATIN, REGGEATON AND MORE)	
HEAVEN AT 7/11 VIDEOGAME CD	
DO YOUR LAUNDRY	
MASSAGE	347 880 1997 c_caycedo@hotmail.com
TOUR NY CITY 5 BOROS	whitney.org/biennial2006/projects/day2day

3 Flyer for *daytoday (día a día)*, 2002–09.

are spiritual entities, sacred beings that nurture and sustain the surrounding ecosystem, including plant, animal, and human life. Caycedo's long-term commitments with specific waterways and their surrounding ecosystems and communities are an essential part of her spiritual fieldwork practice, and a means of gathering materials to make artworks as a way to understand a place and its inhabitants.

It is within this broader context that Caycedo has been developing a complex, multidisciplinary body of work under the title *Be Dammed (Represa/Represión)*, a result of extensive research periods and spiritual fieldwork on the ground. Through materials and images that mimic and critique the mechanics of flow and control of dams and rivers, the artist addresses the privatization of waterways and the social and environmental impact of extractive, large-scale infrastructural projects such as dams and mines. The group of works under *Be Dammed*, which range from collective actions and workshops to videos, sculptures, artist books, and installations, question and subvert the logic of what writer Macarena Gómez-Barris calls the extractivist viewpoint: an aerial perspective that "reduces the representation of living things and entities into commodities."[13] The title of the project in Spanish, *Represa/Represión*, is a play on the words "dam" and "repression," making linguistic and ideological correlations between dam infrastructure and social control.

The video installation *Spaniards Named Her Magdalena, But Natives Call Her Yuma* (2013), made after Caycedo's first visit to El Quimbo Dam, lays the foundations for the project's overall ideological framework (fig. 5). Through visual metaphors of flow and containment, the work establishes the language and aesthetic that has become common to her practice while also shifting the viewer's attention to Indigenous understandings of waterways. The affirmation of one of the river's ancestral names in the title of the work, Yuma, which means "land of friends," recognizes the ancestral traditions and histories of waterways before European colonization. The installation is comprised of a reflective pond, a concrete bench, and a two-channel video projection where images of the free-flowing Yuma as well as dams and reservoirs across Germany are juxtaposed with images of crowds, police barricades, and protests in Berlin (pp. 50–51). Whispering throughout the video in both Spanish and English, Caycedo recounts personal reflections on the relationship between her body, the territory, social control, and resource extraction.[14] In one instance she describes a conversation with Mamo Pedro Juan, a shaman of the Kogui Indigenous community in Santa Marta, Colombia, who states that all waterways are connected and that a dam is akin to a knot in the anus, thereby making connections between dam infrastructure and the body (fig. 6). For the Koguis, and other Indigenous cultures in the Americas, nature is at the center of their spiritual world. Likewise, the spiritual dimension of Caycedo's fieldwork, which foregrounds equivalences between nature and the body, is a guiding principle, where the body allows itself to be moved and shaped by nature's energies, flows, and currents. Caycedo's whispered words in the video, perhaps enacting the silencing of rivers into reservoirs, alongside dual images that reveal the proximities between seemingly distant people, structures, and geographies (e.g., artisanal fisherwoman Zoila Ninco in Colombia and Caycedo in Germany), express how dam infrastructure and its disciplining of nature is also an encroachment on the social body.

In the following year, Caycedo expanded the ideological and visual tenor of her project with *Yuma, or The Land of Friends* (2014), a composite of satellite imagery depicting the construction site of El Quimbo Dam

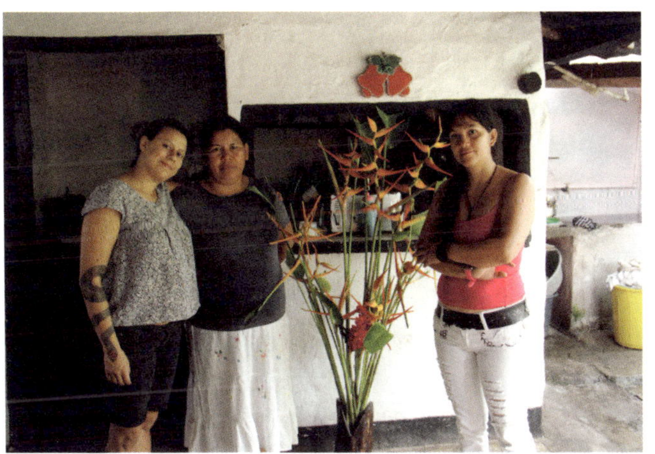

4 From left to right: Carolina Caycedo, Zoila Ninco, and Ximena Chavarro in Zoila's house in La Jagua, Huila, 2014.

(pp. 52–53). The work is made with three different satellite images taken over a six-month period and acquired by Caycedo online, two in color and one in black and white. These images, which show different stages of devastation on the territory caused by the dam's construction, are digitally manipulated by the artist—or rather "eroded" into abstract shapes—to subvert the unobstructed perspective of power from above.[15] The company that sells these images, which are sourced from various privatized satellites, also sells them to corporations such as Emgesa, who use them to plan their destructive engineering projects. Through the acquisition of these images and the renegotiation of their perspective on the territory, *Yuma, or The Land of Friends* dismantles the extractivist viewpoint to reveal the violence inflicted on the territory.[16] If, according to Indigenous philosophies, knowledge is inscribed on the territory, then the construction of dams is tantamount to an active destruction not only of nature, but of the knowledge systems that are embedded within it. Caycedo's work, therefore, can be interpreted as an act of recovery. It not only seeks to raise awareness on social and environmental issues, but also offers an active source of knowledge preservation and a type of visual and material witnessing.

The Western gaze and its logic of extraction—typified by an impersonal and detached view of the territory—is further disrupted with a series of works that Caycedo has titled *Water Portraits* (2016– ; fig. 7). Still under the umbrella of *Be Dammed*, these works are made of long strips of canvas or silk that hang across exhibition spaces, flow from walls and ceilings, and emerge overhead as if defying gravity. The images printed on the fabric are photographs that Caycedo has taken of rivers that have suffered from the effects of extractive technologies. Digitally manipulated to produce pulsating, kaleidoscopic imagery, the fractal images in these works are inspired by the spiritual experiences Caycedo has had with traditional medicine, in particular that of the Yaqui tribe in the Sonora desert in Mexico.[17] While the first water portraits depict one single, repeating fractal image of a river, the most recent works portray the larger visual narrative of a river and its surrounding territory. For instance, the portrait titled *Wanaawna Meets Salty Waters* (2019) depicts the Santa Ana River in Los Angeles, a body of water that has been adversely impacted by settler colonialism, dam construction, and urban development. The work begins by representing the free-flowing river, followed by the construction of the dam and its toxic effects, before culminating at the river's mouth where it meets the Pacific Ocean. Wanaawna is the Indigenous Tongva name of the Santa Ana River. Describing Indigenous creation stories in Southern California, Charles Sepulveda writes that "springs are sacred places where spirits exist. From both their creation stories and lived experience, Acjachemen know that water is sacred and a source of life and healing."[18] Caycedo's water portraits capture this spirit and show a view that is largely ignored and hard to see: the river as a living entity with social and political agency. Like the imagery and visual metaphors of Caycedo's earlier works, the territories and waterways depicted here highlight the complex ecology of human and natural systems as well as her own attempts to renegotiate the damaged and obstructed relations of our human and non-human world.

SPIRITUAL OBJECTS: COSMOTARRAYAS

The series *Cosmotarrayas* (2015–) marks a turning point in Caycedo's project as well as an evolution in her spiritual fieldwork. Having been focused on broader perspectives of environment and geography, Caycedo began shifting her attention to more personal and distinct relations of inhabitance. Described by the artist as "connectors between my community involvement and my studio practice," and based on small-scale everyday gestures, the *Cosmotarrayas* are sculptures made of handmade artisanal fishing nets gathered in the field and filled with related objects.

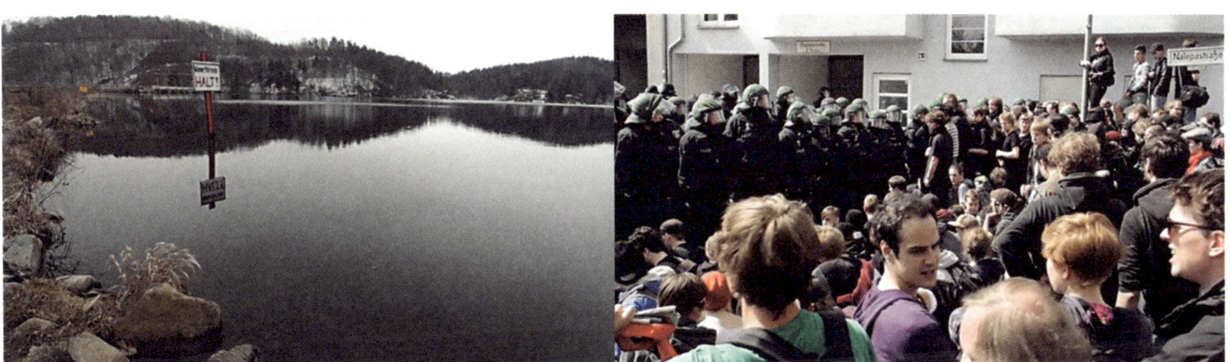

5 Still from *Spaniards Named Her Magdalena, But Natives Call Her Yuma (Los españoles la llamaron Magdalena, pero los indígenas la llaman Yuma)*, 2013.

Their hanging form is a direct reference to the ways that fisherfolk hang their nets from trees to dry (fig. 8). But far from being discrete artworks, Caycedo's *Cosmotarrayas* are a result of affective and embodied relations. Each item used to make the sculpture, including the fishing net that holds the objects contained within, tells the story of a particular place or person: a maker, wearer, or user. As the series title suggests, each sculpture portrays the universe of the person that made and used those objects, and represents the intimate, spiritual, and interdependent relationships that communities have with the river. Oftentimes, these nets are passed on through generations and "embody the tradition of weaving and the profound knowledge of rivers and fish."[19] As an ancestral technology, the net itself, with its porous, flexible, and interconnected yet strong structure, stands in opposition to a dam's industrial and impenetrable concrete construction. And for Caycedo, as well as the fisherfolk, the everyday gesture of casting an *atarraya* ("cast-net" in Spanish), knowing that they probably won't catch any fish, is a political act that affirms the river as a public space and a common good (fig. 9).[20] Drawing from the net's history, the strength of the material, and its continued use, Caycedo's *Cosmotarrayas* are embodiments of resistance to extractive practices and economies.

The first three net sculptures, portraits of the rivers *Yaqui*, *Yuma*, and *Elwha,* were made with nets gifted to the artist by the family of Zoila Ninco, an artisanal fisherwoman and community organizer who has collaborated with Caycedo on several films and performances (figs. 10–11).[21] These nets and the objects they carry (ponchos, instruments, shoes, and wooden

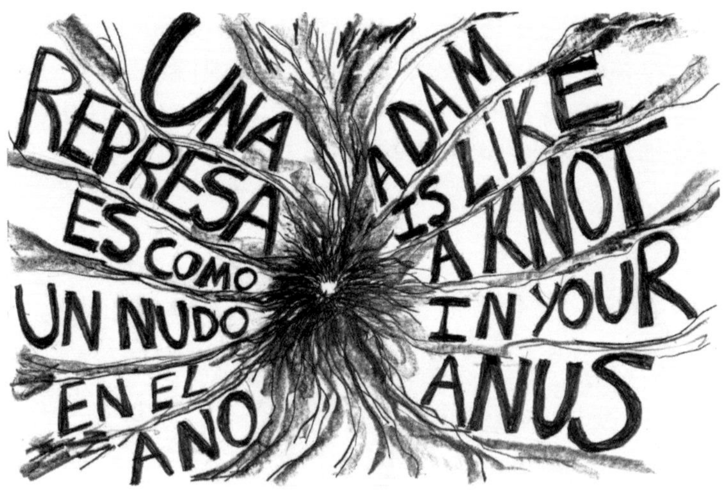

6 *Dam Knot Anus / Nudo represa ano,* 2016. Pencil on paper; 15 1/2 × 20 × 1 1/2 in. (39.37 × 50.80 × 3.81 cm).

staffs) were first used in a performance titled *One Body of Water* (2015), where actors portray three contested rivers in different stages of either privatization or restoration: the Yaqui, Yuma, and Elwha rivers in Mexico, Colombia, and the state of Washington, respectively (pp. 56–57). Once in the studio, however, and dissatisfied with the colors of the net that was to become *Yaqui*, which had the colors of the Colombian flag, Caycedo started hand-dying the nets, a decision that shifted her approach to these objects.

Where sculptures like *Yaqui*, *Elwha*, and *Yuma* reference a previous use in a play, subsequent sculptures explore the affective universe of specific places and people who have been affected by dam construction, and as such embody stories of displacement and resistance. The sculpture *Ver-o-Peso*, for instance, is part of a series created in Brazil for the 2016 Bienal de São Paulo titled *Cosmotarrafas* (p. 22). Caycedo conducted fieldwork in Brazil, specifically around the Doce, Xingu, Paraná, and Ribeira Rivers. The net used to make the sculpture, bought at the Ver-o-peso market in Belém, contains delicate embroideries made by Iris, a woman that Caycedo met and whose town, Barra Longa, was directly affected by the bursting of the Fundão tailings dam at the Germano iron ore mine of the Samarco Mariana Mining Complex. Caycedo had the opportunity to visit this region a year after the dam's collapse and saw first-hand how the toxic mud had contaminated the Doce River and devastated Iris's town.[22] The embroideries contained in *Ver-o-Peso* are visual poems that express the deep-seated sadness felt by Iris and her community. One depicts a crying eye surrounded by a text that reads, "my eyes cry tears of mud," a deeply personal and emotional expression that binds the body and its flowing tears to the pollution of a river that previously sustained life.

These personal stories told through objects and materials also come from the artist herself. In *Undammed/Desbloqueada* (2017), Caycedo implicates her own body in the work, and in doing so makes connections between the handmade net, mining, dams, and the female body (pp. 60–61). Here, a conical net surrounds a copper intrauterine device (IUD), which is suspended above an artisanal gold washing pan holding a Navajo sandstone. This stone, collected by Caycedo in Glen Canyon, is the artist's "own little visual spell" to unblock the Colorado River, which is dammed by both the Hoover and Glen Canyon Dams.[23] These dams not only block the river, but also obstruct the harmony of the four mountains (or entities) that are sacred to the Diné (Navajo). The copper IUD was Caycedo's; she had the device removed when she realized that it was also an obstruction that was blocking the flow of her menses. Caycedo describes the removal as an act of decolonization and speaks about how we must also pay attention to "the infrastructures that exist within us."[24] Through this work, Caycedo argues that acts of control and domination also extend to women's bodies, and by doing so highlights the gender politics of dam construction and environmental justice more broadly. It is no coincidence that women are at the forefront of environmental struggles worldwide, and as a consequence are targets of violence and repression by governments and corporations.

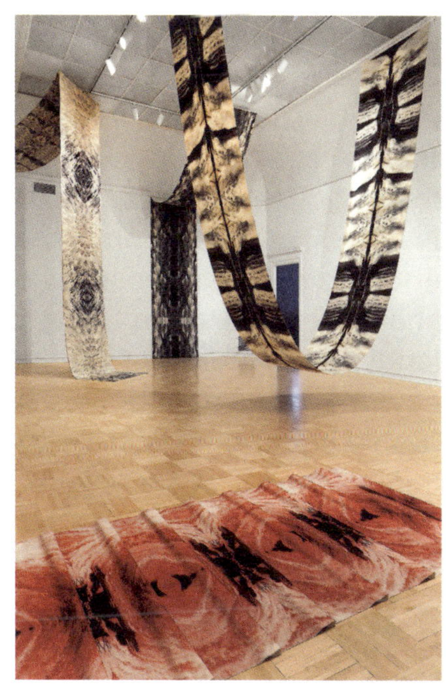

7 Works from the *Water Portrait (Retratos de agua)* series, 2015–16. Dye-sublimation prints on canvas. Installation view of *Between Bodies*, Henry Art Gallery, University of Washington, Seattle, 2018–19.

Caycedo's net sculptures have continued to shift, change, and evolve as she moves through different contexts, ideas, and aesthetic concerns. Some have been created as offerings to spiritual deities such as Oshún—talismans intended to protect its owners, or witchcraft-type visual spells that are also objects of healing. Whereas others have been developed through more abstract explorations of the ideas and perspective shifts that have concerned her. Take *From the Bottom of the River/Desde el fondo del río I* (2019), a dyptich sculpture made of hand-painted glass pieces and artisanal fishing nets that, when combined, resemble a pair of eyes (fig. 12). In these works, the net is reduced in scale and covers a conical form. Affixed to the wall, it returns the viewer's gaze "from the bottom of the river," as the title suggests, inhabiting the perspective of rocks, fish, and other non-human entities. It is a physical incarnation of what Gómez-Barris describes as a submerged, fish-eye perspective, whereby the extractive view from above is subverted by seeing "from the muddied depths" of the river. This underwater perspective also references the thousands of disappeared in Colombia and across the region who have been murdered for defending their territories, and whose bodies remain submerged in rivers throughout Latin America. For Caycedo, it is this gaze that holds us accountable, asking us to inhabit the perspectives of those who have lost their lives in the struggle for environmental justice. Here, we might return to Orlando Fals Borda, who expressed a similar realignment. These sculptures, after all, embody *sentipensante*. Not only do they help us consider new ways of environmental and social thinking, but they also invite us to enter into the life of another, to feel in their world a shared heritage and a responsibility for what connects us.

Indeed, this is true for all of Caycedo's artworks and the rhizomatic structures they engender. Interconnected, distinct, yet constantly overlapping, they share ideas, materials, collaborators, and participants. The open-ended, generous structure of her work challenges the notion of the discrete work of art. It is not that the viewer completes the work with her/his own experiences, but that the work itself and its ideas continue to shift, adapt, and evolve into different but interrelated physical manifestations. It is this borderless condition that invites us to consider the importance of affective relations and exchanges with the spirits, histories, and non-human entities of the lands in which we live. It also encourages us to reassess our needs in relation to capital production, shifting our attention to the knowledge that lies within our bodies, lands, and waterways as a way to deaccelerate global capitalism and its environmental destruction. Rivers teach us that we live in an interdependent global community. Caycedo's spiritual fieldwork asks us to feel and think along these same lines, and to question and resist the infrastructures imposed on us as well as those self-imposed within us.

Inspirado por las comunidades ribereñas de Colombia y por sus formas de hacer y saber, el sociólogo colombiano Orlando Fals Borda acuñó el término *sentipensante* para describir a una persona que conoce tanto a través del corazón como de la mente. Este concepto forma parte de una metodología de investigación más amplia desarrollada durante la década de 1970 que Fals Borda denomina "Investigación-acción participativa" (IAP): una forma de llevar a cabo trabajo de campo que se aleja de los métodos occidentales de observación y recolección de datos para centrarse en formas participativas fundamentadas en los conocimientos de las comunidades campesinas e indígenas. Este método, una sociología desde abajo, se aleja significativamente de los enfoques basados en objetos en tanto que emplea estrategias activistas y permite formas más subjetivas de comprensión.[1] Para Fals Borda, un cuerpo que siente es un cuerpo que piensa y, por tanto, una fuente de conocimiento continua, constante y accesible.

La artista Carolina Caycedo piensa y siente como parte de su metodología artística y se basa en una amplia variedad de fuentes y linajes para crear su obra multidisciplinaria, lo que incluye investigaciones a fondo en "los frentes de la justicia ambiental", así como trabajo de campo con comunidades, donde recoge experiencias, sensaciones y materiales (fig. 1).[2] A diferencia de los métodos de investigación de campo convencionales, en los que una persona observa desde una distancia científica y etnográfica, Caycedo lleva a cabo un "trabajo de campo espiritual", en el que su propio cuerpo y el de otros seres, humanos y no humanos, participan de intercambios afectivos. Caycedo define el trabajo de campo espiritual como:

> Un proceso de desarrollo de relaciones con entidades humanas y no humanas en un lugar (o campo) específico. Al añadir lo espiritual a estas metodologías, insisto en mi propia subjetividad y en la de otros, en no mantener una distancia objetiva en mi estudio de caso, sino en realmente involucrarme en él, sin perder el rigor de lo que significa estar en el campo haciendo trabajo de investigación. Esto es también un reconocimiento de que el trabajo de campo no solo cambia y moldea nuestros pensamientos sobre un tema en particular, sino que tiene la capacidad de moldear nuestro espíritu y entablar lazos de solidaridad entre los académicos o individuos creativos y las comunidades.[3]

Durante este proceso, Caycedo no excluye las metodologías de investigación convencionales, como la investigación de archivo, las entrevistas en persona o la observación meticulosa. En cambio, la artista incluye el rigor de estos enfoques a la vez que construye una geografía de pensamientos y sentimientos compuesta de personas, lugares y entidades no humanas. Se trata, además, de un proceso en el que se crean obras de arte por medio de colaboraciones y relaciones de cuidado comprometidas, un enfoque que desafía las perspectivas racionales y científicas asociadas con las formas de pensamiento occidentales.

Desde la perspectiva de la historia del arte, su obra hace referencia y se nutre de los movimientos de vanguardia que surgieron a lo largo del siglo XIX y el XX. De manera muy similar a la obra de aquellos artistas, la obra de Caycedo amplía nuestra comprensión de lo que es el arte y de lo que puede hacer.[4] Sin embargo, sus métodos y procesos espirituales se alinean más estrechamente con el concepto de *sentipensante* de Fals Borda y la tradición como teoría de Charles Sepulveda: "una comprensión tribal específica Acjachemen y Tongva de las tierras y las aguas en contraposición con la dinámica occidental de la sumisión", donde la naturaleza no está separada ni es distinta de los seres humanos.[5]

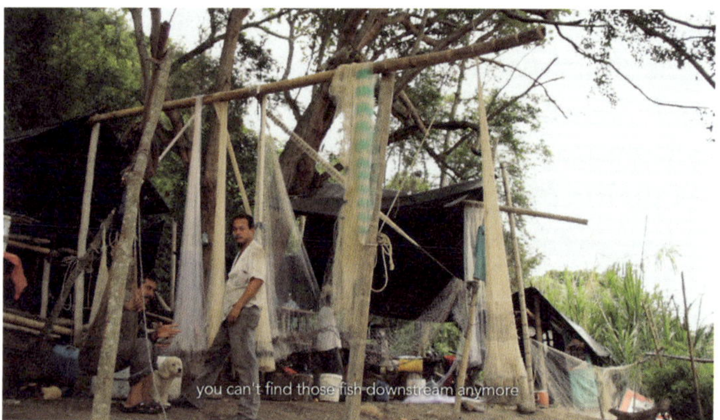

8 Still from *Land of Friends*, 2014. HD video (color, sound); 38 minutes, 10 seconds.

Al rastrear el desarrollo del proceso y la metodología artística de Caycedo a través de obras específicas, comenzando por proyectos de intercambio como *día a día* y culminando con el proyecto a largo plazo de la artista *Be Dammed (Represa/Represión)* (2012–), no solo permite analizar de qué manera su obra ha evolucionado a lo largo del tiempo, avanzando constantemente de formas individuales a otras más colectivas de intercambio afectivo, sino que también pone de relieve los aspectos más experimentales y radicales de su proyecto artístico, que se presta al desarrollo de una conciencia social cada vez más amplia y a nuevos modos de ver desde perspectivas no humanas.

EL TRUEQUE: INTERCAMBIOS Y EXPERIENCIAS FUERA DE LA LÓGICA OCCIDENTAL

La obra de Caycedo está conformada por su experiencia como sujeto transcultural, ya que sus numerosos desplazamientos y relaciones con personas y lugares son fuentes importantes de su práctica artística.[6] Como tal, y como artista que se inspira en los intercambios cotidianos así como en colaboraciones más formales, Caycedo negocia constantemente la imbricación de las esferas de lo público y lo privado, lo íntimo y lo social, desdibujando así las distinciones entre su obra y su vida. Por ejemplo, sus proyectos tempranos se centraban en las relaciones sociales e incorporaban el trueque como manera de establecer economías afectivas de intercambio. En *Museo de la Calle* (1998), Caycedo, como integrante del colectivo artístico Colectivo Cambalache, empleó un pequeño carro de reciclaje llamado *El Veloz* con una "colección intercambiable" para hacer trueques en la calle como forma de investigación de campo en el barrio marginalizado de El Cartucho en Bogotá, Colombia (fig. 2).[7] El colectivo describe el proyecto como "una actividad de intercambio y redistribución informal para promover el reciclaje cultural y un intercambio humanitario ilimitado de bienes y servicios".[8] A medida que intercambiaban objetos con los residentes del lugar, emergió un conocimiento compartido sobre el lugar específico de su transacción, como si estuvieran llevando a cabo una arqueología urbana de las vidas cotidianas de los residentes.[9] Poco interesado en el objeto discreto del arte contemporáneo, *Museo de la Calle* demostró el compromiso de Caycedo con la creación de redes de intercambio fuera de la acumulación de capital y la extracción. En 2002, Caycedo desarrolló aún más este concepto, transformando el acto del trueque en un emprendimiento duradero de sustento propio.

Conocido como *día a día* (2002–09), el proyecto le permitió ganarse la vida fuera de la economía formal del capitalismo global. Durante aproximadamente siete años, Caycedo intercambió su conocimiento, sus talentos y sus habilidades por artículos que necesitaba para vivir, aunque su intención no era solamente poner de relieve la viabilidad de una economía alternativa y no monetaria. También buscaba obtener una comprensión más profunda del lugar y sus gentes. El proyecto comenzó en Viena, Austria, a donde fue invitada por la institución Secession a realizar un proyecto de arte público. Allí, en lugar de intercambiar objetos, Caycedo utilizó su propio conjunto de habilidades (que incluía bailar salsa, cortar el pelo, cocinar, dibujar retratos y "leer un libro en voz alta", entre otras destrezas) para negociar y obtener cosas que quería o necesitaba, como vino, jabón y un lugar donde ducharse. Para destacar las varias posibilidades de intercambio, se publicaron dos listas distintas en línea, que se distribuyeron en formato de volantes ("CAROLINA DA" y "TÚ DAS"; fig. 3). Los intercambios en sí tuvieron lugar en línea o en su "oficina central" temporal y móvil, una furgoneta marrón Ford de 1964 que condujo por toda Viena. El proyecto, que existió fuera de las estructuras de consumo y acumulación del capitalismo, no solo se basaba en los conceptos de confianza mutua, intimidad y el compartir, sino que pedía a los participantes que reconsideraran las nociones de valor con respecto a objetos, bienes, servicios y experiencias.[10]

Durante sus siete años de duración, *día a día* siguió evolucionando y se llevó a cabo en distintas ciudades e instituciones del mundo. Al describir el proyecto mientras se encontraba realizando una residencia en el espacio g727 en Los Ángeles en 2009, cuando el proyecto estaba llegando a su fin, Caycedo afirmó:

> Comprendí que lo que he estado haciendo hasta ahora en esta ciudad ha sido tejer un tapiz de experiencias y personas. Y no quiero decir tejer un tapiz completamente nuevo, sino más bien incorporar un nuevo color, un nuevo hilo a un rico y complejo tejido de redes comunitarias, organizaciones sin fines de lucro, individuos conscientes, colectivos artísticos, habitantes anárquicos y pensadores revolucionarios que comparten.[11]

Al escribir acerca de *día a día*, Caycedo explica: "quiero entenderlo como una forma de desobediencia y de evasión del control al estar en constante movimiento".[12] De diversas formas, los conceptos de movimiento y flujo han existido por mucho tiempo en la vida personal y en la práctica artística de Caycedo. En sus proyectos de trueque, sus movimientos a través de ciudades, países y continentes reflejan sus vivencias como inmigrante y mujer mestiza en Europa y los Estados Unidos. Estos proyectos expresan, al final, el hecho de que, a pesar de los bloqueos y las obstrucciones, las personas y los ríos son entidades soberanas con derecho a la autodeterminación. Prestando atención a este concepto y cuidando las relaciones existentes del tejido social, uno puede comenzar a rastrear un método de trabajo que, con el tiempo, terminaría siendo la base de un proyecto artístico mucho más amplio, que se ha desarrollado a lo largo del tiempo, en diversos medios y geografías, y que está compuesto de una variedad cada vez mayor de redes sociales y ambientales.

BE DAMMED (REPRESA/REPRESIÓN)

Tras finalizar los proyectos de trueque, Caycedo se enfocó hacia formas más colectivas de intercambio, que incluyen tanto entidades humanas como no humanas. Además, su proceso se ha vuelto cada vez más espiritual, marcado por un renovado interés en el río que enmarcó su adolescencia y la constante expansión de su red de participantes, colaboradores y contribuidores (fig. 4). Mientras estudiaba un Máster en Bellas Artes en Los Ángeles, Caycedo leyó un artículo escrito por el activista Jonathan Luna, en el que se describían las controversias e injusticias que rondaban la construcción de la represa El Quimbo, la primera represa hidroeléctrica propiedad de una corporación transnacional en Colombia. La construcción de la represa destruyó los ecosistemas locales y desplazó a comunidades cuyo sustento dependía de la agricultura y la pesca artesanal. En el artículo, Luna describía cómo el río Magdalena, la principal vía navegable de Colombia y la fuerza vital más importante para los valles fértiles que lo rodean, se rebeló contra la corporación transnacional Emgesa inundando sus orillas y erosionando el dique que evitaba su flujo natural. Caycedo quedó particularmente impactada por el hecho de que el río Magdalena se hubiese activamente rehusado a ser desviado. En ese momento, las comunidades locales, al igual que Caycedo, comprendieron que el río en

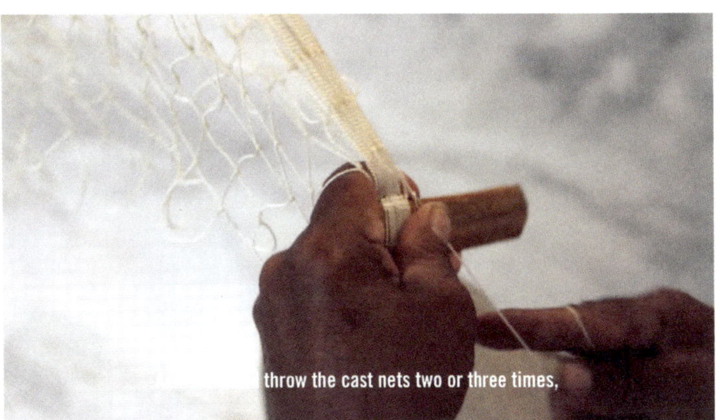

9 Still from *Huila's Bleeding*, 2014. HD video (color, sound); 12 minutes.

sí tiene agencia social y política. Para la mayoría de las culturas indígenas del continente americano, los ríos y los canales que conectan las diversas biosferas son entidades espirituales, seres sagrados que nutren y sustentan los ecosistemas circundantes, que incluyen la vida vegetal, animal y humana. Los compromisos a largo plazo que Caycedo ha establecido con ciertos ríos y sus ecosistemas y comunidades son componentes esenciales de su trabajo de campo espiritual, y una manera de reunir materiales para hacer obras de arte como una forma de entender un lugar y sus habitantes.

Es dentro de este contexto más amplio que Caycedo ha ido desarrollando una obra compleja y multidisciplinaria bajo el título *Be Dammed*, resultado de periodos de investigación exhaustiva y de trabajo de campo espiritual in situ. Por medio de materiales e imágenes que imitan y critican los mecanismos de flujo y control de las represas y los ríos, la artista aborda la cuestión de la privatización de los ríos navegables y del impacto social y ambiental que tienen los proyectos de infraestructura extractivista a gran escala, como represas y minas. El conjunto de obras comprendidas bajo el título *Be Dammed*, que abarcan desde acciones colectivas y talleres a videos, esculturas, libros de artista e instalaciones, cuestionan e invierten la lógica de lo que la autora Macarena Gómez-Barris llama el punto de vista extractivista: una perspectiva aérea que "reduce la representación de seres y entidades vivas a materias primas".[13] El título del proyecto en español, *Represa/Represión*, es un juego de palabras, que establece correlaciones lingüísticas e ideológicas entre la infraestructura de la represa y el control social.

La video instalación *Spaniards Named Her Magdalena, But Natives Call Her Yuma (Los españoles la llamaron Magdalena, pero los indígenas la llaman Yuma)* (2013), creada tras la primera visita de Caycedo a la represa El Quimbo, sienta las bases para el marco ideológico general del proyecto (fig. 5). Por medio de metáforas visuales de flujo y contención, la obra establece el lenguaje y la estética que terminarían siendo comunes a su práctica, mientras que también centra la atención del espectador en maneras indígenas de comprender las vías fluviales. El uso de uno de los nombres ancestrales del río en el título de la obra, Yuma, que significa "tierra de los amigos", reconoce las tradiciones ancestrales y las historias de los ríos antes de la colonización europea. La instalación está compuesta de un estanque brillante, un banco de cemento y una

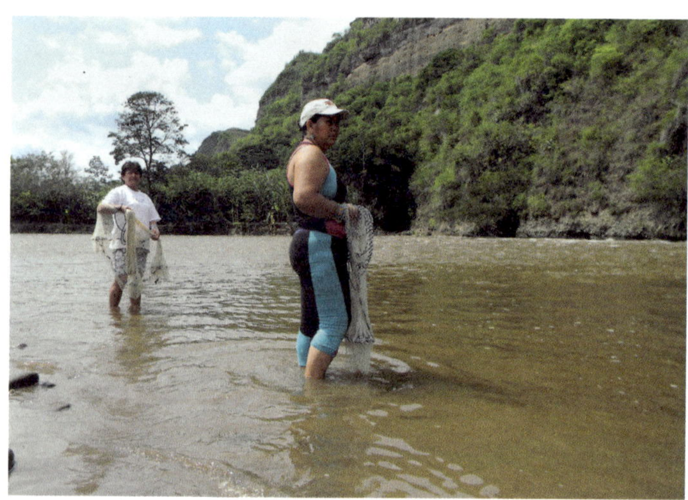

10 Cecilia Torres and Zoila Ninco fishing during the La Jagua Geochoreography final event at the Las Peñas beach, Magdalena River at La Jagua, Huila, 2014.

proyección de video de dos canales donde las imágenes de un Yuma que fluye libremente, así como de represas y embalses en Alemania, se yuxtaponen con imágenes de multitudes, barricadas de la policía y protestas en Berlín (pp. 50–51). Susurrando a lo largo del vídeo tanto en español como en inglés, Caycedo nos cuenta sus reflexiones personales sobre la relación entre su cuerpo, el territorio, el control social y la extracción de recursos.[14] En un momento describe una conversación con Mamo Pedro Juan, un chamán de la comunidad indígena Kogui de Santa Marta, Colombia, que afirma que todos los ríos están conectados y que una represa es semejante a un nudo en el ano, estableciendo así conexiones entre la infraestructura de una represa y el cuerpo (fig. 6). Para los Koguis y otras culturas indígenas de las Américas, la naturaleza es el centro de su mundo espiritual. De manera semejante, la dimensión espiritual del trabajo de campo de Caycedo, que pone en primer plano las equivalencias entre la naturaleza y el cuerpo, es una guía, en donde el cuerpo se deja mover y moldear por las energías, los flujos y las corrientes de la naturaleza. Las palabras que Caycedo susurra en el video, que quizás representen el silenciamiento de los ríos que han sido convertidos en embalses, junto con las imágenes duales que revelan la cercanía que existe entre pueblos, estructuras y geografías en apariencia distantes (p. ej., la pescadora artesanal Zoila Ninco en Colombia y Caycedo en Alemania) expresan cómo la infraestructura de la represa y su disciplinamiento de la naturaleza es también una invasión del cuerpo social.

Al año siguiente, Caycedo amplió el tenor ideológico y visual de su proyecto con *Yuma, or The Land of Friends (Yuma, o Tierra de los amigos)* (2014), una amalgama de imágenes satelitales en la que puede verse la construcción de la represa El Quimbo (pp. 52–53). La obra está realizada con tres imágenes satelitales distintas tomadas durante un periodo de seis meses y que Caycedo adquirió en línea: dos a color y una en blanco y negro. Estas imágenes, que muestran las distintas etapas de devastación del territorio causada por la construcción de la represa, han sido manipuladas digitalmente por la artista—o, más bien, "erosionadas" en formas abstractas—para subvertir la perspectiva del poder, que ofrece una vista aérea sin obstrucciones.[15] La empresa que vende estas imágenes, que provienen de varios satélites privados, también se las vende a corporaciones como Emgesa, que las utilizan para planificar sus destructivos proyectos de ingeniería. Por medio de la adquisición de estas imágenes y de la renegociación de su perspectiva sobre el territorio, *Yuma, o Tierra de los amigos* desmantela el punto de vista extractivista para revelar la violencia que se inflige sobre el territorio.[16] Si, según las filosofías indígenas, el conocimiento se inscribe en el territorio, entonces la construcción de represas supone una destrucción activa no solo de la naturaleza sino también de los sistemas de conocimiento que la integran. Por tanto, la obra de Caycedo puede interpretarse como un acto de recuperación. No solo busca concientizar sobre problemas sociales y ambientales, sino que también ofrece una fuente activa de preservación del conocimiento y un tipo de testimonio visual y material.

La mirada occidental y su lógica de extraer—caracterizada por una visión impersonal y desconectada del territorio—se ve aún más alterada con una serie de obras que Caycedo ha titulado *Water Portraits (Retratos de agua)* (2016– ; fig. 7). Estas obras, que siguen formando parte de *Be Dammed (Represa/Represión)*, están compuestas de largas tiras de lienzo o seda que cuelgan a través de espacios de exposición, fluyen desde paredes y techos, y emergen desde lo alto como si desafiaran la gravedad. Las imágenes impresas en el tejido son fotografías que Caycedo ha tomado de ríos que han sufrido los efectos de las tecnologías de extracción. Manipuladas digitalmente para producir imágenes pulsantes y caleidoscópicas, las imágenes fractales de estas obras están inspiradas en las experiencias espirituales que Caycedo ha tenido con la medicina tradicional, en particular con la de la tribu Yaqui en el desierto de Sonora en México.[17] Si bien en los primeros retratos de agua se representa una única imagen fractal repetida de un río, sus obras más recientes retratan la narrativa visual más amplia de un río y el territorio que lo rodea. Por ejemplo, el retrato titulado *Wanaawna Meets Salty Waters (Wanaawna se encuentra con aguas saladas)* (2019) representa el río Santa Ana de Los Ángeles, un cuerpo de agua que se ha visto negativamente afectado por el colonialismo, la construcción de represas y el desarrollo urbano. La obra comienza representando un río que fluye libremente para seguir con la construcción de una represa y sus efectos tóxicos, culminando en la desembocadura del río en el Océano Pacífico. Wanaawna es el nombre indígena que le dan los Tongva al río Santa Ana. Al describir los relatos de creación de los indígenas del sur de California, Charles Sepulveda escribe que "los manantiales son lugares sagrados donde existen los espíritus. Tanto por sus relatos de creación como por sus vivencias, los Acjachemen saben que el agua es sagrada y una fuente de vida y sanación".[18] Los retratos de agua de Caycedo capturan este espíritu y muestran una perspectiva en gran medida ignorada y difícil de ver: que el río es una entidad viva que tiene agencia social y política. Al igual que las imágenes y las metáforas visuales presentes en las obras tempranas de Caycedo, los territorios y ríos representados aquí ponen de relieve la compleja ecología de los sistemas humanos y naturales, así como sus propios intentos de renegociar las relaciones dañadas y obstruidas de nuestro mundo humano y no humano.

OBJETOS ESPIRITUALES: COSMOTARRAYAS

La serie *Cosmotarrayas* (2015–) marca un punto de inflexión en el proyecto de Caycedo, así como una evolución en su trabajo de campo espiritual. Habiéndose centrado previamente en perspectivas más amplias sobre el medioambiente y la geografía, Caycedo comenzó a prestar atención a relaciones habitacionales más personales y diversas. Descritas por la artista como "conectores entre mi participación

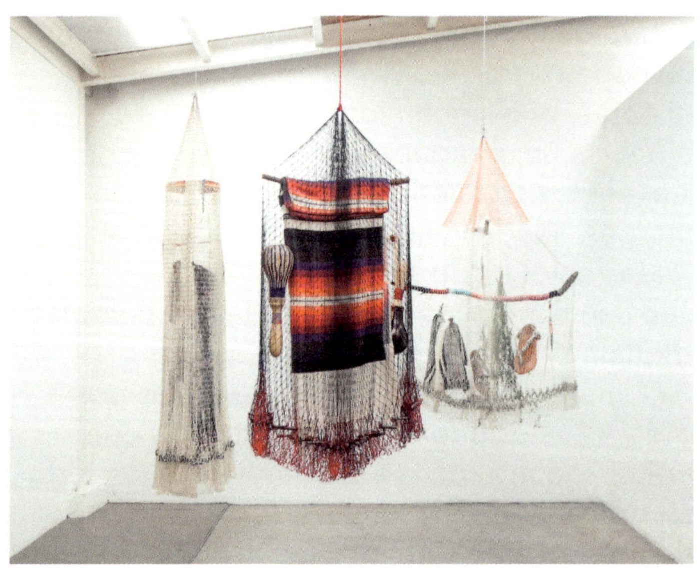

11 Installation view of *Entre Caníbales*, Instituto de Visión, 2016. Works shown, from left to right: *Cosmotarraya Elwha*, 2016; *Cosmotarraya Yaqui*, 2016; and *Cosmotarraya Yuma*, 2016.

comunitaria y mi práctica de estudio", y basadas en pequeños gestos cotidianos, las *Cosmotarrayas* son esculturas hechas de redes de pesca artesanales recolectadas en el campo y llenas de objetos relacionados. La forma en que cuelgan refiere directamente a las maneras en que los pescadores cuelgan sus redes de los árboles para que se sequen (fig. 8). Sin embargo, lejos de ser obras de arte autónomas, las *Cosmotarrayas* de Caycedo son resultado de relaciones afectivas y corporales. Cada objeto utilizado para crear la escultura, incluida la red de pesca que sostiene los objetos, cuenta la historia de un lugar o una persona particular: un creador, un portador o un usuario. Como sugiere el título de la serie, cada escultura retrata el universo de la persona que creó y utilizó esos objetos, y representa las relaciones íntimas, espirituales e interdependientes que las comunidades establecen con el río. A menudo, estas redes se pasan de generación en generación y "encarnan la tradición del tejido y el profundo conocimiento de los ríos y los peces".[19] Como tecnología ancestral, la propia red, con su estructura porosa, flexible e interconectada, y aún así fuerte, se opone a la construcción de cemento, industrial e impenetrable, que es la represa. Y, para Caycedo, así como para los pescadores, el gesto diario de lanzar una atarraya ("esparavel" en otras regiones), sabiendo que probablemente no haya peces que pescar, es un acto político que afirma que el río es un espacio público y un bien común (fig. 9).[20] Inspiradas en su historia, la fuerza del material y su uso continuo, las *Cosmotarrayas* de Caycedo son encarnaciones de la resistencia a las prácticas y economías extractivas.

Las primeras tres esculturas de redes de pesca, retratos de los ríos *Yaqui*, *Yuma* y *Elwha*, fueron creadas con redes obsequiadas a la artista por la familia de Zoila Ninco, una pescadora artesanal y organizadora comunitaria que ha colaborado con Caycedo en varios videos y performances (figs. 10–11).[21] Estas redes y los objetos que contienen (ponchos, instrumentos, zapatos y bastones de madera) se utilizaron por primera vez en una performance titulada *One Body of Water* (*Un cuerpo de agua)* (2015), donde los actores representaron tres ríos disputados en distintas etapas de privatización o restauración: los ríos Yaqui, Yuma y Elwha de México, Colombia y el estado de Washington, respectivamente (pp. 56–57). Sin embargo, una vez en el estudio, insatisfecha con los colores de la red que se convertiría en *Yaqui*, que tenía los colores de la bandera colombiana, Caycedo comenzó a teñir las redes a mano, decisión que alteró su aproximación a estos objetos.

Si bien las esculturas *Yaqui*, *Elwha* y *Yuma* hacen referencia a su uso previo en una performance, las esculturas posteriores exploran el universo afectivo de personas y lugares específicos que han sido afectados por la construcción de la represa y, como tales, encarnan historias de desplazamiento y resistencia. Por ejemplo, la escultura *Ver-o-Peso* forma parte de una serie creada en Brasil para la bienal de São Paulo de 2016, titulada *Cosmotarrafas* (p. 22). Caycedo condujo trabajos de campo en Brasil, específicamente en la zona de los ríos Doce, Xingu, Paraná y Ribeira. La red utilizada para crear la escultura, comprada en el mercado Ver-o-peso de Belém, contiene delicados bordados creados por Iris, una mujer a la que Caycedo conoció y cuyo pueblo, Barra Longa, había sido directamente afectado por el estallido de la represa de relave Fundão de la mina de mineral de hierro Germano, perteneciente al complejo minero Samarco Mariana. Caycedo tuvo la oportunidad de visitar esta región un año después del colapso de la represa y vio con sus propios ojos cómo el lodo tóxico había contaminado el río Doce y devastado el pueblo de Iris.[22] Los bordados en la obra *Ver-o-Peso* son poemas visuales que expresan la profunda tristeza que sienten Iris y su comunidad. Uno representa un ojo que llora rodeado de un texto que dice "mis ojos lloran lágrimas de lodo", una expresión profundamente personal y emotiva que vincula el cuerpo y sus lágrimas con la contaminación del río que previamente había sustentado la vida.

Estas historias personales contadas a través de objetos y materiales también se extienden a la propia artista. En *Undammed / Desbloqueada* (2017), Caycedo implica su propio cuerpo en la escultura y, al hacerlo, establece conexiones entre la red hecha a mano, la minería, las represas y el cuerpo de la mujer (pp. 60–61). Aquí, una red cónica rodea un dispositivo intrauterino de cobre (DIU), suspendido sobre una batea artesanal para lavar oro, sobre la que vemos una piedra arenisca navajo. Esta piedra, que Caycedo recolectó en el cañón Glen, es el "pequeño hechizo visual" de la artista para desbloquear el río Colorado, que está interrumpido por las represas Hoover y Glen Canyon.[23] Estas represas no solo bloquean el río, sino que también obstruyen la armonía de las cuatro montañas (o entidades) sagradas para los Diné (navajo). El DIU de cobre era de Caycedo, quien hizo que le retiraran el dispositivo cuando se dio cuenta de que también era una obstrucción que bloqueaba el flujo de su menstruación. Caycedo describe la extracción como un acto de descolonización y habla sobre cómo también debemos prestar atención a "las infraestructuras que existen dentro de nosotros".[24] En esta obra, Caycedo sostiene que los actos de control y dominación también se extienden a los cuerpos de las mujeres y, al hacerlo, pone de relieve las políticas de género relativas a la construcción de represas y la justicia medioambiental más ampliamente. No es coincidencia que las mujeres estén al frente de la lucha medioambiental en todo el mundo y que, como consecuencia, sean blanco de violencia y represión por parte de gobiernos y corporaciones.

Las esculturas de redes de Caycedo han continuado cambiando, modificándose y evolucionando a medida que la artista atraviesa distintos contextos, ideas y preocupaciones estéticas. Algunas han sido creadas como ofrendas a deidades espirituales como Oshún, talismanes que tienen por objetivo proteger a sus dueños o hechizos visuales semejantes a los de la brujería, que funcionan también como objetos de sanación.

12 *From the Bottom of the River/ Desde el fondo del río I*, 2019. Diptych, hand-painted blown glass, artisanal fishing net, and lead weights; 77 1/5 × 24 4/5 × 5 9/10 in. (196 × 63 × 15 cm).

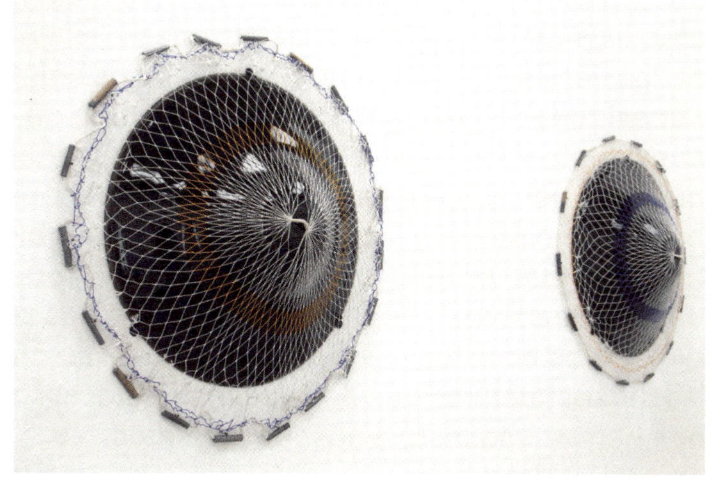

Mientras que otras han sido desarrolladas a través de exploraciones más abstractas de las ideas y los cambios de perspectiva que le han interesado. Por ejemplo, consideremos *From the Bottom of the River/ Desde el fondo del río I* (2019), una escultura díptica hecha de piezas de vidrio pintadas a mano y redes de pesca artesanales queal combinarlas parecen un par de ojos (fig. 12). En estas obras, la red se reduce en escala y recubre una forma cónica. Fijada a la pared, regresa la mirada del espectador "desde el fondo del río", como sugiere el título, habitando la perspectiva de las rocas, los peces y otras entidades no humanas. Es una encarnación física de lo que Gómez-Barris describe como una perspectiva de ojo de pez sumergida, donde la vista aérea de extracción se ve subvertida al ver ahora "desde las profundidades cenagosas" del río. Esta perspectiva sumergida también hace referencia a los miles de desaparecidos en Colombia y en toda la región, que han sido asesinados por defender sus territorios y cuyos cuerpos continúan sumergidos en ríos de toda Latinoamérica. Para Caycedo, esta es la mirada que nos hace responsables, que nos pide que ocupemos las perspectivas de aquellos que han perdido sus vidas en la lucha por la justicia medioambiental. Aquí, retomamos a Orlando Fals Borda, quien expresó un realineamiento similar. Estas esculturas, después de todo, encarnan el concepto de *sentipensante*. No sólo nos ayudan a considerar nuevas formas de pensamiento ambiental y social, sino que nos invitan a entrar en la vida del otro, a sentir en su mundo un legado compartido y una responsabilidad por lo que nos conecta.

De hecho, esto se aplica a todas las obras de Caycedo y a las estructuras rizomáticas que engendran. Interconectadas, distintas y aún así constantemente solapadas, comparten ideas, materiales, colaboradores y participantes. La estructura de su obra, de carácter libre y generoso, desafía la noción de la obra de arte autónoma. No es que el espectador complete la obra con sus propias experiencias, sino que la obra en sí y sus ideas no dejan de cambiar, adaptarse y evolucionar hacia manifestaciones físicas distintas pero relacionadas. Es esta condición ilimitada la que nos invita a considerar la importancia de las relaciones y los intercambios afectivos con los espíritus, las historias y las entidades no humanas de las tierras que habitamos. También nos anima a reevaluar nuestras necesidades en relación con la producción de capital, redirigiendo nuestra atención hacia el conocimiento que habita en nuestros cuerpos, nuestras tierras y nuestros ríos como una manera de desacelerar el capitalismo global y la destrucción medioambiental. Los ríos nos enseñan que vivimos en una comunidad global interdependiente. El trabajo de campo espiritual de Caycedo nos pide que sintamos y pensemos en estos mismos términos, y que cuestionemos y resistamos las infraestructuras que nos han impuesto, así como aquellas que nos hemos impuesto a nosotros mismos.

1 Jafte Dilean Robles Lomeli and Joanne Rappaport, "Imagining Latin American Social Science from the Global South: Orlando Fals Borda and Participatory Action Research," *Latin American Research Review*, Latin American Studies Association, September 28, 2018. https://larrlasa.org/articles/10.25222/larr.164/.

2 Carolina Caycedo and Catalina Lozano, "Nunca Fuimos Modernas," *Terremoto*, September 3, 2018. https://terremoto.mx/article/nunca-fuimos-modernas/.

3 Carolina Caycedo, email exchange with the author, February 19, 2020.

4 Caycedo's approach as a visual artist has an antecedent in artists who cull ideas from the experiential. Artists Hélio Oiticica, Lygia Clark, and María Teresa Hincapié are all influential figures. Oiticica's *Parangolés*, for example, were inspired by *vivências* or lived experiences; the body was not only used as a support for the work, but was fully incorporated into it.

5 Charles Sepulveda, "Our Sacred Waters: Theorizing *Kuuyam* as a Decolonial Possibility," *Decolonization: Indigeneity, Education & Society* 7, no. 1 (2018): 40–58.

6 Born in London to Colombian parents, Caycedo experienced from a very young age the complexities of being an immigrant. Caycedo's parents decided to move back to Colombia after her brother was born, a decision prompted by law changes under the conservative rule of Margaret Thatcher that required at least one parent of a child born in the UK to be a citizen.

7 The Colectivo Cambalache has had as members a number of prominent artists through the years, including Adriana García Galán, Raimond Chaves, Alonso Gil, and Federico Guzmán.

8 Carolina Caycedo et al., Cambalache Statement.

9 Cartucho was a neighborhood in the center of Bogotá that was occupied in the 1980s by drug traffickers and later indigents and social outcasts. Soon after it became the most violent and dangerous neighborhood in Colombia, where life on the street and informal economies of trade and exchange dominated daily life. There, Colectivo Cambalache dragged a cart similar to the ones used by local garbage collectors and recyclers, which they named *El Veloz*, and exchanged objects. The project, whose starting point was Bogotá, then extended to San Juan, Ljubljana, Seville, and Barcelona, where objects from each city were constantly exchanged and circulated.

10 Caycedo has compared *daytoday* to the Hxaro system of delayed and non-equivalent gift exchange practiced by the !Kung peoples in southern Africa. Through this system, the creation of affective networks becomes more important than the items exchanged as lifetime bonds are established between those who participate in the trade.

11 Carolina Caycedo, "DAYTODAY in L.A. Blog," in *DAYTODAY 2002–2009* (Los Angeles: g727, 2009), 55.

12 Carolina Caycedo, "I Could Do With a Little More Chaos Myself," in *DAYTODAY 2002–2009* (Los Angeles: g727, 2009), 74.

13 Macarena Gómez-Barris, "Inverted Visuality: Against the Flow of Extractivism," *Journal of Visual Culture* 15 (2016): 29–31.

14 When Caycedo uses the word "territory" she is not only referring to the land itself, but also the people, plants, animals, and diverse ecosystems that live on and are nurtured by the land, as well as their social and political dimension. It stands in opposition to the word "landscape," which implies a Western gaze that is detached and separate from nature.

15 The use of digital mapping tools and satellite images by Caycedo was also a practical choice; she was in Berlin at the time and it was the only way to follow developments from afar. This physical constraint is, in a way, evidence of how the body and its distance to the site equally inform the materiality of the work.

16 The view of the satellite (not unlike that of a military drone) also underscores the violence that results from the militarization of these extractive zones in Colombia and other Latin American countries, which has led to the assassination of environmental leaders and activists.

17 In one such instance, Caycedo, invited by the tribe to take part in the ceremony of the toad, had a spiritual experience where she felt the dry banks of the river beneath her body and started to weep. A toad then spoke to her, saying that it was very important for women to cry as the tears of women bring water to the dry banks of the river. She then saw a mountain with the profile of a woman who looked at her, and it felt as though all the women of the world were looking at her at the same time. These kinds of visions are described by the Yaqui people as "painting." This suggests that color, and visual images more broadly, can be the conduits for spiritual experiences that generate knowledge of a specific place.

18 Sepulveda, "Our Sacred Waters: Theorizing *Kuuyam* as a Decolonial Possibility," 44.

19 Carolina Caycedo, "Genealogy of Nets," unpublished manuscript.

20 Because it obstructs the natural flow of a river, dam construction affects spawning and migrating fish, causing significant reductions (and at times extinction) of local fish populations. In addition to affecting the free passage of fish, the stagnant water in dam reservoirs also impacts water temperature and oxygenation. When cold water is released from a dam reservoir, it can have devastating effects for native fish populations downstream.

21 The *atarraya* first appeared in Caycedo's work during the last scenes of the video *Spaniards Named Her Magdalena, But Natives Call Her Yuma* (2013), where artisanal fisherwoman and community organizer Zoila Ninco is seen casting her net into the Cuacua-Sauza River.

22 All of the nets in this series are dyed with colors that reference this toxic mud: red, black, and brown.

23 Caycedo, email exchange with the author, February 19, 2020.

24 Carolina Caycedo and Jeffrey De Blois, "The River as a Common Good: Carolina Caycedo's Cosmotarrayas," Institute of Contemporary Art/Boston. Accessed February 7, 2020. https://www.icaboston.org/publications/river-common-good-carolina-caycedos-cosmotarrayas.

1 Jafte Dilean Robles Lomeli y Joanne Rappaport,"Imaginando las ciencias sociales latinoamericanas desde el Sur global: Orlando Fals Borda y la Investigación-acción participativa," Latin American Research Review, Asociación de Estudios Latinoamericanos, 28 de septiembre de 2018. https://larrlasa.org/articles/10.25222/larr.164/.

2 Carolina Caycedo y Catalina Lozano, "Nunca fuimos modernas", Terremoto, 3 de septiembre de 2018. https://terremoto.mx/article/nunca-fuimos-modernas/.

3 Carolina Caycedo, intercambio de correos electrónicos con la autora, 19 de febrero de 2020.

4 El enfoque de Caycedo como artista visual tiene antecedentes en artistas que extraen ideas de la experiencia. Los artistas Hélio Oiticica, Lygia Clark y María Teresa

Hincapié son todas figuras de gran influencia. Por ejemplo, los Parangolés de Oiticica se inspiraron en las vivências; el cuerpo no solo se utilizaba como soporte para la obra, sino que se incorporaba por completo a ella.

5 Charles Sepulveda, "Nuestras aguas sagradas: Teorizando Kuuyam como una posibilidad decolonial", Decolonization: Indigeneity, Education & Society 7, n.° 1 (2018): 40–58.

6 Nacida en Londres en el seno de una familia colombiana, Caycedo experimentó desde temprana edad las complejidades de ser inmigrante. Los padres de Caycedo decidieron regresar a Colombia tras el nacimiento de su hermano, una decisión motivada por los cambios legales aprobados por el gobierno conservador de Margaret Thatcher, que requerían que al menos uno de los padres de un niño nacido en el Reino Unido fuera ciudadano del país.

7 El Colectivo Cambalache ha contado entre sus miembros con varios artistas destacados a lo largo de los años, incluidos Adriana García Galán, Raimond Chaves, Alonso Gil y Federico Guzmán.

8 Carolina Caycedo et al., Declaración Cambalache.

9 El Cartucho era un barrio en el centro de Bogotá que fue ocupado en la década de 1980 por traficantes de drogas y más tarde, por indigentes y marginados sociales. Pronto se convirtió en el barrio más violento y peligroso de Colombia, un lugar en el que la vida en las calles y las economías informales de comercio e intercambio dominaban la vida cotidiana. Allí, el Colectivo Cambalache arrastraba un carro similar a los que utilizaban los recicladores y cartoneros locales, al que llamaron *El Veloz* y con el que intercambiaban objetos. El proyecto, cuyo punto de partida fue Bogotá, luego se extendió a San Juan, Ljubljana, Sevilla y Barcelona, donde continuaron intercambiando y circulando objetos de cada ciudad.

10 Caycedo ha comparado su día a día con el sistema Hxaro de reciprocidad aplazada y no equivalente practicado por los pueblos !kung del sur de África. A través de este sistema, la creación de redes afectivas es más importante que los artículos que se intercambian, ya que se establecen vínculos de por vida entre las partes que participan del intercambio.

11 Carolina Caycedo, "Blog DÍA A DÍA en L.A.", en DÍA A DÍA 2002–2009 (Los Ángeles: g727, 2009), 55.

12 Carolina Caycedo, "No me vendría mal un poquito más de caos", en DÍA A DÍA 2002–2009 (Los Ángeles: g727, 2009), 74.

13 Macarena Gómez-Barris, "Visualidad invertida: Contra el flujo del extractivismo," Journal of Visual Culture 15 (2016): 29–31.

14 Cuando Caycedo usa la palabra "territorio" no solo se refiere a la tierra en sí misma sino también a la gente, las plantas, los animales y los diversos ecosistemas que viven y son nutridos por la tierra, así como a su dimensión sociopolítica. Se opone a la palabra "paisaje", que implica una mirada occidental desconectada y alejada de la naturaleza.

15 El uso de herramientas de mapeo digital y de imágenes satelitales por parte de la artista fue también una elección práctica; se encontraba en Berlín en esa época y era la única manera de realizar un seguimiento de los avances del proyecto desde lejos. Esta limitación física, en cierto sentido, evidencia de cómo el cuerpo y su distancia de un lugar informan de igual manera la materialidad de la obra.

16 La vista satelital (que no se aleja mucho de la que ofrece un drone militar) también pone de relieve la violencia resultante de la militarización de estas zonas de extracción en Colombia y otros países latinoamericanos, que ha llevado al asesinato de líderes y activistas que defendían el medio ambiente.

17 En una ocasión, Caycedo, invitada por la tribu a tomar parte en la ceremonia del sapo, tuvo una experiencia espiritual donde sintió las orillas secas del río bajo su cuerpo y comenzó a llorar. Luego, un sapo le habló y le dijo que era muy importante que las mujeres lloren, ya que sus lágrimas llevan agua a las orillas del río. Luego, vio una montaña con perfil de mujer que la miraba y tuvo la sensación de que todas las mujeres del mundo la miraban al mismo tiempo. El pueblo Yaqui describe este tipo de visiones como "pintura". Ello sugiere que el color, y las imágenes visuales en general, pueden conducir a experiencias espirituales que generan conocimiento de un lugar específico.

18 Sepulveda, "Nuestras aguas sagradas: Teorizando Kuuyam como una posibilidad decolonial", 44.

19 Carolina Caycedo, "Genealogía de las redes", manuscrito no publicado.

20 Dado que obstruye el flujo natural de un río, la construcción de una represa afecta a los peces en sus periodos de desove y migración, lo que provoca una reducción significativa (en ocasiones, una extinción) de las poblaciones de peces locales. Además de afectar el libre paso de los peces, el agua estancada en los embalses de la reserva también produce un impacto sobre la temperatura y la oxigenación del agua. Cuando se libera agua fría de un embalse, puede tener un efecto devastador para las poblaciones de peces nativas río abajo.

21 La atarraya apareció por primera vez en la obra de Caycedo durante las últimas escenas del video *Los españoles la llamaron Magdalena, pero los indígenas la llaman Yuma* (2013), donde vemos a la pescadora artesanal y organizadora comunitaria Zoila Ninco lanzar su red en el río Cuacua-Sauza.

22 Todas las redes de esta serie están teñidas con colores que hacen referencia a este lodo tóxico: rojo, negro y marrón.

23 Caycedo, intercambio de correos electrónicos con la autora, 19 de febrero de 2020.

24 Carolina Caycedo y Jeffrey De Blois, "El río como bien común: las Cosmotarrayas de Carolina Caycedo", Institute of Contemporary Art/Boston. Visitado el 7 de febrero de 2020. https://www.icaboston.org/publications/river-common-good-carolina-caycedos-cosmotarrayas.

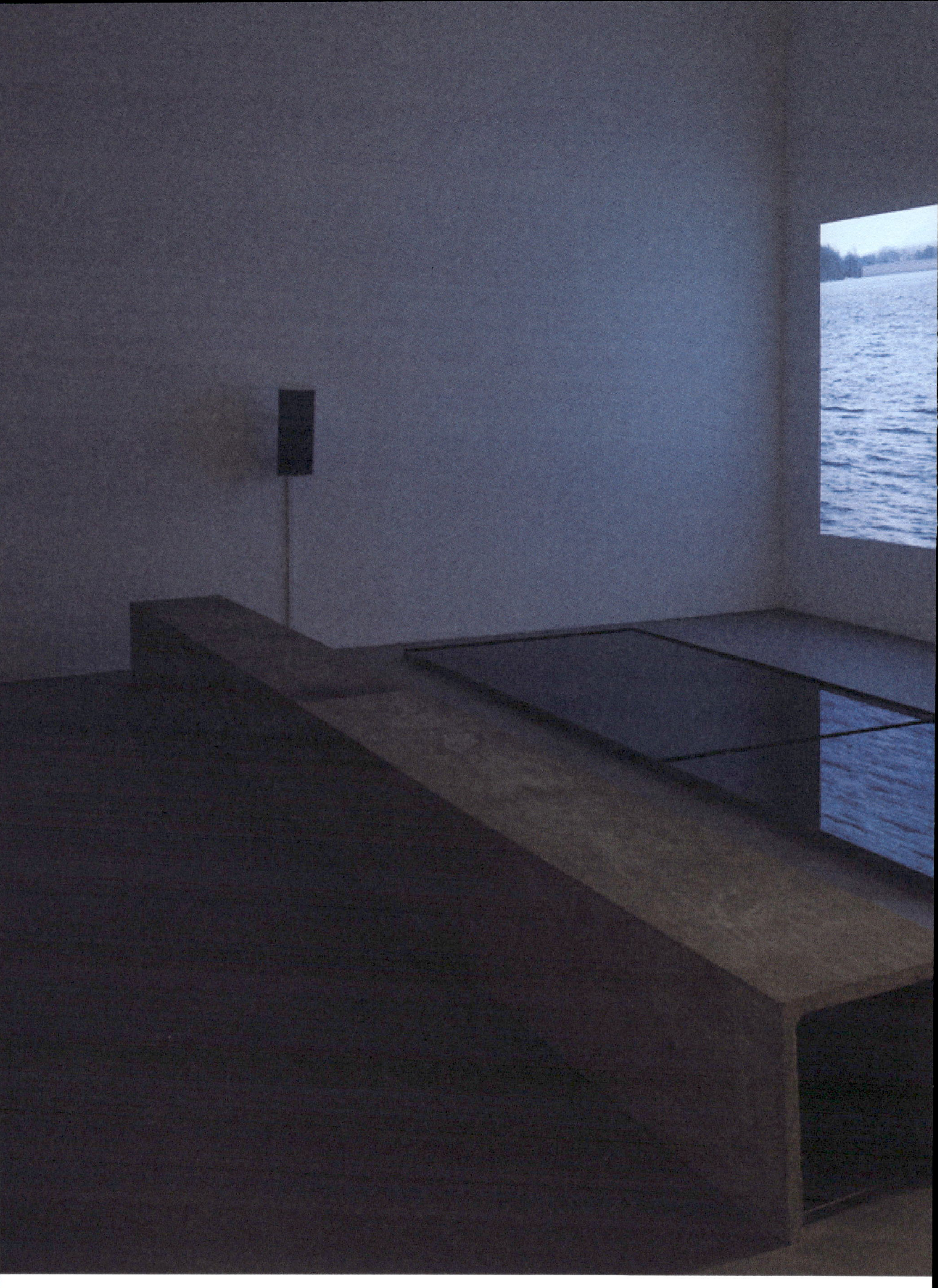

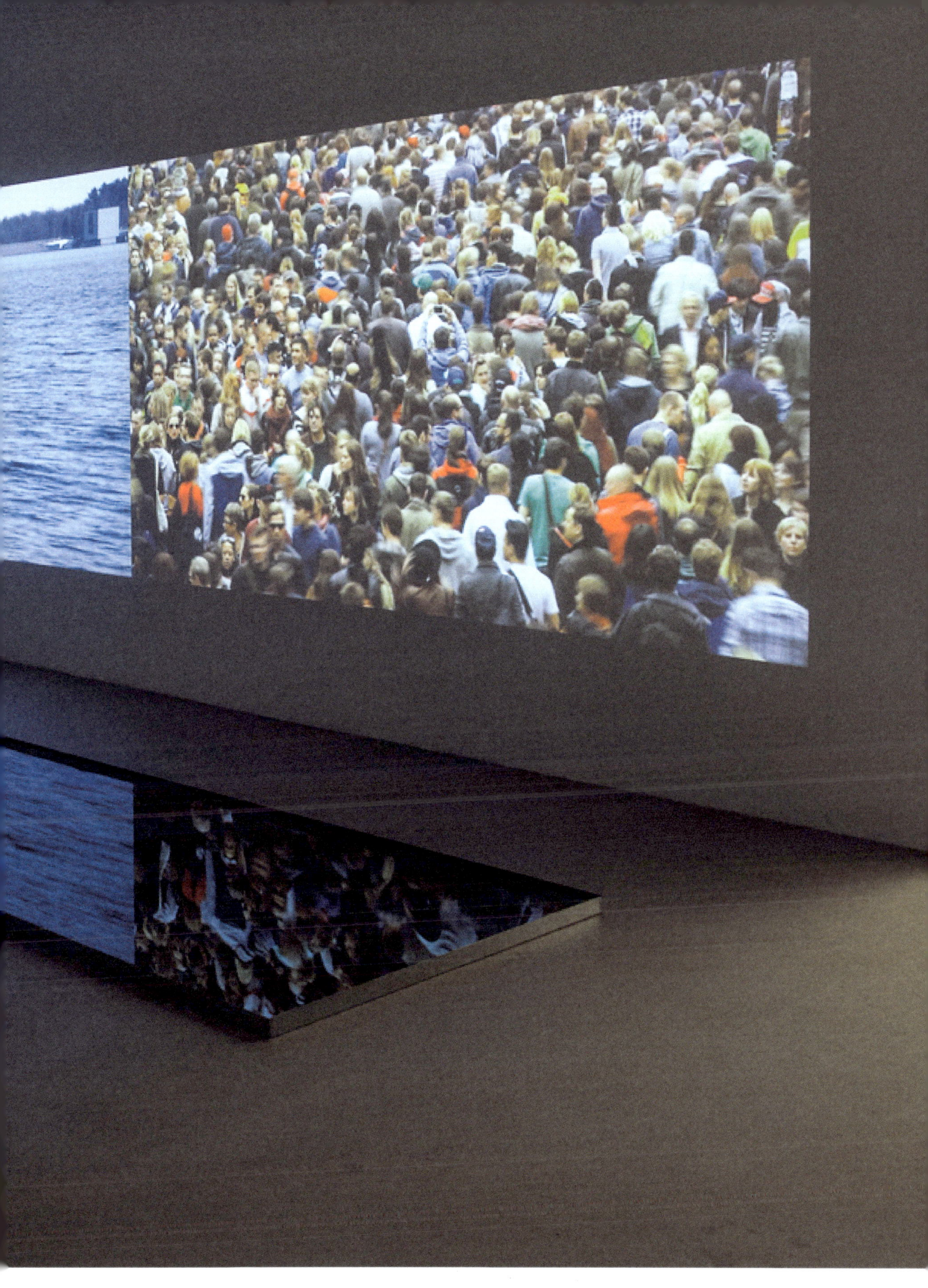

Installation view of *Carolina Caycedo: The headlong stream is termed violent but the river bed hemming it in is termed violent by no one,* DAAD Galerie, Berlin, 2013–14. Work shown: *Spaniards Named Her Magdalena, But Natives Call Her Yuma,* 2013. Two-channel HD video installation (color, sound); 27 min.

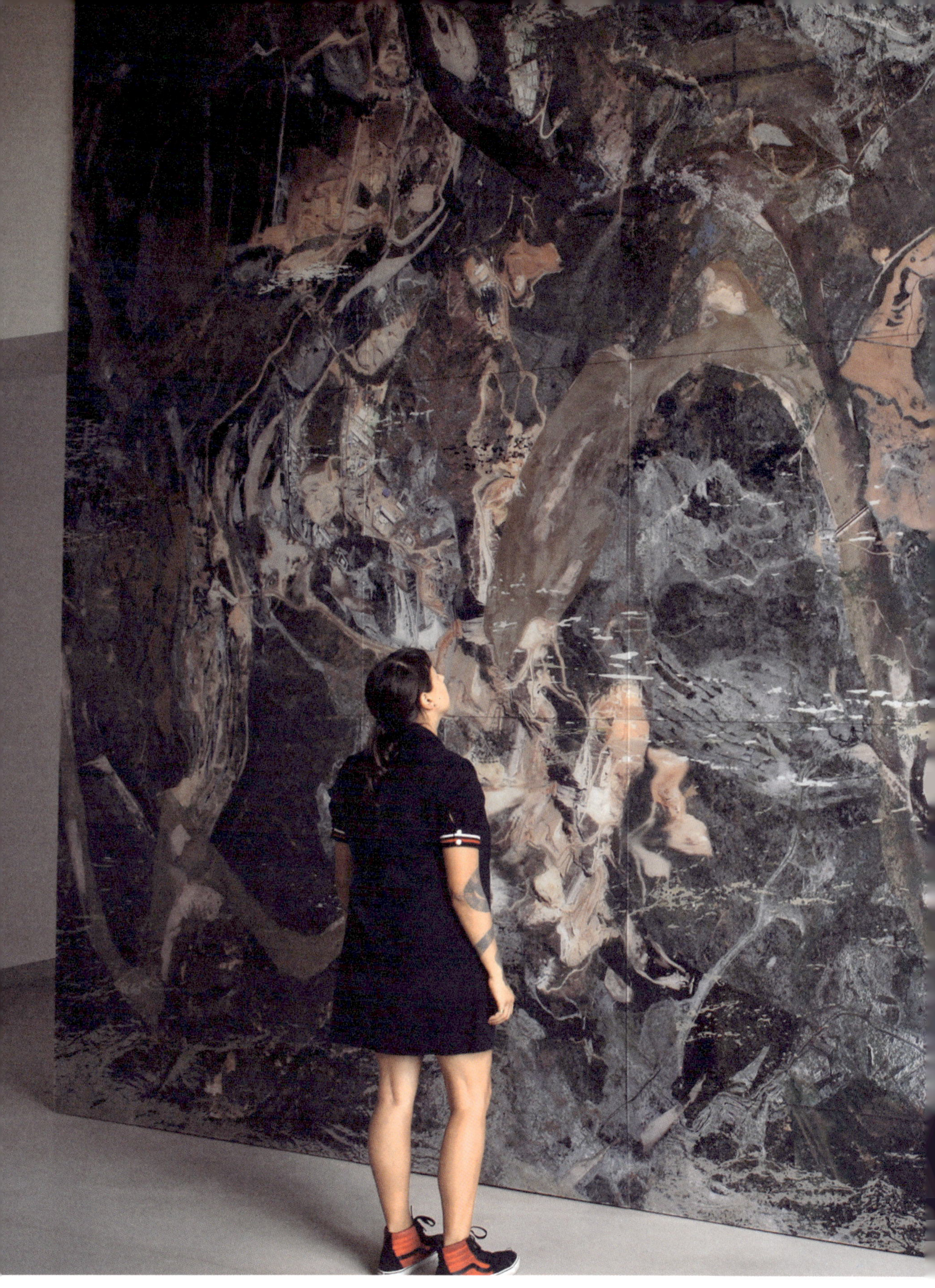

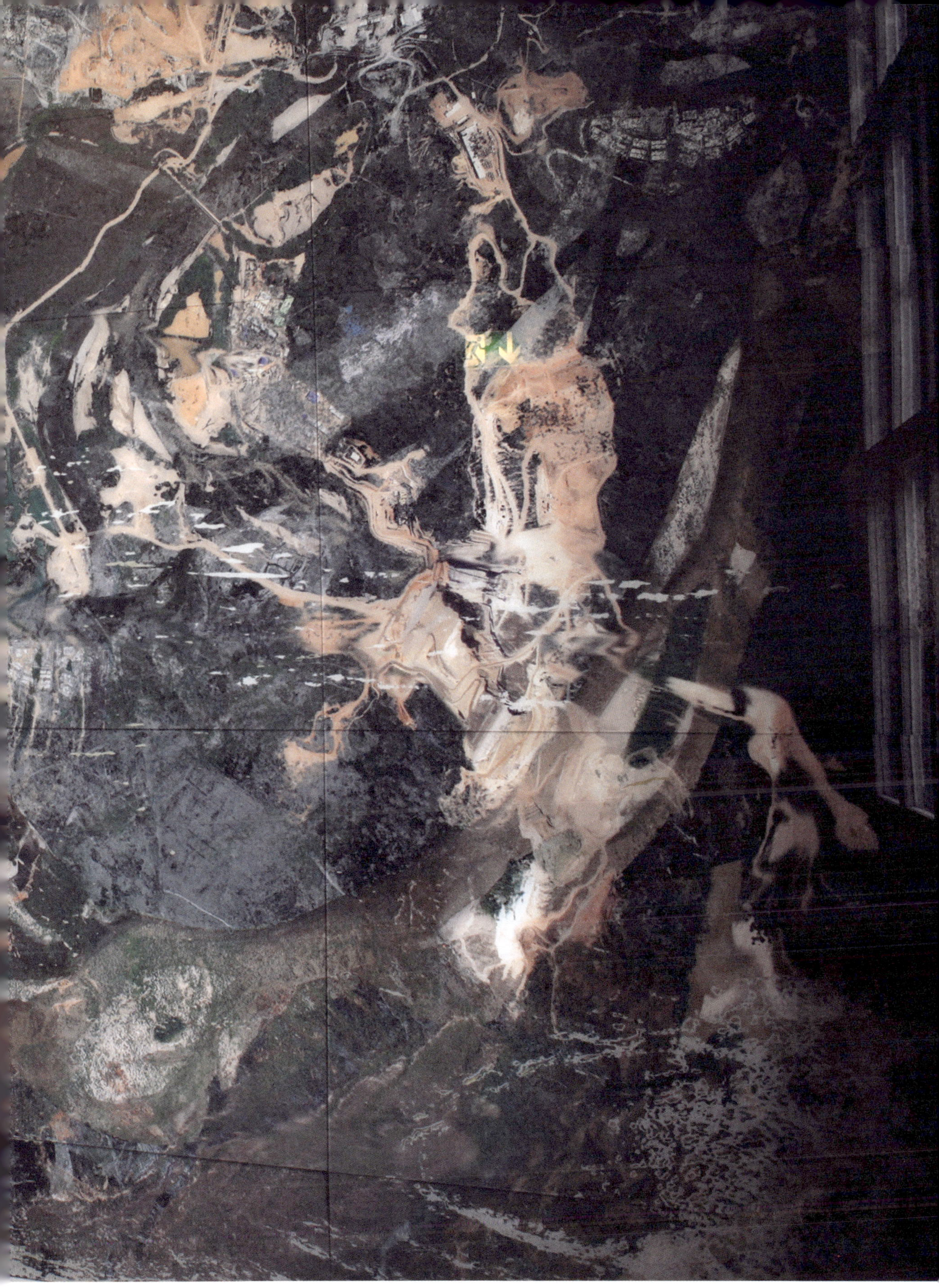

Installation view of 8th Berlin Biennale for Contemporary Art, Museen Dahlem, 2014. Work shown: *Yuma, or the Land of Friends*, 2014. Digital prints on glass, and satellite images; mural: 19 × 15 1/2 ft. (5.80 × 4.73 m).

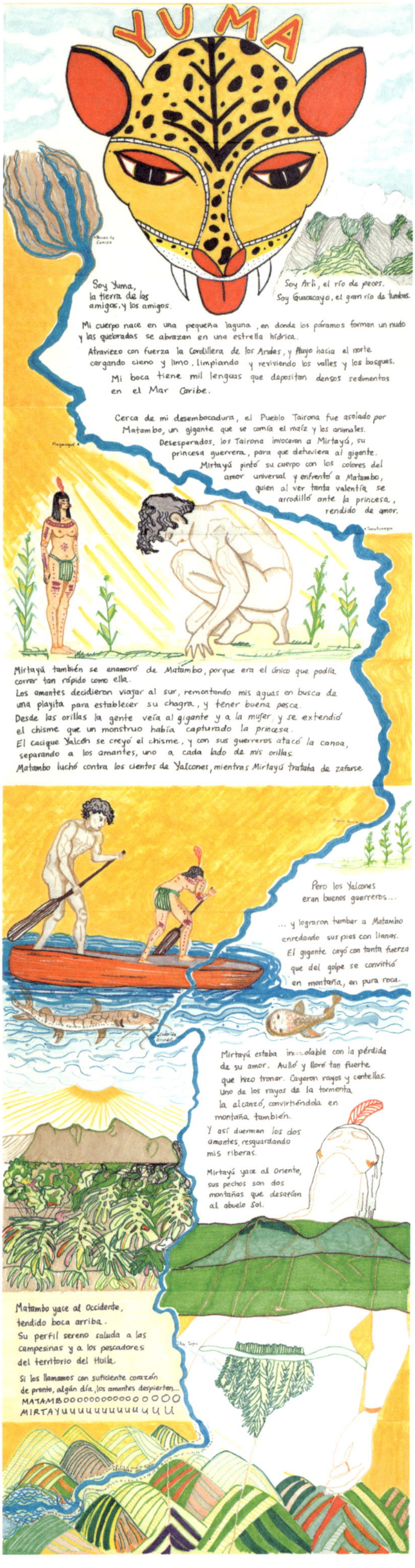

YUMA

Soy Yuma,
la tierra de las
amigas, y los amigos.

Soy Arli, el río de peces.
Soy Guacacayo, el gran río de tumbas.

Mi cuerpo nace en una pequeña laguna, en donde los páramos forman un nudo y las quebradas se abrazan en una estrella hídrica.

Atravieso con fuerza la Cordillera de los Andes, y fluyo hacia el norte cargando cieno y limo, limpiando y reviviendo los valles y los bosques.

Mi boca tiene mil lenguas que depositan densos sedimentos en el Mar Caribe.

Cerca de mi desembocadura, el Pueblo Tairona fue asolado por Matambo, un gigante que se comía el maíz y los animales.
Desesperados, los Tairona invocaron a Mirtayú, su princesa guerrera, para que detuviera al gigante.
Mirtayú pintó su cuerpo con los colores del amor universal y enfrentó a Matambo, quien al ver tanta valentía se arrodilló ante la princesa, rendido de amor.

Mirtayú también se enamoró de Matambo, porque era el único que podía correr tan rápido como ella.
Los amantes decidieron viajar al sur, remontando mis aguas en busca de una playita para establecer su chagra, y tener buena pesca.
Desde las orillas la gente veía al gigante y a la mujer, y se extendió el chisme que un monstruo había capturado la princesa.
El cacique Yalcón se creyó el chisme, y con sus guerreros atacó la canoa, separando a los amantes, uno a cada lado de mis orillas.
Matambo luchó contra los cientos de Yalcones, mientras Mirtayú trataba de zafarse

Pero los Yalcones
eran buenos guerreros...

... y lograron tumbar a Matambo enredando sus pies con lianas.
El gigante cayó con tanta fuerza que del golpe se convirtió en montaña, en pura roca.

Mirtayú estaba inconsolable con la pérdida de su amor. Aulló y lloró tan fuerte que hizo tronar. Cayeron rayos y centellas.
Uno de los rayos de la tormenta la alcanzó, convirtiéndola en montaña también.

Y así duermen los dos amantes, resguardando mis riberas.

Mirtayú yace al Oriente, sus pechos son dos montañas que desafían al abuelo Sol.

Matambo yace al Occidente, tendido boca arriba.
Su perfil sereno saluda a las campesinas y a los pescadores del territorio del Huila.

Si los llamamos con suficiente corazón de pronto, algún día, los amantes despierten...
MATAMBOOOOOOOOOOOOOOOO
MIRTAYUUUUUUUUUUUUUU

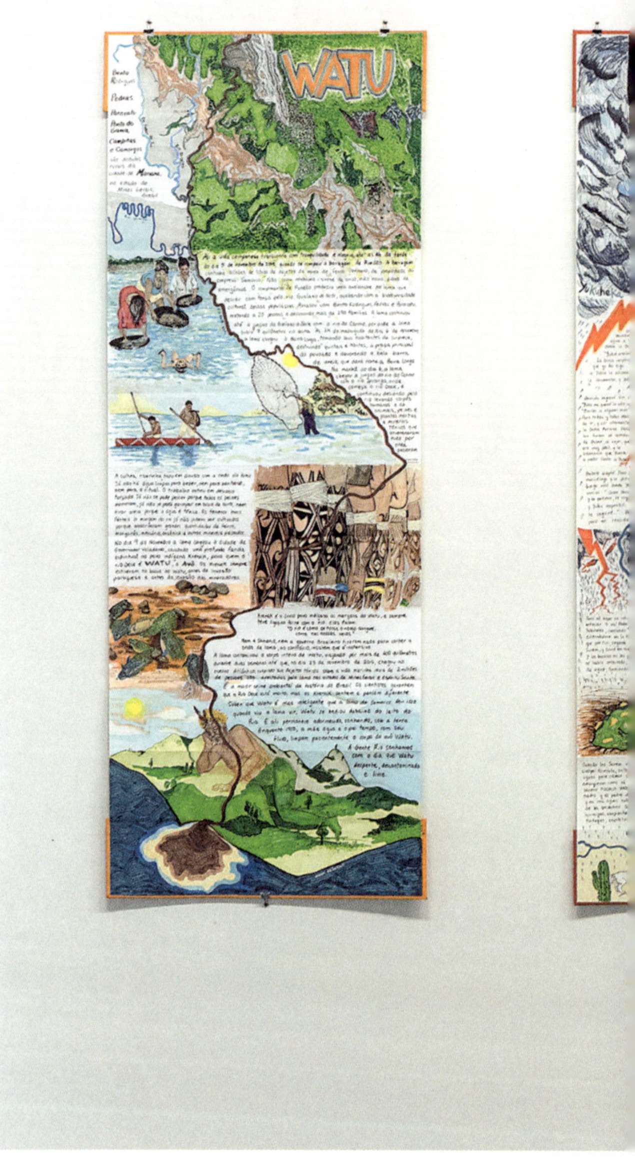

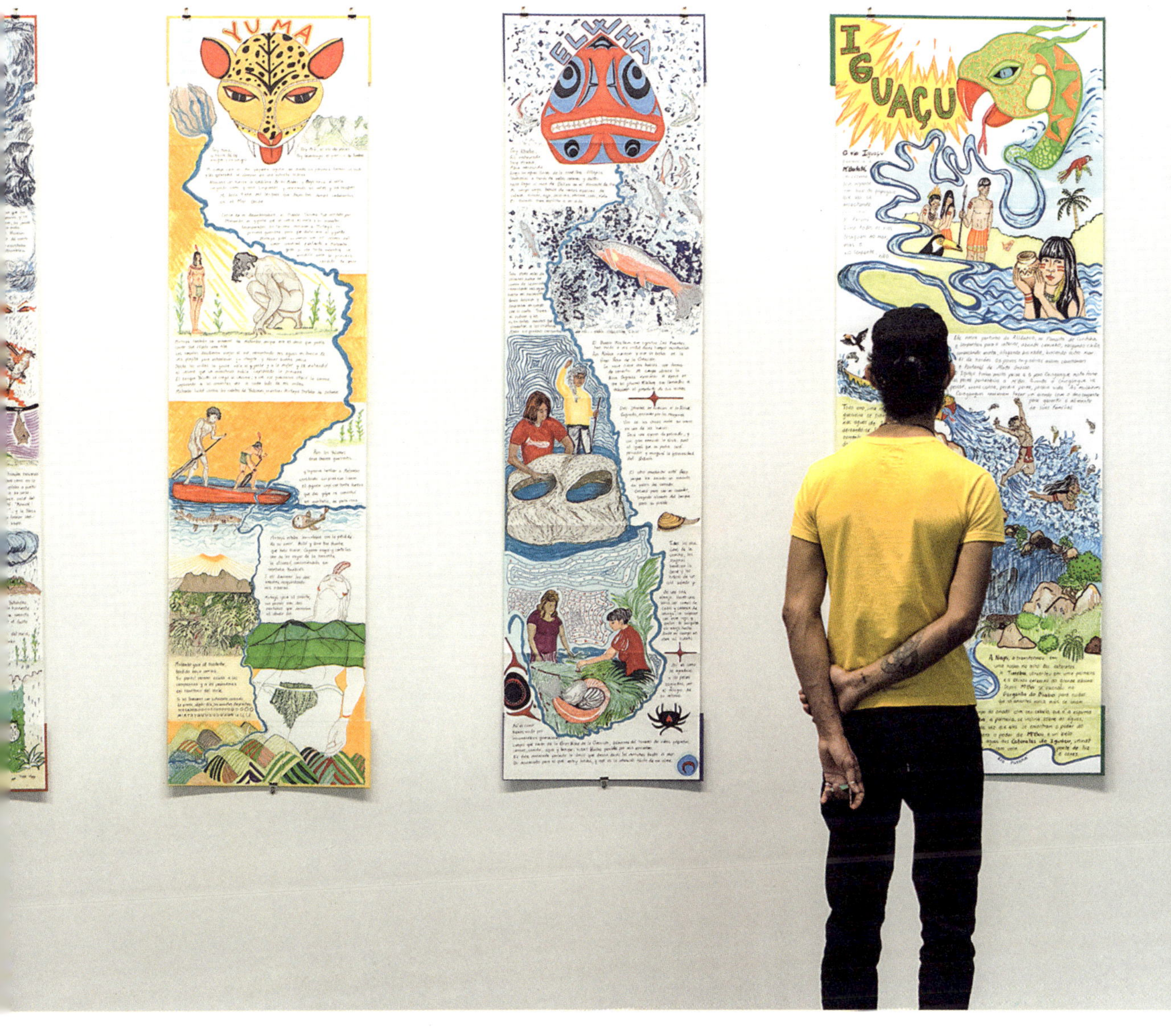

← *Yuma*, 2016, from the *River Book* series (2016–).

↑ Installation view of *Incerteza Viva (Live Uncertainty)*, 32nd Bienal de São Paulo, 2016. Works shown, from left to right: *Watu, Yaqui, Yuma, Elwha, and Iguaçu*, all 2016, from the *River Book* series (2016–). Marker on Canson paper; dimensions variable.

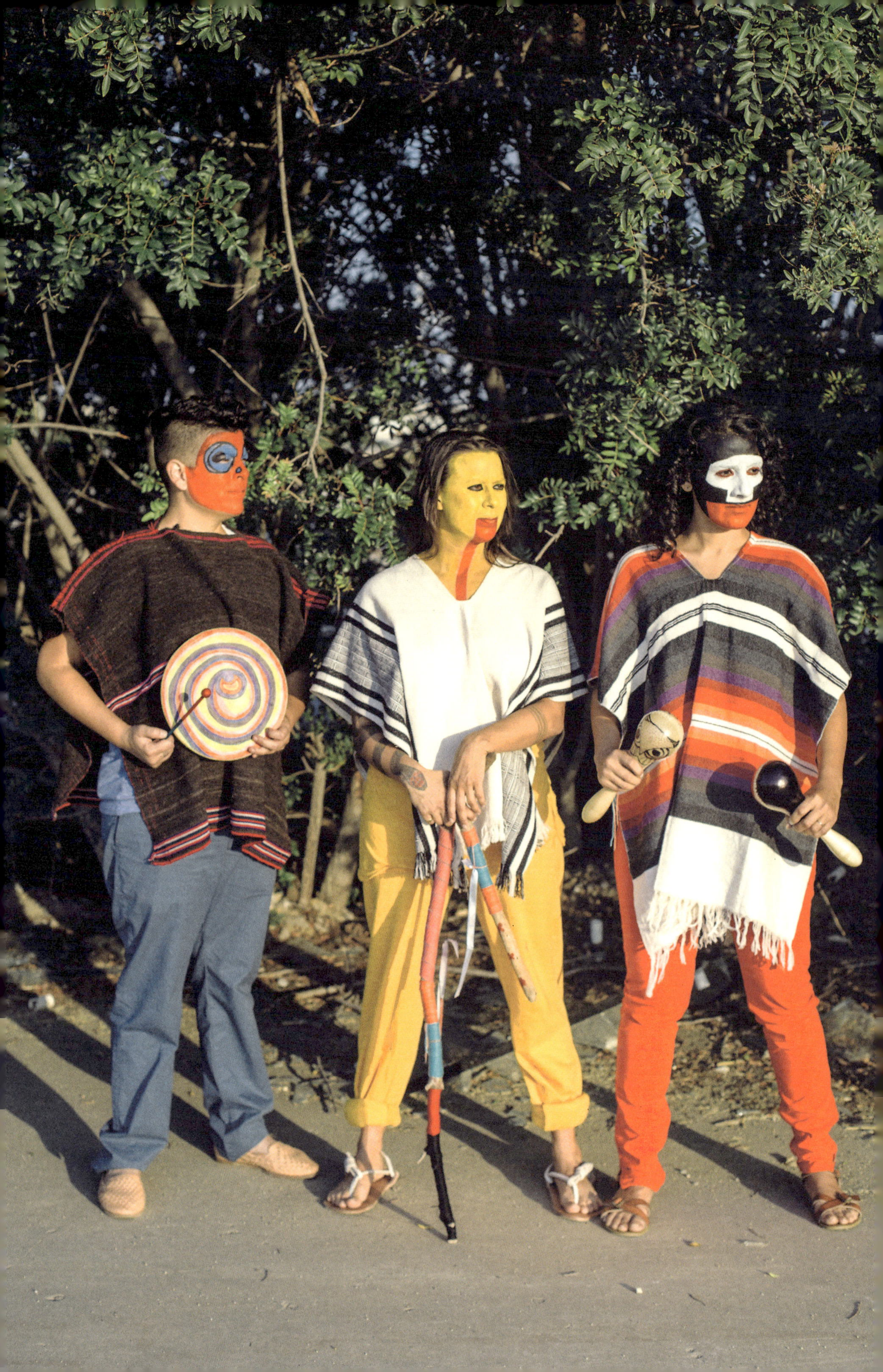

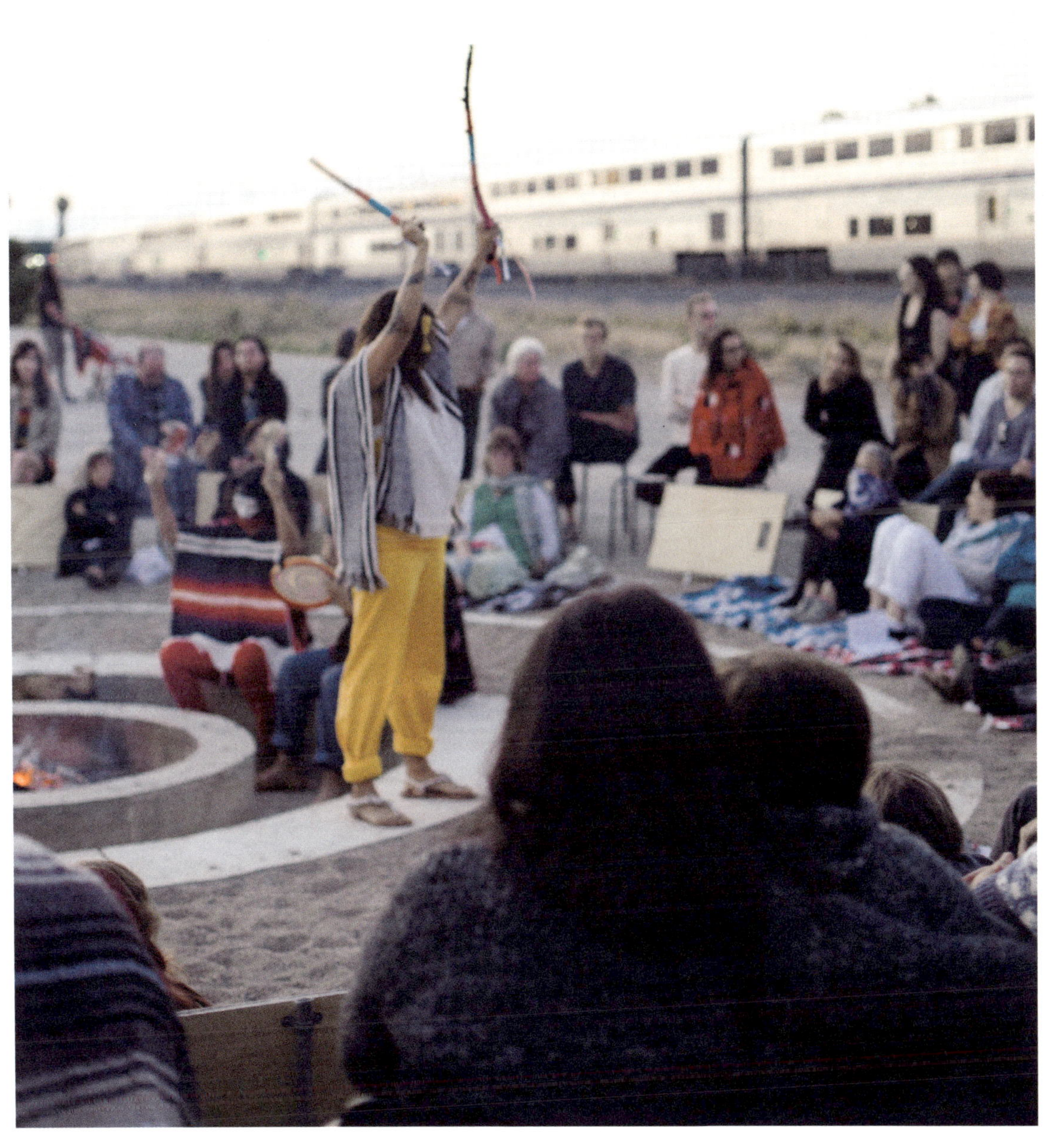

One Body of Water, 2015. Performance by: Karen Anzoategui, Carolina Caycedo, and Mireya Lucio. Writing Consultant/Editor: Brynn Saito.

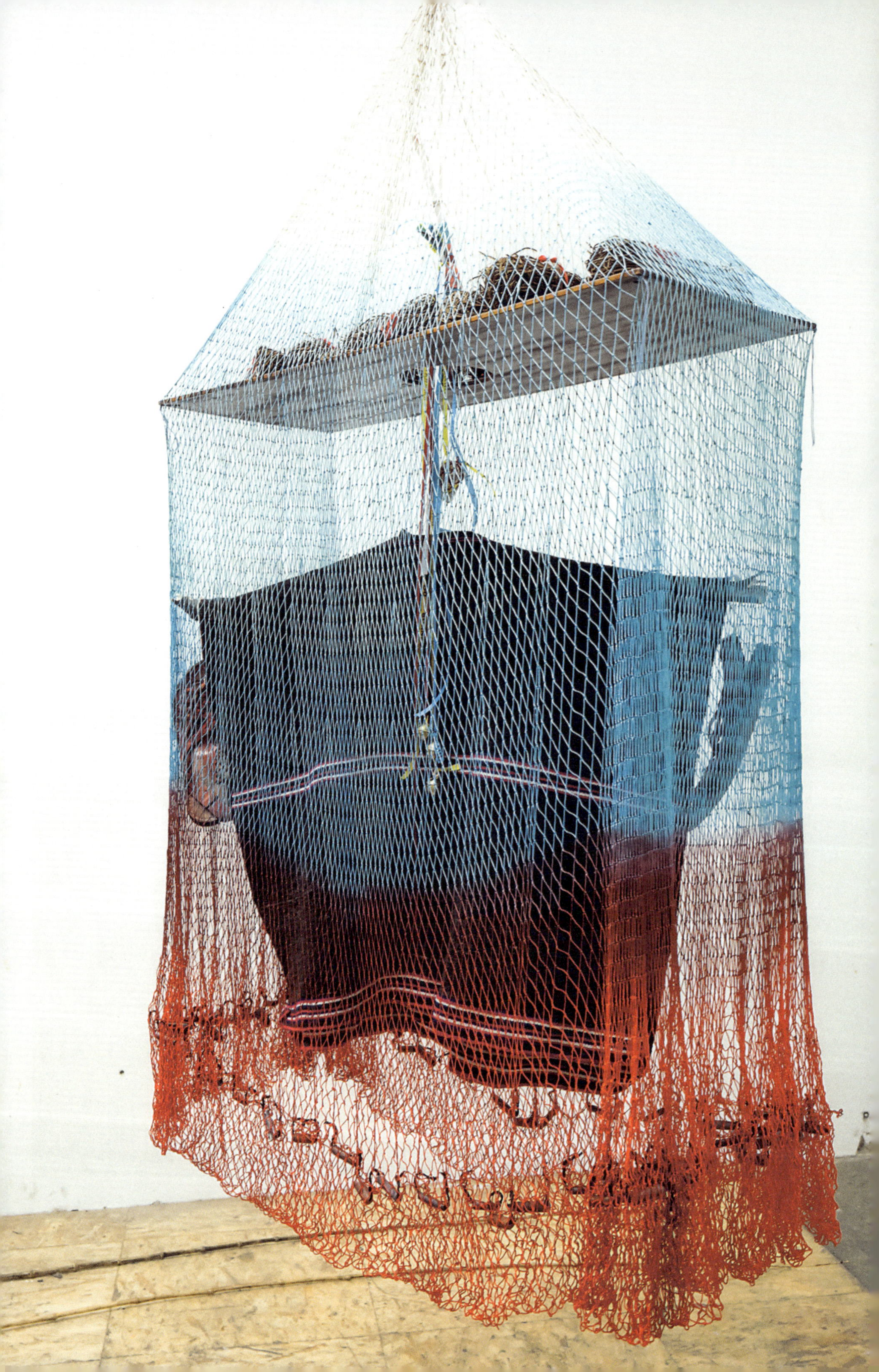

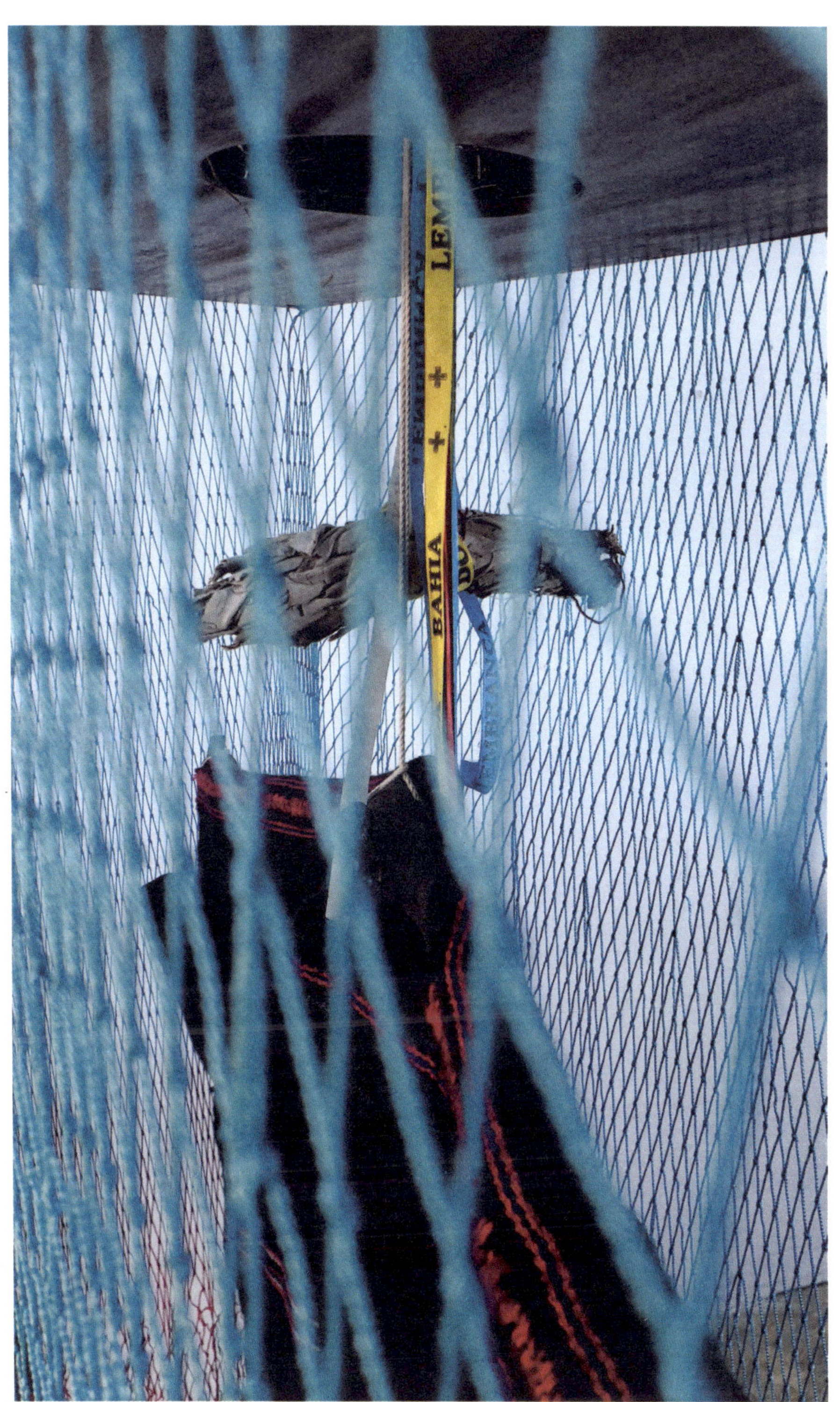

Cosmotarraya Elwha, 2016–20. Installation view in the artist's studio.

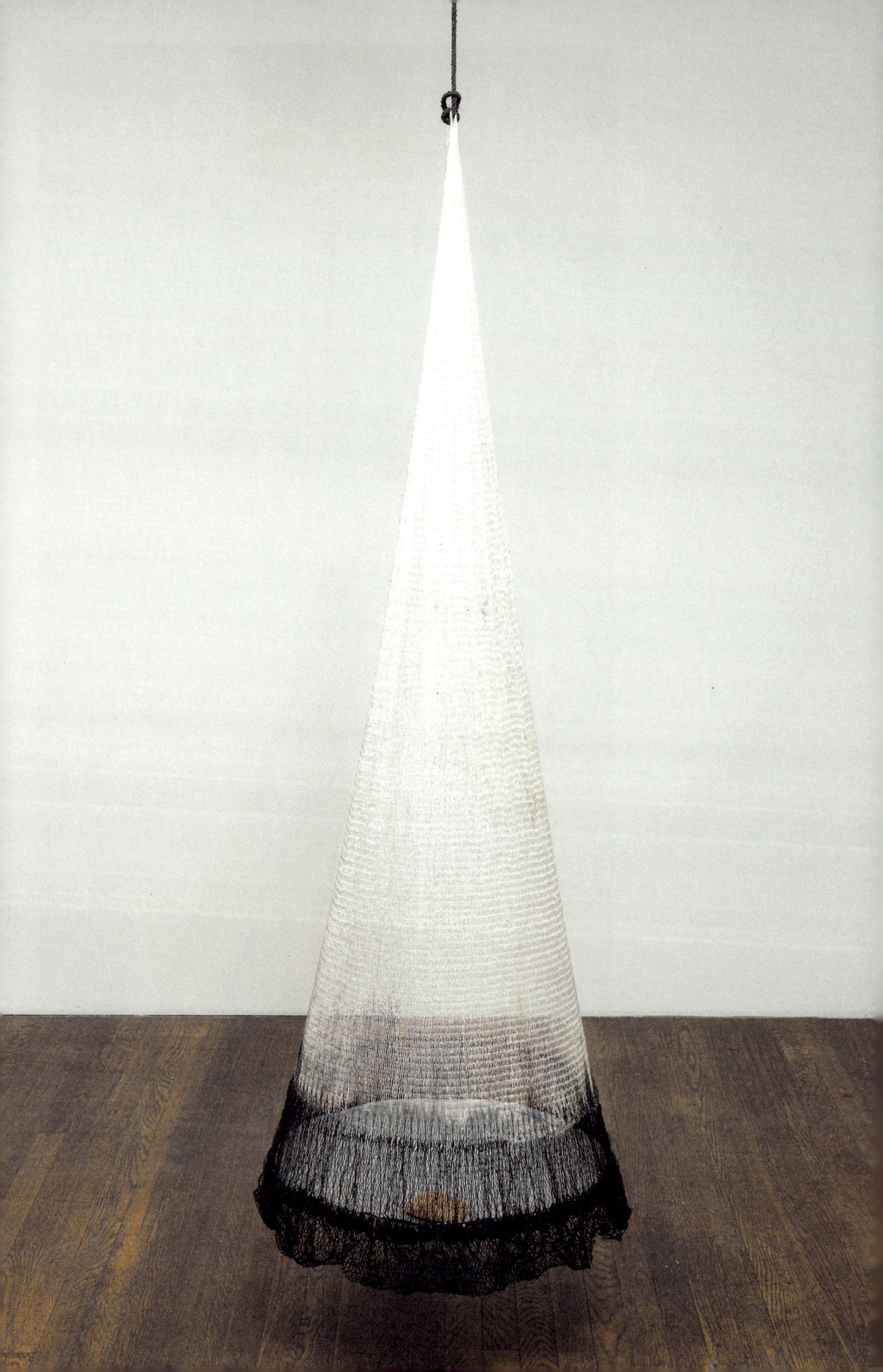

Installation views of *Carolina Caycedo: Hunger as Teacher / El Hambre Como Maestra*, Commonwealth and Council, Los Angeles, 2017. Work shown: *Undammed / Desbloqueada*, 2017.

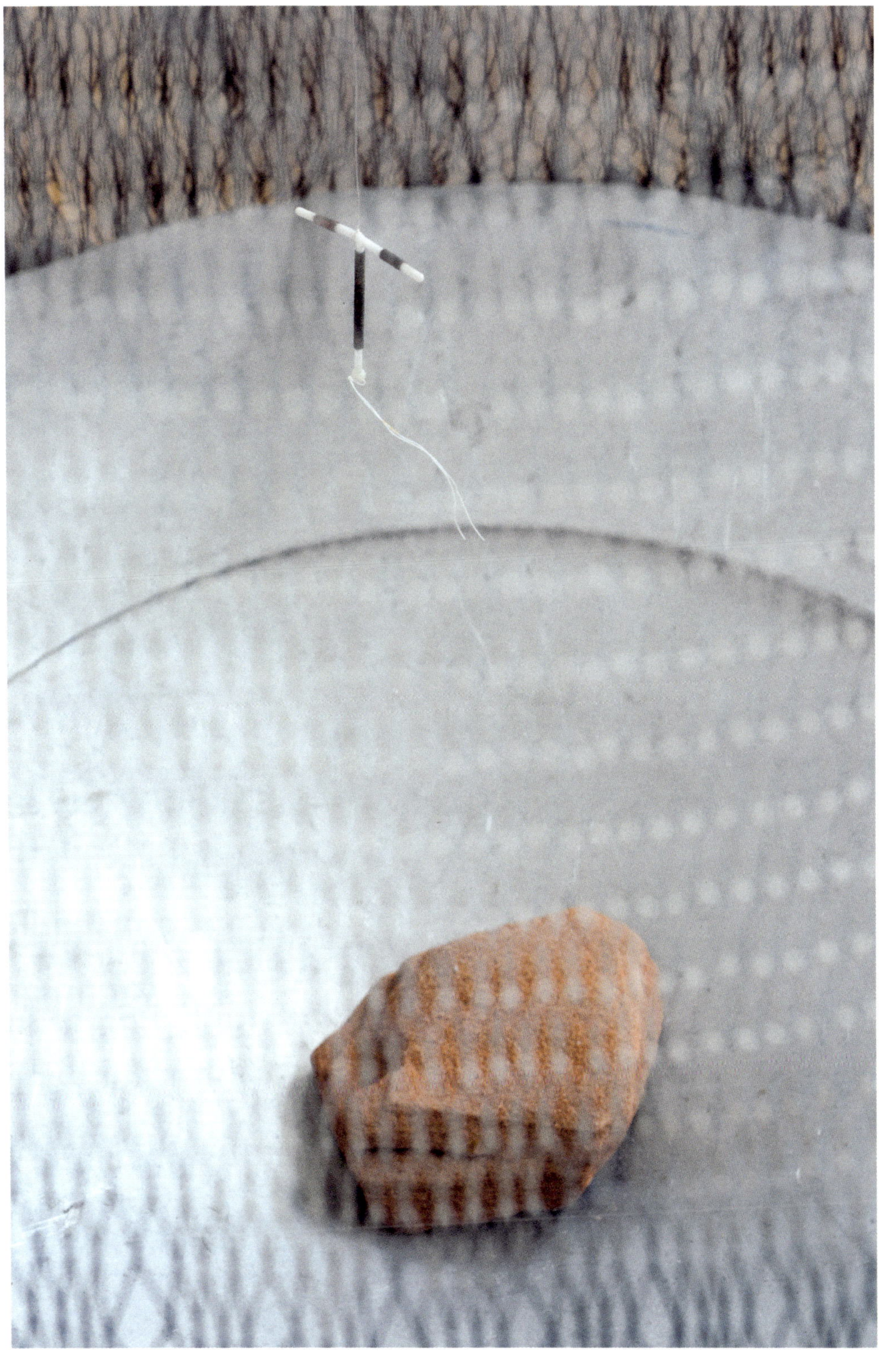

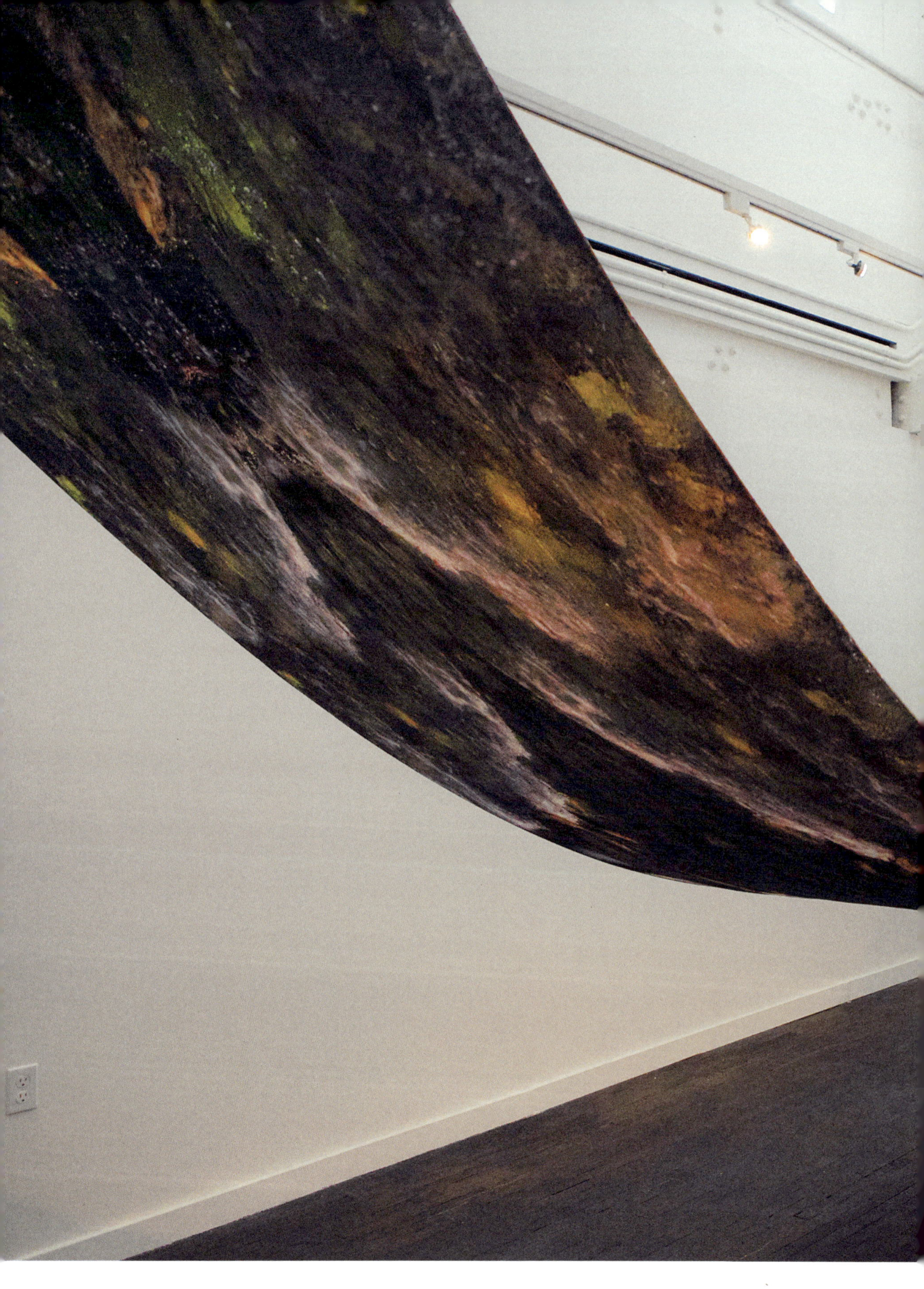

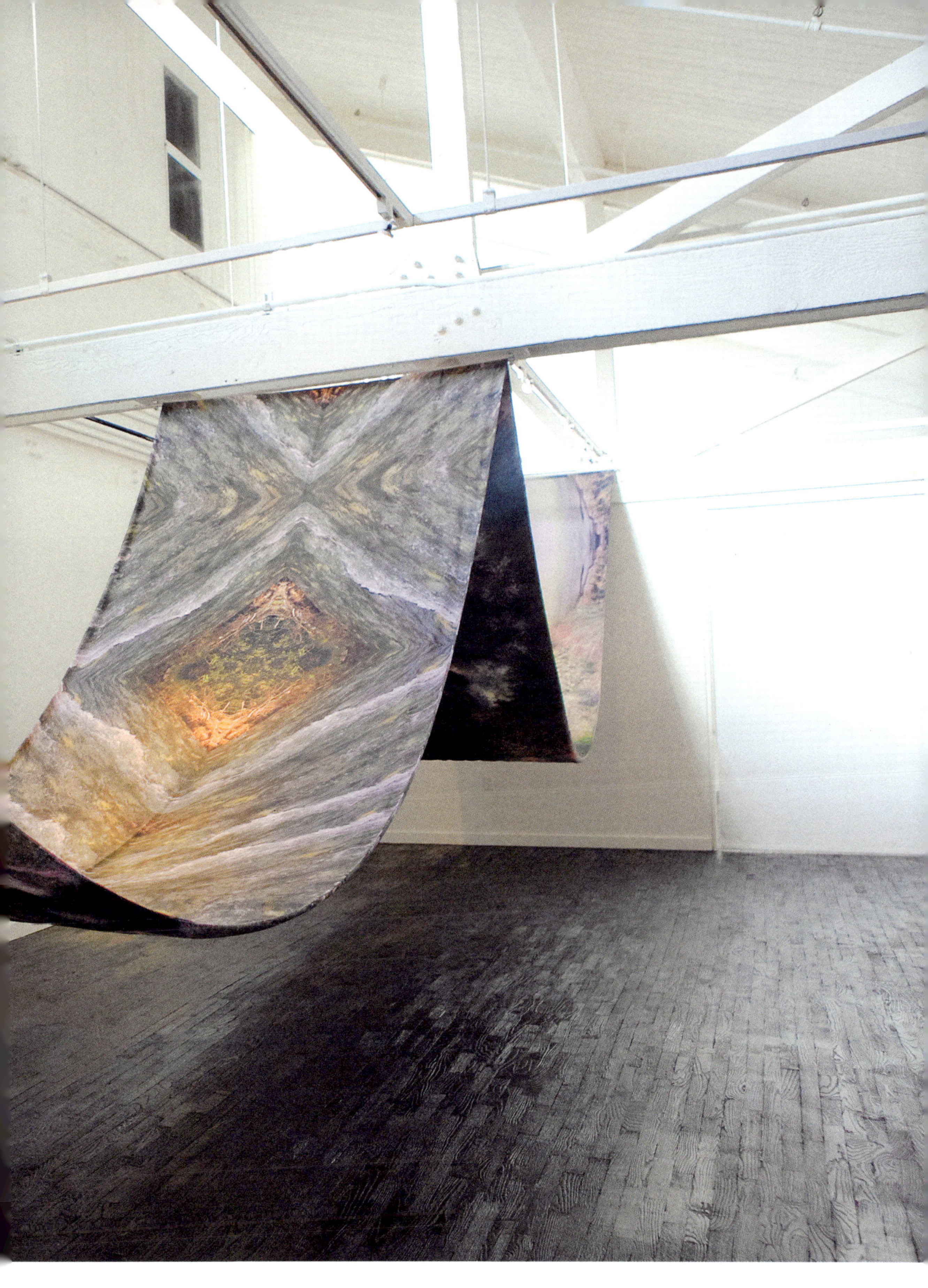

Installation view of *Carolina Caycedo: Wanaawna, Rio Hondo and Other Spirits*, Orange County Museum of Art, Santa Ana, CA, 2019–20. Work shown: *San Gabriel*, 2019.

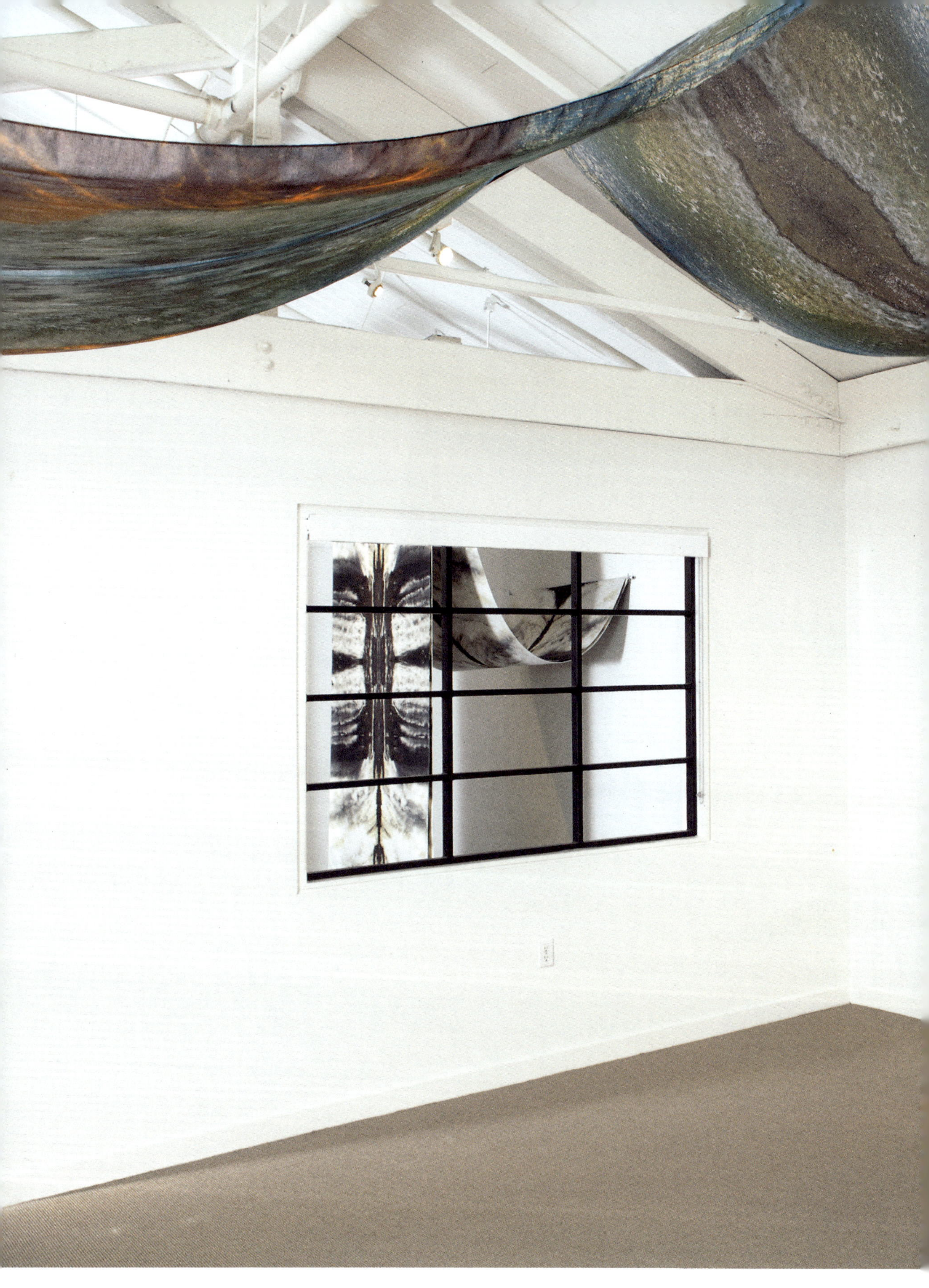

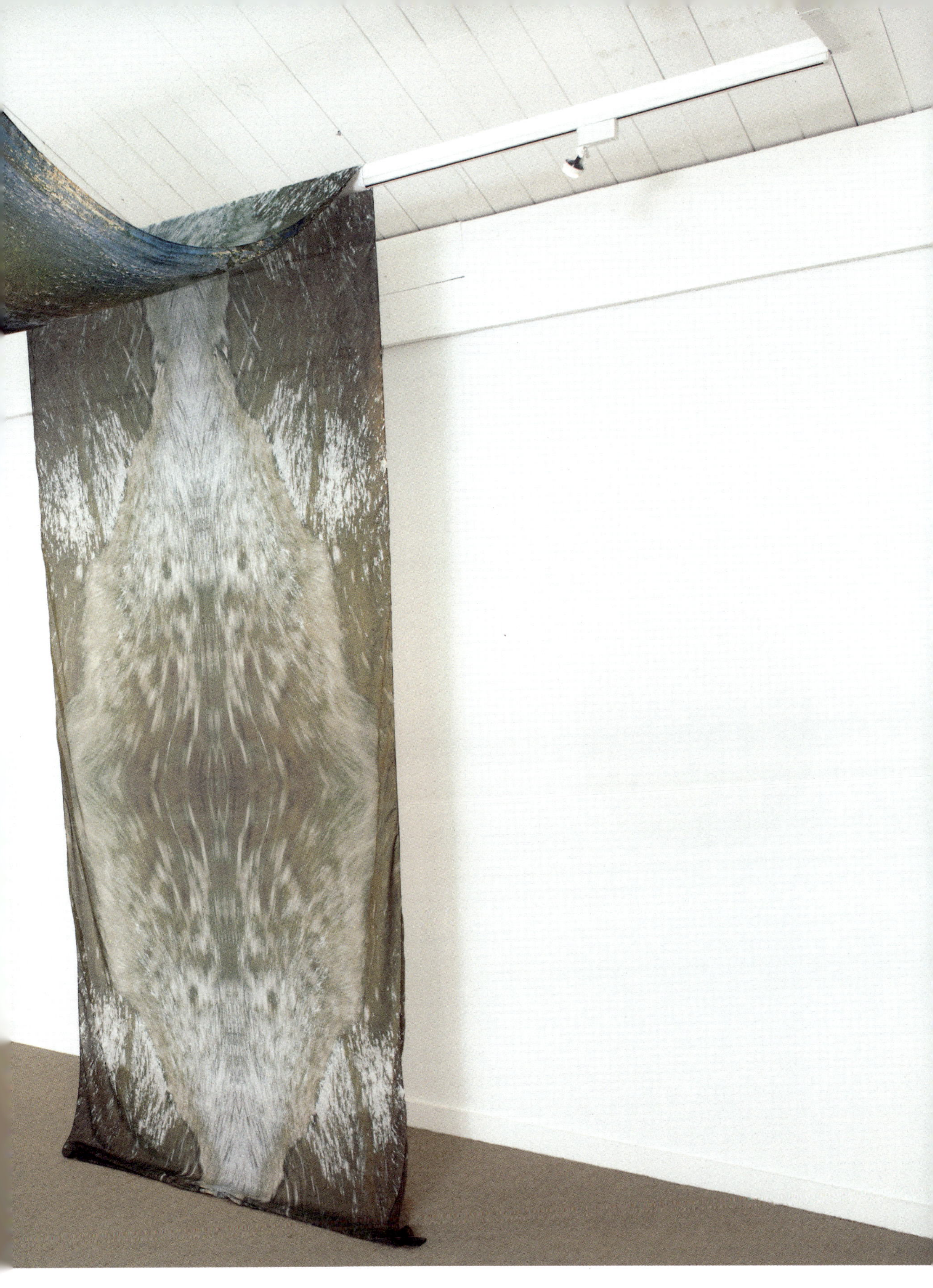

Installation view of *Carolina Caycedo: Wanaawna, Rio Hondo and Other Spirits*, Orange County Museum of Art, Santa Ana, CA, 2019–20. Work shown: *Wanaawna Meets Salty Waters*, 2019.

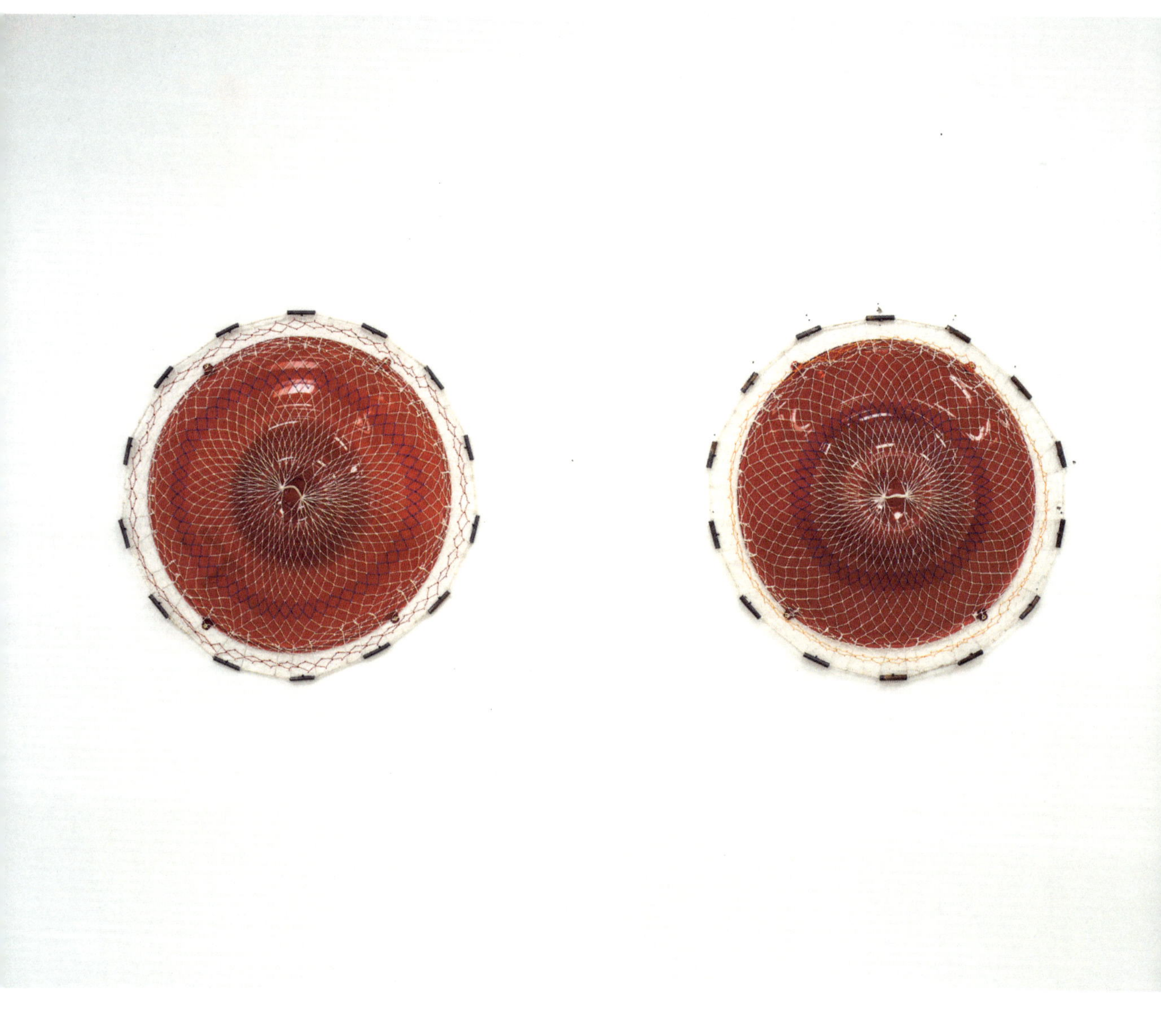

From the Bottom of the River/Desde el fondo del río III 2020, 2020.
Courtesy of the artist and Nada and Michael Gray.

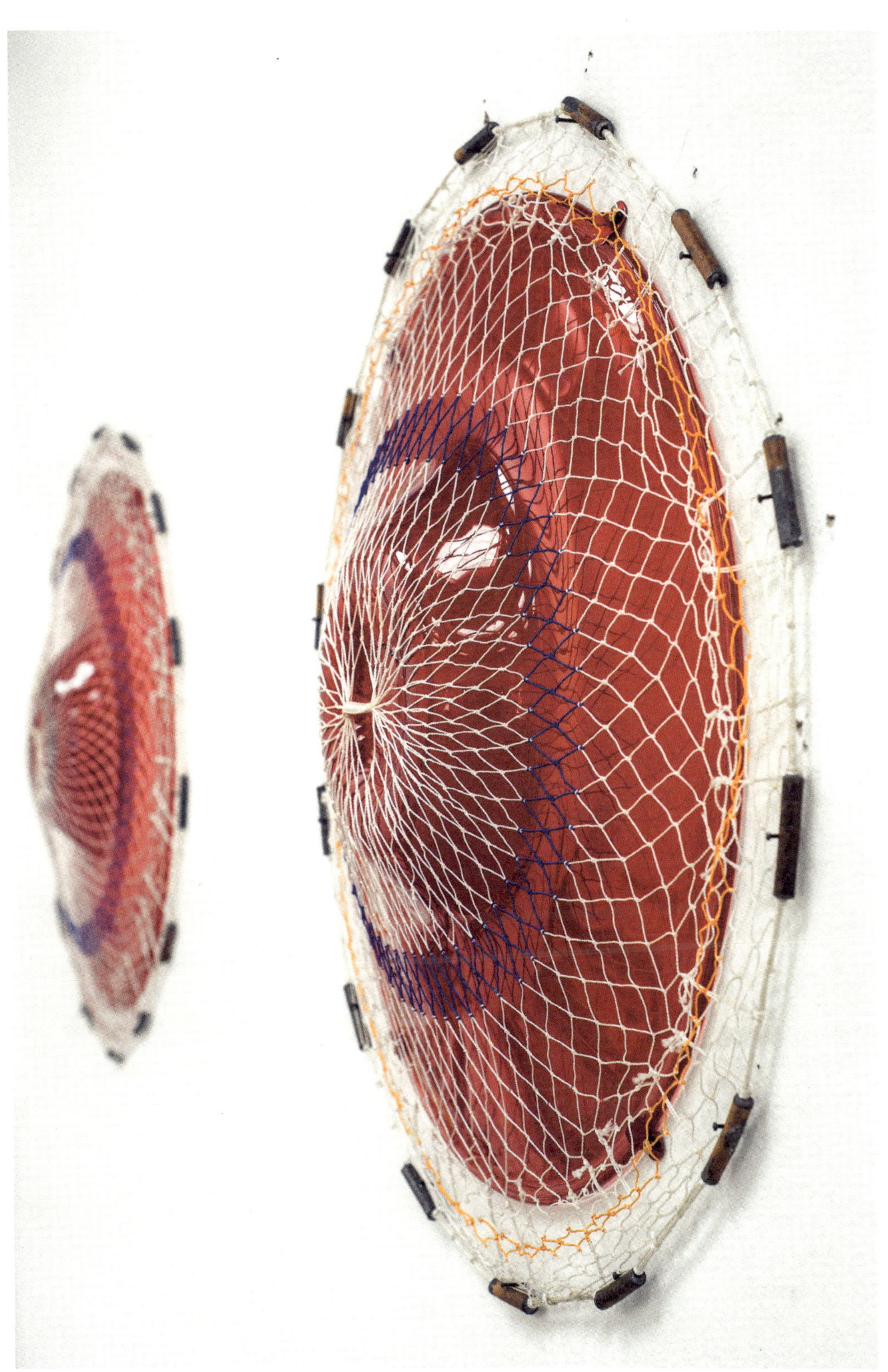

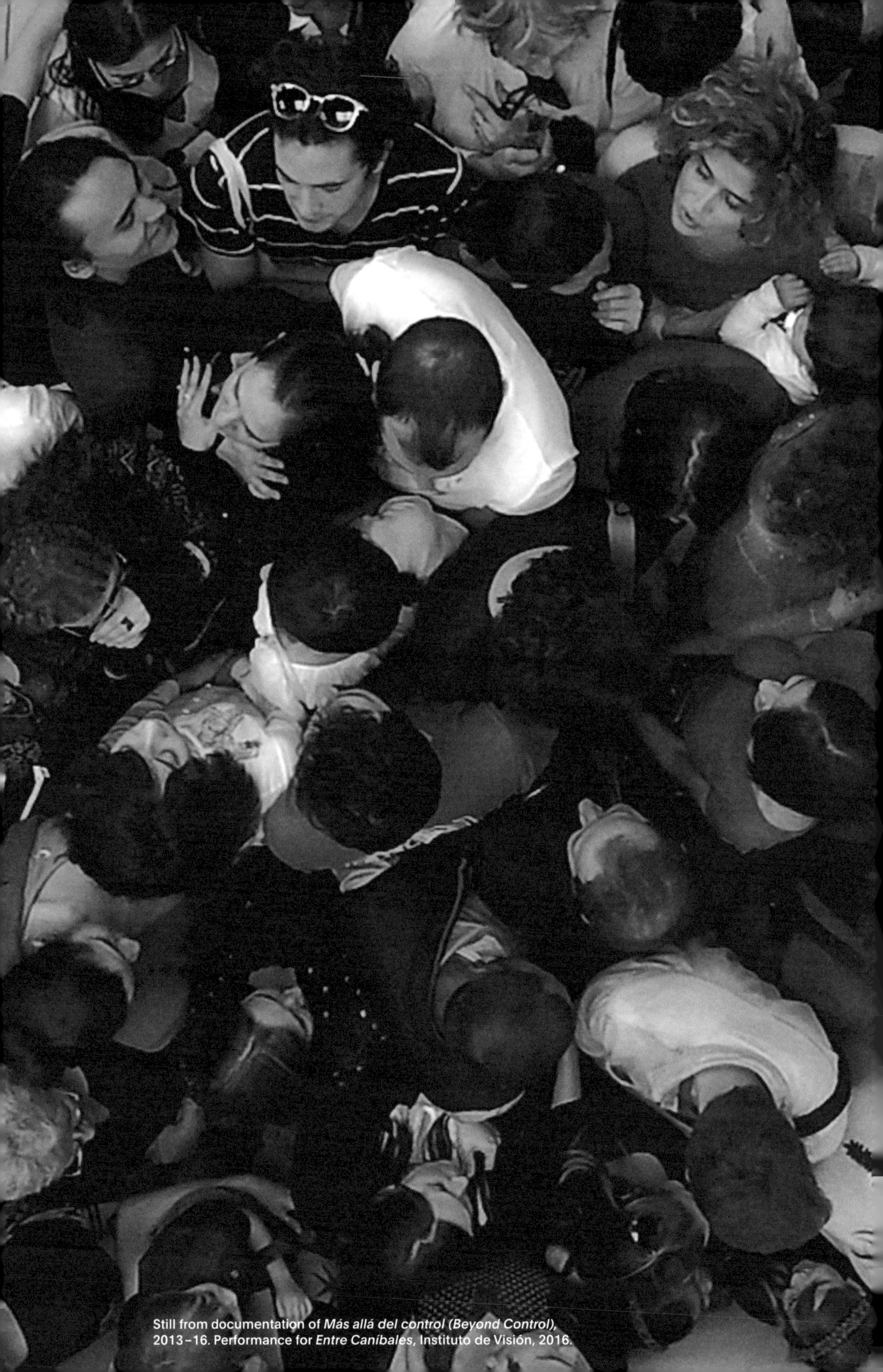

Still from documentation of *Más allá del control (Beyond Control)*, 2013–16. Performance for *Entre Caníbales*, Instituto de Visión, 2016.

Flow, Containment, Collectivity, and Resistance: The Geochoreographies of Carolina Caycedo

Flujo, contención, colectividad y resistencia: las Geocoreografías de Carolina Caycedo

Pilar Tompkins Rivas

During the opening reception of Caycedo's exhibition *Be Dammed* in November 2013, Caycedo and vocalist Karen Adelman broke the loud chatter of the event with a call and response to Mohana, a Colombian water deity of the Mami Wata tradition. Their voices carried over the crowd in the intimate gallery as a cluster of dancers grouped together to form a human arrow, which they used to bifurcate the guests. The dancers then broke their formation and flowed rapidly through the gallery, swishing with the force and movement of a river while Mohana was again invoked through a visceral call. Without forewarning, the performers quickly encircled the exhibition's guests, forming a cordon to physically press the attendees into a corner. Nervous laughter gave way to an awkward shuffling of bodies. Tension in the air rose and a slight claustrophobia set in. Caycedo held the group in this contained state almost until the point of panic. Then, she and Adelman called out, "Mohana! Mohana!"—summoning the spirit of the water goddess—before transitioning their hands from positions of restraint to calming touches on the shoulder. Everyone in the group took a shared breath. Nervousness subsided into calm, and the configuration of bodies was released slowly back into the room (fig. 1).

First performed within the context of an art gallery and later on the beach of the Los Angeles River basin, *Beyond Control* was not only an early performance within Caycedo's larger project *Be Dammed,* it also laid the foundation for what would ultimately become her *Geochoreographies*. Caycedo has long focused her attention on forms of art making that support communities as well as those that formulate new and inventive networks of belonging and care. With *Geochoreographies,* Caycedo takes these modes of art making and merges them into mobile acts of resistance, bringing objects, performers, and environments together in opposition to national and corporate controls. As performers, objects, and meanings coalesce around a specific choreography, the human form becomes a site of political agency, where the relationship of body and landscape is reinforced, and the cultural and spiritual memory of a territory and its people is fortified. With *Beyond Control,* Caycedo began highlighting the possibility of resistance through a kind of collective movement and call-to-action, juxtaposing crowd control strategies and military methods of tactical restraint, which she refers to as "choreographies of power," with a spiritual invocation. The movements of the performers mirrored the forms of containment imposed on free-flowing bodies of water while the call to Mohana offered a kind of release from that very constraint. These actions, although removed from the specific landscapes represented in her other works, highlighted the ideas and gestures that would become central to Caycedo's far-reaching and critical project.

While *Beyond Control* saw Caycedo speak to complex issues through collaborative means, it wasn't until the artist began working with collectives in Colombia—specifically those engaged in immediate forms of resistance to El Quimbo Dam—that she started conceptualizing transdisciplinary approaches to support and engage the communities in crisis.[1] In 2014, the artist spent six months living and working with four communities directly affected by the development of El Quimbo Dam. It was during this period that Caycedo's *Geochoreographies* began taking shape and developing their own definition as she refocused her performance-based *Be Dammed* works to center around community-driven processes. Working with the Jaguos Por El Territorio Collective, Caycedo facilitated a series of movement-based workshops that explored

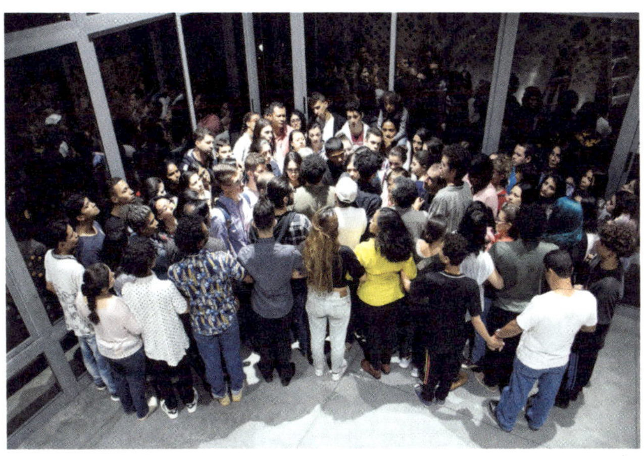

1 *Más allá del control (Beyond Control),* 2013–19. Performance for the exhibition *PASADO TIEMPO FUTURO. Arte en Colombia en el siglo XXI,* Museo de Arte Moderno de Medellín (MAMM), 2019.

circus, dance, performance, puppetry, theater, and video.[2] Although the elements of Caycedo's earlier performance were still visible, these *Geochoreographies* involved more complex negotiations between the landscape and the body. Expanded to include established community resistance techniques forwarded by the pedagogies of Paulo Freire and rooted in engagement practices found in Augusto Boal's Theater of the Oppressed, Caycedo and her collaborators focused on awareness-building and recognizing imbalances of power, leading exercises that stimulated dialogue through movements, words, and actions. For instance, participants would hold hands to form *caracols*—coiled and spiral-like snail shapes—to link their bodies in space (fig. 2). They also formed snaking lines, moving in unison through the shallow waters of the river, and created large puppet masks attached to fishing nets to march through rural and urban settings.

These actions centered around the notion that everyday gestures are expressions of knowledge and culture and constitute an archive of shared memory and corporeal language. The action of casting a fishing net, for instance, is more than throwing open an *atarraya,* as they are known in Colombia. Rather, the gesture itself is a physical expression of resistance against the threat of corporate, political, and military power and represents an embodied form of knowledge indicative of sustainable fishing practices passed down through generations. Caycedo refers to these forms as "everyday *geochoreographies*"—gestures and methods that inform the larger, more performative and organized actions that make up her *Geochoreographies.* In the artist's words, "A *geochoreography* aesthetically imprints a living image on the landscape, producing an expansive notion of the body and its location. Expanding the body helps to avert fear, and to counter physical and psychological displacement…Everyday *geochoreographies* humanize the landscape, countering the dehumanizing effects of the dam.[3] The actions developed and practiced during these workshops, understood simultaneously as methodologies and epistemologies, can move freely between the various forms of Caycedo's art practice and as such represent tools that can be implemented across both local and international contexts. They traverse languages of daily movement, inform mobilized acts of resistance, are a kind of visual art unto themselves, and are expressions of a political process. In this way, *Geochoreographies* allow for a flow between the daily acts of memory and resistance and the philosophic and aesthetic principles guiding Caycedo's art.

In 2015, Caycedo returned to Colombia to work with participants of the 2014 workshops, specifically with members of the Paraguay village within the municipality of Oporapa—the site of one of the dams of the master plan for the Magdalena River—to develop an action in support of their constitutional political process to challenge extractivist projects.[4] Developed collaboratively with the community members and environmental activist groups Descolonizando La Jagua and Ríos Vivos Colombia, *Geochoreography Oritoguaz* (2015) saw participants use their own bodies to spell out their opposition to the invasive mechanisms of the state, thus underscoring the body as a political tool and as an extension of the land itself. With their figures, the collective wrote the words *Ríos Vivos* ("Living Rivers") and *Yuma Resiste* ("Yuma Resist") to mark their presence in defense of the land before its flooding by the Oporapa Dam (fig. 3). Through collective action, this iteration of Caycedo's *Geochoreographies* saw community members actualize an elemental aspect of how Caycedo has come to define these works; specifically, how participants expanded their forms to communicate a shared language of resistance. With their image and their voice imprinted on the territory, they were, as Caycedo suggests, "humanizing the landscape." While documented by video, aerial photography, and existing within a shared space of memory and experience, this group action was not contained within the realm of performance art, but instead existed somewhere between activism and art, emphasizing the expansive possibilities inherent to the human form.

As Caycedo began translating this series from the Magdalena River to other parts of the globe, she started using objects as tools of engagement and pedagogy. From her use of *atarraya* fishing nets to her *Water Portraits* series, Caycedo embraced the multiple roles these types of objects served and continue to serve; they are instruments for discussion, devices for performers and the public to activate, as well as independent artworks. Her *Serpent River Book* (2017), for instance, is not only an art object and a teaching tool, it is also intended to be worn by participants in *Geochoreographies,* draped over shoulders as they carry the unfolding book throughout a space (fig. 4). Like most of her objects, Caycedo intended the book to be used in different capacities, allowing for multiple points of engagement and multiple narratives. Although distinct in certain ways, this mutable quality is reminiscent of the Brazilian Neo-Concrete movement, which Caycedo has often cited as inspiration for her practice.

The Neo-Concrete artists, in particular Hélio Oiticica and Lygia Pape, advocated for a symbiotic space where the poetic could interact with and exist alongside the political.[5] Art forms such as paintings and sculptures were deconstructed, reinvented, and engaged by the viewer. Oiticica's *Parangolés* (1964) are exemplars of this tradition (fig. 5). These multi-colored capes functioned as wearable paintings, activated through the movements of the people who wore them.[6] Sometimes embroidered with hidden words, these purposefully cheap and vibrant materials would enliven the environment of the wearer and bring a vision of Oiticica's art to a public that was otherwise constrained and controlled by the fixed systems of the world. Similarly, Lygia Pape used art objects as a way to unify people and create a collective experience outside of the normal social order. Her seminal work *Divisor* (1968), for example, consisted of a massive piece of white fabric with numerous holes for the heads of participants to poke through (fig. 6). As they draped the fabric over themselves, the space between spectator and artwork dissolved, creating a shared social body. Oiticica described the piece as not being rooted in "aesthetic novelties or curious 'artistic' developments," but rather, "proposing transformations in a repressive world."[7]

In her *Geochoreographies,* Caycedo incorporates *atarrayas* and the fabric of her water portraits in much the same way as these Neo-Concrete forms were used. During *Geochoreographies* in art spaces and museums that introduce diverse audiences to the central issues of her work, as seen in *Atarrayas* (2015–17, presented in Bogotá, Caracas, and Medellín; p. 12) and *Sankofa* (2019, presented in Berlin), Caycedo often employs a fishing net to physically connect participants to each other. Stretched between the hands of workshop participants, the nets become catalysts for discussing symbolic and physical networks, such as those proposed by Indigenous cosmologies or the earth's intricate water systems. Even in some of Caycedo's earlier pieces, including *Resiste* (2009) and *Mujeres en Mi* (2010; pp. 88–89), evidence of Oiticica and Pape's influence is quite clear.[8] Both works are meant to hang as sculptures or be worn by one or more people, and like the work of Caycedo's predecessors, they are meant to foster connections between individuals to stimulate notions of solidarity, collectivity, and resistance to repression. What's more,

Caycedo is building on these art historical traditions by allowing these objects to communicate the experiences tied to and emanating from specific places with audiences existing outside those sites, bringing what were previously hyper-local *Geochoreographies* into a much broader context.

Of course, Caycedo builds on these traditions in more ways than one. Neo-Concrete Art, and the lineages it stems from such as Concrete Art and Constructivism, carried implicit political tones that were often in direct reaction to the social and political climate of the time. Caycedo's work can be regarded as similarly reactive, but at the same time her practice is not explicitly tied to the present, nor is it exclusively future-oriented. Like other works in Caycedo's oeuvre, her *Geochoreographies* can also take on the valence of recuperation, particularly in the way of lost, overlooked, or damaged histories. In addition to advocacy for the present and future, these works create spaces, movements, and objects wherein the memories of lives and movements lost can be recovered and preserved. Nowhere is this more evident than in the video work *Apariciones / Apparitions* (2018), in which Caycedo contends with the erasures that have resulted through the processes and legacies of colonialism (pp. 98–99). Structured around a *geochoreography* that moves throughout the Huntington in San Marino, California, the piece

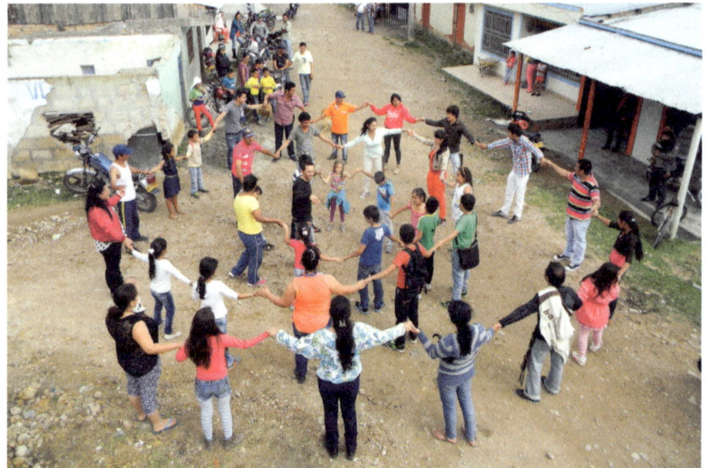

2 Performance view, *Geocoreografías Oporapa*, 2014. Collective action.

reconceptualizes spaces within the institution's gardens, library, and museum by performing African and Indigenous spiritual and dance practices. Commissioned as part of a collaboration between the Huntington and the Vincent Price Art Museum at East Los Angeles College, Caycedo's *geochoreography* functions to brown and queer the historically white spaces of the Huntington and implements decolonizing strategies to make bodies of color and non-binary bodies visible.

The institution, established by railroad magnate Henry Huntington in 1919, was built in the San Gabriel River basin, a territory and watershed the Tongva people and their ancestors have inhabited for thousands of years. For the performance itself, Caycedo worked with dancer, educator, and choreographer Marina Osthoff Magalhães to develop gestures inspired by the Candomblé religion and the goddess Oxúm, a deity of water, pleasure, fertility, and sexuality. While enacting these gestures—which included rituals of labor such as tilling land, washing gold in a river, or shaking the entire body (as when a deity, or *orixá*, mounts a mortal)—black, brown, and queer dancers, dressed in Oxúm's signature color of deep gold, inhabited the institution's spaces in evocative, unconventional ways, recapturing the museum's grounds and collections as sites for ritual, enjoyment, and divination. Caycedo also used *atarrayas* within this work as performative and symbolic tools. As dancers draped their bodies with the nets or folded together in embraces underneath them, a link was drawn between the historical utility of the object and the decolonizing acts being performed. The video also interweaves historic images of Indigenous groups native to California to speak to the legacies of colonized territories. Informed by the Aymara aphorism "Qhip nayr uñtasis sarnaqapxañani," which roughly translates to "looking back to walk forth," Caycedo's work introduces a present in which the past refuses to be silenced.

Through collaboration, research, activism, and movement-based practices, Caycedo's *Geochoreographies* traverse the complex and interconnected forms of political, physical, and psychological struggles impacting regions affected by corporate and state subjugation. *Geochoreographies* couple landscape and the human form, operate within activist and community-centered platforms, and foreground critical struggles affecting rural, native communities on local levels and the impact those territories have on the world we live in. Across the many sites that these works unfold, Caycedo engages with a history of performance art, including the genealogies of Neo-Concrete participatory objects and actions, while at the same time expanding beyond this contemporary framework to incorporate a repertoire of diverse forms of embodied knowledge that often derive from humankind's relationship to nature and geography. The contexts in which her *Geochoreographies* are enacted—either at contested sites or within the realm of international art spaces—are opportunities to address globally urgent issues of ecology, the divestment of neoliberal practices that threaten land and people, and to foreground Indigenous political positions and alternative methods for sustainable living. Here, we find an artistic practice that not only expands the canon of art but does so in a way that bridges the ancestral and the contemporary with movements and gestures that form in resistance to the damaging and complicit powers of our world.

Durante la inauguración de la exposición *Be Dammed (Represa/Represión)* en noviembre de 2013, Caycedo y la cantante Karen Adelman interrumpieron el fuerte murmullo del evento con un llamado y respuesta a Mohana, deidad colombiana del agua proveniente de la tradición Mami Wata. Sus voces resonaron sobre la multitud en la intimidad de la galería a la vez que los bailarines se agruparon para formar una flecha humana, que usaron para bifurcar a los invitados. Los bailarines luego rompieron su formación y fluyeron rápidamente por la galería, avanzando con la fuerza y el movimiento susurrante de un río mientras se volvía a invocar a Mohana con un canto visceral. Sin previo aviso, los intérpretes rodearon rápidamente a los invitados de la exposición, formando una hilera para apretujarlos contra un rincón. La risa nerviosa dio lugar a una incómoda reorganización de los cuerpos. El ambiente se puso más tenso y una ligera sensación de claustrofobia se apoderó de los presentes. Caycedo mantuvo al grupo en este estado de contención casi hasta cundir el pánico. Luego, ella y Adelman gritaron: "¡Mohana! ¡Mohana!", invocando el espíritu de la diosa del agua antes de que sus manos pasaran de sostener posiciones restrictivas a dar tranquilizadoras palmaditas en el hombro. Todos respiraron hondo a la vez. El nerviosismo dio paso a la calma, y la configuración de los cuerpos fue poco a poco devuelta al resto de la sala (fig. 1).

Interpretada primero en el contexto de una galería de arte y, más tarde, en una playa de la cuenca del río Los Ángeles, la performance *Beyond Control (Más allá del control)* no solo fue una de las primeras en formar parte del proyecto más amplio de Caycedo, *Represa/Represión*, sino que además sentó las bases de lo que terminaría por convertirse en sus *Geochoreographies (Geocoreografías)*. Caycedo lleva mucho tiempo dedicada a formas de creación artística que apoyan a diversas comunidades, además de aquellas que formulan nuevas e ingeniosas redes de pertenencia y cuidado. Con *Geocoreografías*, Caycedo toma estos modos de creación artística y los fusiona en actos móviles de resistencia, uniendo objetos con artistas y entornos en oposición al control nacional y corporativo. A medida que se fusionan los intérpretes, objetos y significados en una coreografía específica, la forma humana se convierte en lugar de agencia política, donde se refuerza la relación del cuerpo con el paisaje y se fortifica la memoria cultural y espiritual de un territorio y su pueblo. Con *Más allá del control*, Caycedo comenzó a poner de relieve la posibilidad de la resistencia a través de una especie de movimiento colectivo y llamado a la acción, yuxtaponiendo estrategias de control de multitudes y métodos militares de restricción táctica, a los que denomina "coreografías del poder", con una invocación espiritual. Los movimientos de los bailarines imitaban las formas de restricción impuestas a los cuerpos de agua que fluyen libremente, mientras que el llamado a Mohana ofrecía una especie de liberación de esa misma restricción. Estas acciones, aunque se encuentran alejadas de los paisajes específicos representados en otras de sus obras, ponían de relieve las ideas y los gestos que terminarían siendo centrales al proyecto de Caycedo, de carácter crítico y amplio alcance.

Si bien en *Más allá del control* Caycedo abordó cuestiones complejas a través de medios colaborativos, no fue hasta que la artista comenzó a trabajar con colectivos en Colombia—en especial con aquellos que ponían en práctica formas de resistencia inmediatas en la represa El Quimbo—que comenzó a conceptualizar enfoques transdisciplinarios para apoyar y entablar relaciones con comunidades en crisis.[1] En 2014, la artista pasó seis meses viviendo y trabajando con cuatro comunidades directamente afectadas por el desarrollo de la represa El Quimbo. Fue durante este período que las *Geocoreografías* de Caycedo comenzaron a cobrar forma y a desarrollar su propia definición a medida que la artista reorientó sus obras de performance *Represa/Represión* para centrarlas en procesos llevados a cabo por la comunidad. Trabajando con el colectivo Jaguos Por El Territorio, Caycedo dictó una serie de talleres basados en el movimiento en los que se exploraban técnicas del circo, la danza, la performance, el arte de las marionetas, el teatro y el video.[2] A pesar de que todavía eran

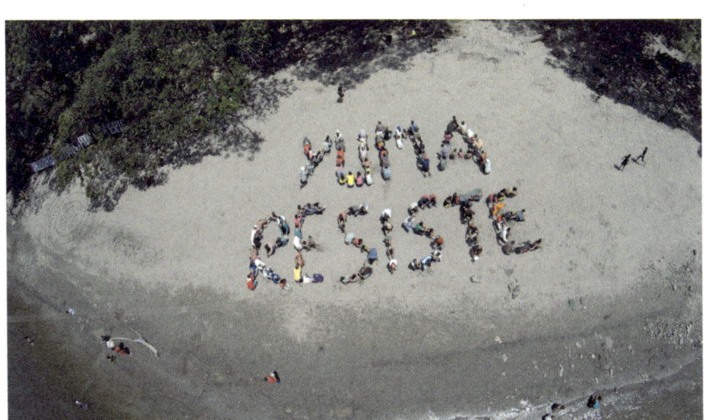

3 Performance view, *Yuma Resiste* from *Geocoreografías Oritoguaz*, 2015. Collective action.

visibles los elementos de las performances anteriores de Caycedo, estas *Geocoreografías* suponían negociaciones más complejas entre el paisaje y el cuerpo. Ampliadas para incluir técnicas establecidas de resistencia comunitaria promovidas por la pedagogía de Paulo Freire y arraigadas en las prácticas de participación del Teatro del oprimido de Augusto Boal, Caycedo y sus colaboradores se centraron en desarrollar conciencia y reconocer desequilibrios de poder, liderando ejercicios que estimularan el diálogo a través de los movimientos, las palabras y las acciones. Por ejemplo, los participantes se daban la mano para formar *caracoles*—formas enroscadas como una espiral—para unir sus cuerpos en el espacio (fig. 2). También formaban líneas serpenteantes, que se movían al unísono en las aguas poco profundas del río, y creaban máscaras de marionetas de gran tamaño sujetas a redes de pesca para marchar por espacios rurales y urbanos.

Estas acciones giraban en torno a la idea de que los gestos cotidianos son expresiones del conocimiento y la cultura y de que constituyen un archivo de recuerdos compartidos y lenguaje corporal. El acto de lanzar una red de pesca, por ejemplo, va más allá de simplemente echar una atarraya abierta, como se las conoce en Colombia. En su lugar, el gesto mismo es una expresión física de resistencia contra la amenaza del poder corporativo, político y militar, encarnando una forma de conocimiento indicativo de prácticas de pesca sustentables transmitidas de generación en generación. Caycedo llama a estas formas "*geocoreografías cotidianas*", es decir, gestos y métodos sobre los que se basan las acciones organizadas más formativas y de mayor alcance que componen sus *Geocoreografías.* Según la artista: "Una *geocoreografía* imprime estéticamente una imagen viva en el paisaje, produciendo una noción expansiva del cuerpo y su ubicación. Ampliar el cuerpo ayuda a evitar el miedo y contrarrestar el desplazamiento físico y psicológico... Las *geocoreografías* cotidianas humanizan el paisaje, oponiéndose a los efectos deshumanizantes de la represa".[3] Las acciones desarrolladas y practicadas durante estos talleres, comprendidas simultáneamente como metodologías y epistemologías, pueden moverse libremente entre varias formas de la práctica artística de Caycedo y, como tales,

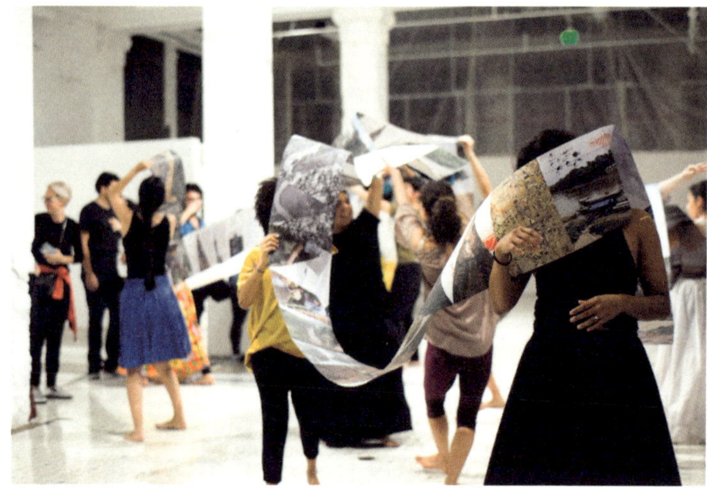

4 *Rio de todos, Rio de nadie (River of Everyone, River of No One)*, 2017. With Marina Magalhãs, Isis Avalos, and Samad Guerra. Workshop and *Serpent River Book* activation, Main Museum of Los Angeles Art.

representan herramientas que pueden implementarse tanto en contextos locales como internacionales. Son acciones que atraviesan los lenguajes del movimiento cotidiano, informan actos movilizados de resistencia, son una suerte de arte visual para sí mismas y son expresiones de un proceso político. De este modo, las *Geocoreografías* permiten un fluir entre los actos diarios de memoria y resistencia y los principios filosóficos y estéticos que guían el arte de Caycedo.

En 2015, Caycedo regresó a Colombia para trabajar con los participantes de los talleres impartidos en el 2014, específicamente, con los miembros del poblado paraguayo que se encontraba en la municipalidad de

Oporapa—ubicación de una de las represas del plan maestro para el río Magdalena—para desarrollar una acción en apoyo a su proceso político constitucional para desafiar proyectos extractivistas.[4] Desarrollada en colaboración con miembros de la comunidad y los grupos activistas ambientalistas Descolonizando La Jagua y Ríos Vivos Colombia, la *Geochoreography Oritoguaz (Geocoreografía Oritoguaz)* (2015) vio a sus participantes utilizar sus propios cuerpos para deletrear su oposición a los mecanismos invasivos del Estado, enfatizando así el cuerpo como herramienta política y como extensión de la propia tierra. Con sus figuras, el colectivo escribió las palabras "ríos vivos" y "Yuma resiste" para marcar su presencia en defensa de la tierra antes de su inundación por la represa Oporapa (fig. 3). A través de la acción colectiva, la repetición de las *Geocoreografías* de Caycedo vio a los miembros de la comunidad materializar un aspecto fundamental de la manera en que Caycedo ha llegado a definir estas obras; en especial, la manera en que los participantes ampliaron sus formas para comunicar un lenguaje compartido de resistencia. Con su imagen y su voz imprimidas sobre su territorio, estaban, como sugiere Caycedo, "humanizando el paisaje". Si bien se documentó con video y fotografía aérea, y existió dentro de un espacio compartido de memoria y experiencia, esta acción grupal no formó parte de la esfera del arte de la performance, sino que, en su lugar, existió en un punto intermedio entre el activismo y el arte, poniendo de relieve las amplias posibilidades que son inherentes a la forma humana.

A medida que Caycedo comenzó a traducir esta serie del río Magdalena a otras partes del mundo, empezó a utilizar objetos como herramientas de participación y pedagogía. Desde su uso de las redes de pesca como la atarraya hasta su serie *Water Portraits (Retratos de agua)*, Caycedo aprovechó las distintas funciones que desempeñaron y continúan desempeñando este tipo de objetos; son instrumentos para el debate, dispositivos para ser activados por los artistas y el público, así como obras de arte independientes. Su *Serpent River Book (Libro Río Serpiente)* (2017), por ejemplo, no es solo un objeto de arte y una herramienta pedagógica, sino que también está pensado para que los participantes de las *Geocoreografías* lo lleven sobre sus hombros mientras despliegan el libro a través de un espacio (fig. 4). Como con la mayoría de sus objetos, Caycedo quería que el libro se utilizara de distintas formas, permitiendo múltiples puntos de participación y múltiples narrativas. Aunque es único en cierta manera, esta cualidad mutable recuerda el movimiento neoconcreto brasileño, que Caycedo ha señalado a menudo como inspiración para su práctica.

Los artistas neoconcretos, en particular Hélio Oiticica y Lygia Pape, defendían un espacio simbiótico donde lo poético pudiera interactuar y coexistir con lo político.[5] Se deconstruyeron y reinventaron formas de arte como la pintura y la escultura para incorporar la participación del espectador. Los *Parangolés* (1964) de Oiticica son ejemplos de esta tradición (fig. 5). Estas capas multicolor funcionaban como pinturas que podían llevarse puestas y que se activan por medio de los movimientos de las personas que las usaban.[6] Estos materiales deliberadamente baratos y vibrantes, que a veces llevaban bordadas palabras ocultas, animaban el mundo de su portador y permitían disfrutar del arte de Oiticica a un público que, de otra manera, estaba constreñido y controlado por los sistemas fijos del mundo. De manera similar, Lygia Pape utilizó objetos de arte para unificar al pueblo y crear una experiencia colectiva fuera del orden social normal. Su trascendental obra *Divisor* (1968), por ejemplo, consistía de un inmenso trozo de tela blanca con numerosos agujeros por donde los participantes debían meter la cabeza (fig. 6). Al colgarse la tela sobre el cuerpo, se disolvía el espacio entre espectador y obra de arte, creando un cuerpo social compartido. Oiticica dijo que la pieza no estaba arraigada en "novedades estéticas o desarrollos 'artísticos' curiosos", sino que, más bien, la obra "proponía transformaciones en un mundo represivo".[7]

En sus *Geocoreografías*, Caycedo incorpora atarrayas y las telas de sus retratos de agua de manera muy similar a como se utilizaron estas formas del arte neoconcreto. Durante las *Geocoreografías* que se llevan a cabo en espacios de arte y museos—que presentan las cuestiones centrales de su obra ante públicos diversos, como fue el caso de *Atarrayas* (2015–17, presentada en Bogotá, Caracas y Medellín; p. 12) y *Sankofa* (2019, presentada en Berlín)—Caycedo suele emplear una red de pesca para conectar físicamente a los participantes. Estiradas entre las manos de los participantes del taller, las redes se convierten en catalizadores para debatir redes simbólicas y físicas, como las que proponen las cosmologías indígenas o como los complejos sistemas acuáticos de la Tierra. Incluso en algunas de las piezas más tempranas de Caycedo, como *Resiste* (2009) y *Mujeres en mí* (2010; pp. 88–89), es bastante clara la influencia de Oiticica y Pape.[8] Ambas obras están pensadas para colgarse como esculturas o para ser utilizadas por una o varias personas y, al igual que las obras de los predecesores de Caycedo, están pensadas para fomentar conexiones entre los individuos y estimular las nociones de solidaridad, colectividad y resistencia a la represión. Es más, Caycedo está ampliando estas tradiciones de la historia del arte al permitir que estos objetos comuniquen experiencias ligadas y provenientes de lugares específicos con públicos que existen fuera de esos sitios, construyendo puentes simbólicos entre lo que antes eran *Geocoreografías* hiperlocales con un contexto mucho más amplio.

Por supuesto que Caycedo amplía estas tradiciones en más de una forma. El arte neoconcreto, y los linajes de los que se origina, como el arte concreto y el constructivismo, poseía un tono político implícito que, a menudo, suponía una reacción directa al clima sociopolítico de la época. La obra de Caycedo también puede entenderse como un arte reactivo, pero, a la vez, su práctica no está explícitamente ligada al presente ni tampoco se orienta de forma exclusiva al futuro. Como otras piezas de la obra de Caycedo, sus *Geocoreografías* también pueden adoptar valencias de recuperación, en particular, en forma de historias perdidas, ignoradas o dañadas. Además de defender el presente y el futuro, estas obras crean espacios, movimientos y objetos donde pueden recuperarse y preservarse los recuerdos de vidas y movimientos perdidos. Y en ningún lado es esto más evidente que en su video *Apariciones / Apparitions* (2018), en el que Caycedo se enfrenta con la supresión que ha resultado

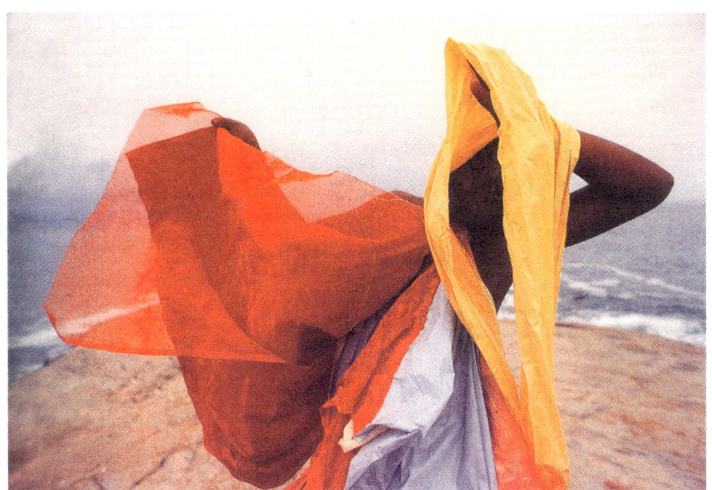

5 Hélio Oiticica, *Parangolé P4 Cape 1*, 1964.

de los procesos y legados del colonialismo (pp. 98–99). La pieza, estructurada alrededor de una *geocoreografía* que se mueve por el Huntington en San Marino, California, reconceptualiza espacios dentro de los jardines, en la biblioteca y el museo de la institución interpretando danzas y prácticas espirituales de tradiciones africanas e indígenas. Comisionada como parte de una colaboración entre el Huntington y el Vincent Price Art Museum de East Los Angeles College, la *geocoreografía* de Caycedo funciona para convertir estos espacios históricamente blancos en marrones y *queer*, e implementa estrategias descolonizadoras para hacer visibles los cuerpos de color y no binarios.

Esta institución, establecida por el magnate de los ferrocarriles Henry Huntington en 1919, se construyó en la cuenca del río San Gabriel, territorio que el pueblo Tongva y sus ancestros habían habitado durante miles de años. Para la performance, Caycedo trabajó con la bailarina, educadora y coreógrafa Marina Osthoff Magalhães para desarrollar gestos inspirados por la religión candomblé y la diosa Oxúm, deidad del agua, el placer, la fertilidad y la sexualidad. Al representar esto gestos—que incluían rituales de trabajo como labrar la tierra, lavar oro en el río o sacudir el cuerpo (como ocurre cuando una deidad, u *orixá*, monta a un mortal)—los bailarines negros, marrones y *queer*, vestidos con el característico color dorado intenso de Oxúm, ocuparon los espacios de la institución de formas evocadoras y poco convencionales para recuperar las tierras y las colecciones del museo como sitios de ritual, disfrute y adivinación.

Caycedo también usó atarrayas en esta obra como herramientas performativas y simbólicas. Mientras los bailarines envolvían sus cuerpos con las redes o se entregaban a un abrazo cubiertos por ellas, se establecía un vínculo entre la actividad histórica del objeto y los actos descolonizadores que se estaban llevando a cabo. El video también intercala imágenes históricas de grupos indígenas nativos de California para mostrar los legados de los territorios colonizados. Basada en el aforismo aymara "Qhip nayr uñtasis sarnaqapxañani", que significa algo así como "mirar hacia atrás para avanzar", la obra de Caycedo introduce un presente en el que el pasado se rehúsa a ser silenciado.

A través de la colaboración, la investigación, el activismo y las prácticas basadas en el movimiento, las *Geocoreografías* de Caycedo atraviesan las complejas formas interconectadas de las luchas políticas, físicas y

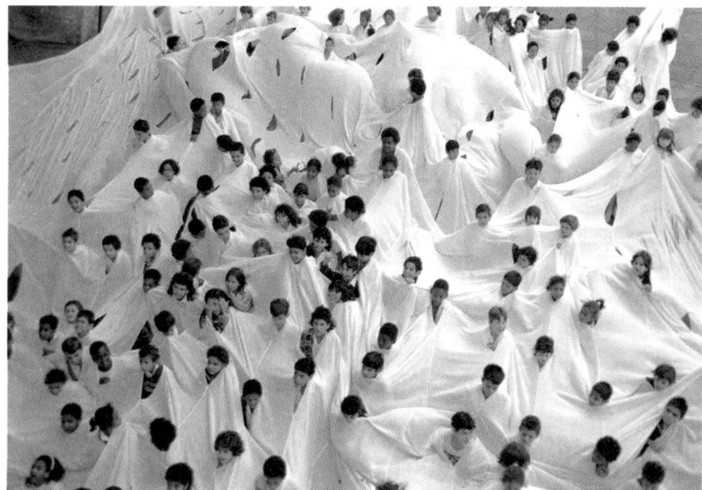

6 Lygia Pape, *Divisor (Divider)*, 1968. Performance at the Museu de Arte Moderna, Rio de Janeiro, 1990.

psicológicas que impactan las regiones afectadas por la subyugación corporativa y estatal. Las *Geocoreografías* unen el paisaje con la forma humana, operan en plataformas activistas y centradas en la comunidad, y ponen de relieve luchas cruciales que afectan a comunidades indígenas rurales a nivel local pero también a nivel internacional, en términos del impacto que esos territorios tienen en el mundo en que vivimos. En todos los sitios en que se despliegan estas obras, Caycedo entabla relaciones con una historia del arte de la performance, incluidas las genealogías de objetos y acciones participativas neoconcretas, a la vez que va más allá de este marco contemporáneo para incorporar un repertorio de diversas formas de conocimiento desde el cuerpo que suelen derivar de la relación de la humanidad con la naturaleza y la geografía. Los contextos en los que se activan sus *Geocoreografías*—ya sea en lugares disputados como en la esfera de los espacios del arte internacional—son oportunidades para abordar problemas ecológicos urgentes a nivel mundial y el despojo de las prácticas neoliberales que amenazan al territorio y los pueblos, así como para destacar el posicionamiento político de los pueblos indígenas y métodos alternativos para vivir de forma sustentable. Aquí, hallamos una práctica artística que no solo amplía el canon del arte sino que además lo hace de una manera que conecta lo ancestral y lo contemporáneo con movimientos y gestos que se forman en resistencia a los poderes dañinos y cómplices de nuestro mundo.

1 El Quimbo Dam is situated along the Magdalena River, which connects the Caribbean coast to the interior of Colombia and Ecuador. The river has been significant since the pre-Columbian era as a stronghold of early civilizations, later as a navigation route during the Spanish conquest of the Americas, and in contemporary times as a cultural and economic backbone of the region. With the river now diverted and channeled through the dam, its watershed is in the process of becoming geographically and ecologically corporatized while local, native communities are being forcibly and nefariously displaced.

2 Other artists with expertise in these areas were invited to collaborate and implement the workshops, and a series of actions–some symbolic, some performative–took place in each of the four municipalities as an outgrowth of the process.

3 Carolina Caycedo, "Geochoreographies," http://carolinacaycedo.com/geochoreographies-2015.

4 Email exchange with Carolina Caycedo, June 30, 2020.

5 Ferreira Gullar, "Manifesto Neoconcreto," *Jornal do Brasil*: Suplemento Dominical (Rio de Janeiro, Brazil), March 21–22, 1959.

6 They were famously activated by Rio de Janeiro's Mangueira Samba School to create movement-based group experiences. Hélio Oiticica, "Parangolé: da anti-arte as apropriações ambientais de Oiticica," *GAM: Galeria de Arte Moderna* (Rio de Janeiro, Brasil), no. 6 (May 1967): 27–31.

7 Hélio Oiticica, "Ligia Pape," in: *Lygia Pape* (Rio de Janeiro: Galeria Maison de France, 1975). [Translation by the author.]

8 Caycedo describes *Resiste*, a Venezuelan flag altered with images and text calling to "resist," specifically as a *parangolé* while in *Mujeres en Mi*—a series of four sculptures made up of clothes donated by women and embroidered with the names of sixty-four Latin American and Latinx women artists (including Neo-Concrete leaders Lygia Pape and Lygia Clark)—direct reference is made to this particular art history.

1 La represa El Quimbo se encuentra situada a lo largo del río Magdalena, que conecta la costa del Caribe con el interior de Colombia y Ecuador. El río ha tenido gran importancia desde épocas precolombinas como baluarte de civilizaciones antiguas y, más tarde, como ruta de navegación durante la conquista española de las Américas; en tiempos contemporáneos, también ha sido el pilar cultural y económico de la región. Ahora, con el río desviado y canalizado por la represa, su cuenca se encuentra en un proceso de corporativización tanto geográfica como ecológica, mientras que las comunidades indígenas locales están siendo desplazadas de manera forzosa e indigna.

2 Otros artistas con experiencia en estas áreas fueron invitados a colaborar e implementar los talleres y, en cada una de las cuatro municipalidades, se llevaron a cabo una serie de acciones—algunas simbólicas, otras performativas—como resultado del proceso.

3 Carolina Caycedo, "Geocoreografías", http://carolinacaycedo.com/geochoreographies-2015.

4 Intercambio de correos electrónicos con Carolina Caycedo, 30 de junio de 2020.

5 Ferreira Gullar, "Manifiesto Neoconcreto", *Jornal do Brasil*: Suplemento Dominical (Río de Janeiro, Brasil), 21–22 de marzo de 1959.

6 Como es bien sabido, fueron movilizados por la Escuela de Samba Mangueira de Río de Janeiro para crear experiencias grupales basadas en el movimiento. Hélio Oiticica, "Parangolé: da anti-arte as apropriações ambientais de Oiticica", *GAM: Galería de Arte Moderna* (Río de Janeiro, Brasil), n.° 6 (mayo de 1967): 27–31.

7 Hélio Oiticica, "Ligia Pape", en: *Lygia Pape* (Río de Janeiro: Galería Maison de France, 1975). [Traducción del autor.]

8 Caycedo describe *Resiste*, una bandera de Venezuela alterada con imágenes y texto que insta a "resistir", específicamente como un *parangolé,* mientras que en *Mujeres en mí*—una serie de cuatro esculturas compuestas de ropas donadas por mujeres y bordadas con nombres de sesenta y cuatro artistas mujeres latinas y latinoamericanas (incluidas las líderes neoconcretas Lygia Pape y Lygia Clark)—se hace referencia directa a esta historia del arte particular.

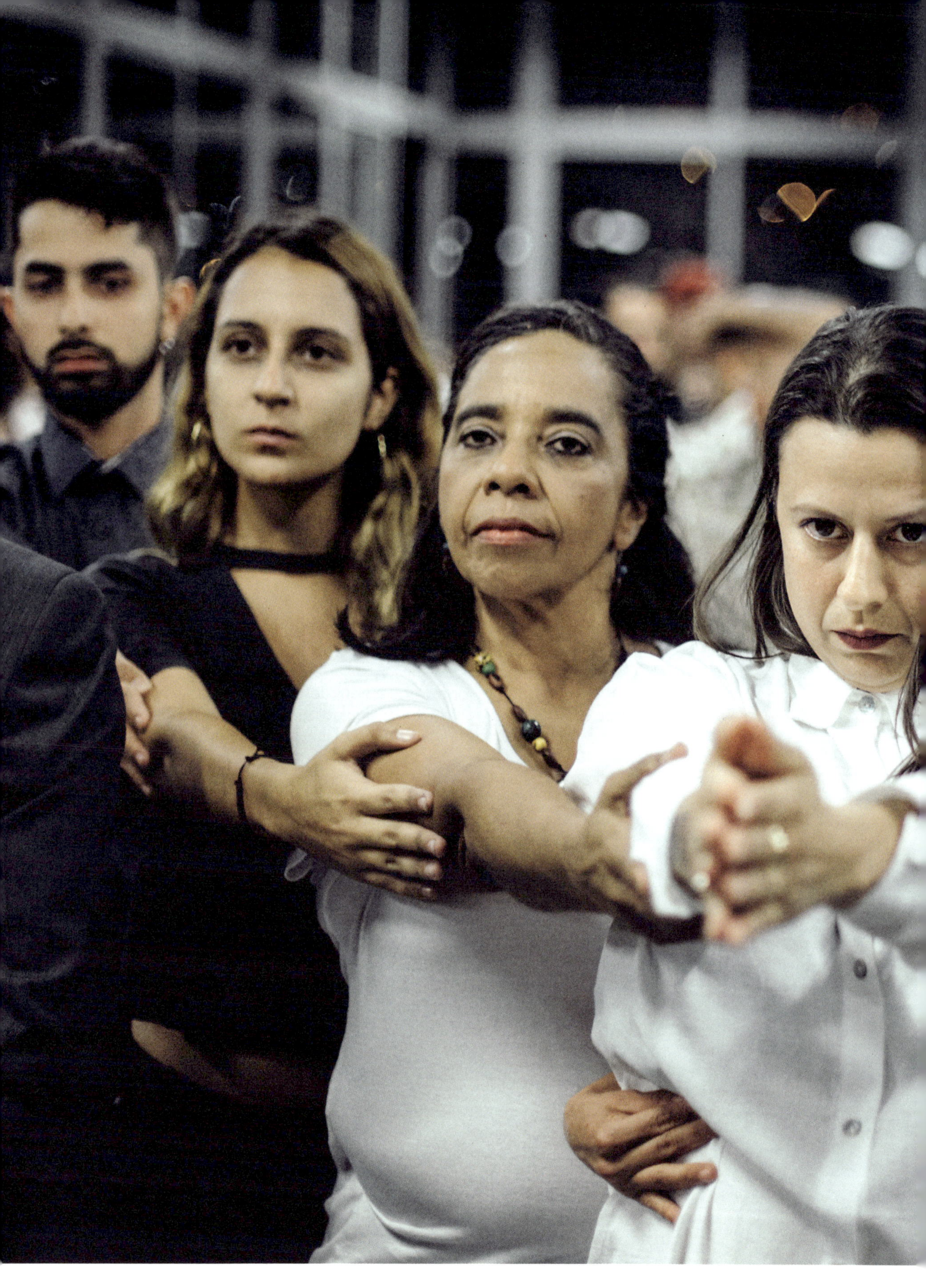

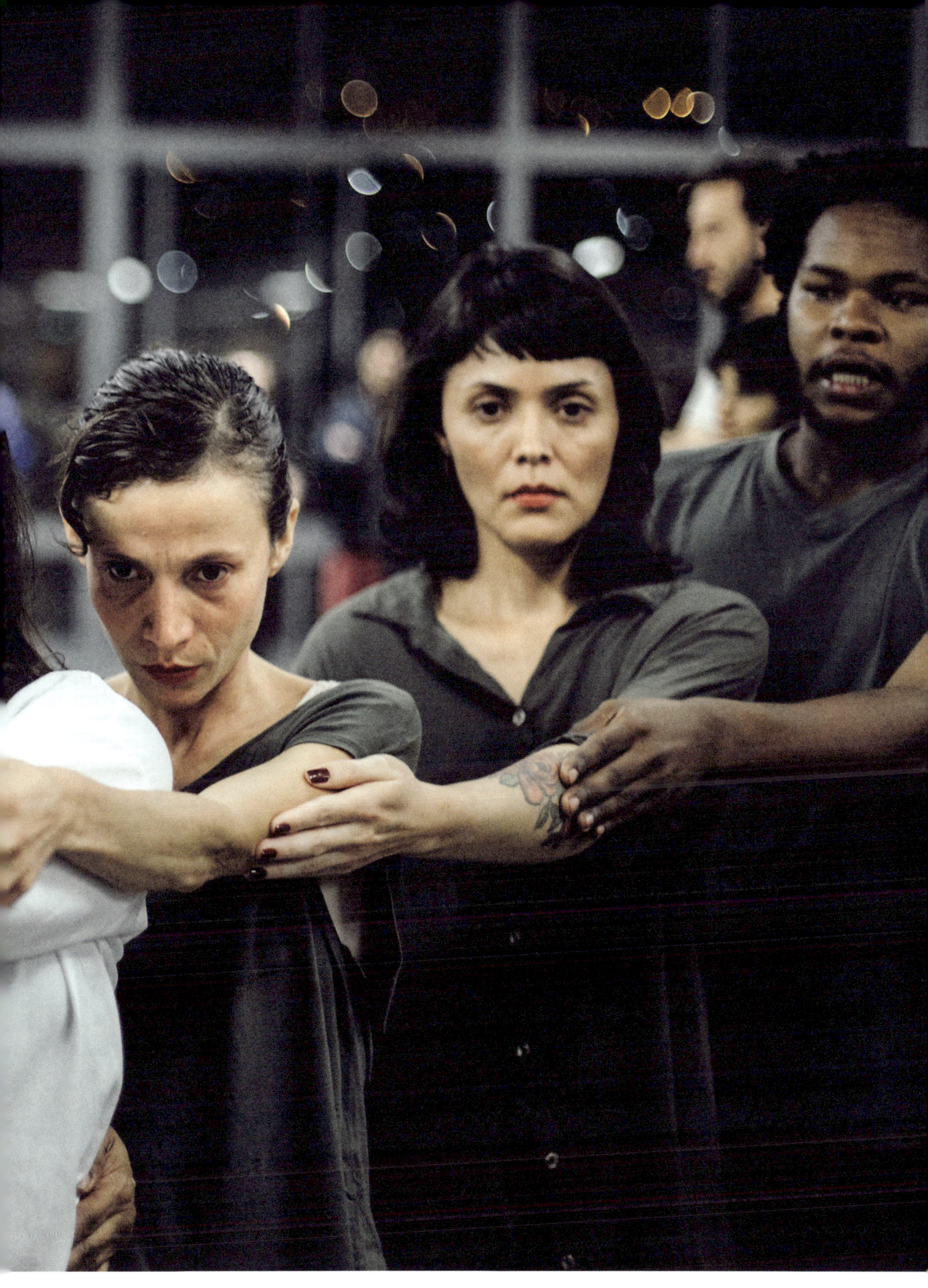

Más allá del control (Beyond Control), 2013–19. Performance for the exhibition *PASADO TIEMPO FUTURO. Arte en Colombia en el siglo XXI*, Museo de Arte Moderno de Medellín (MAMM), 2019. Performed by: Jean Paul Saumon, Carolina Villalba Castaño, Jesús Mosquera Mosquera, Mari Luz Gil, Vanessa Vahos, Adriana María Diosa Colorado, and Oscar Manuel Zuluaga Uribe ("El Juglar").

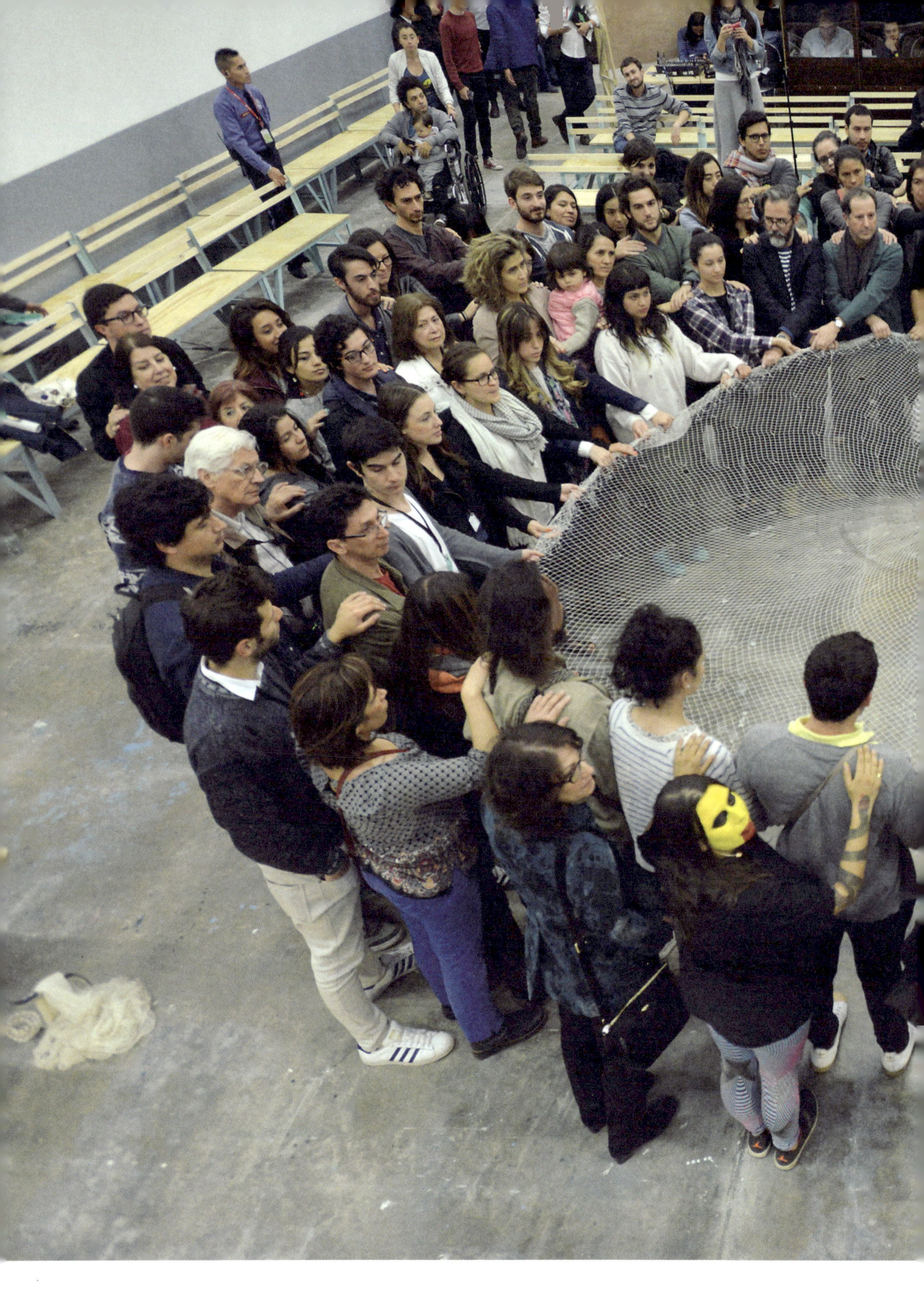

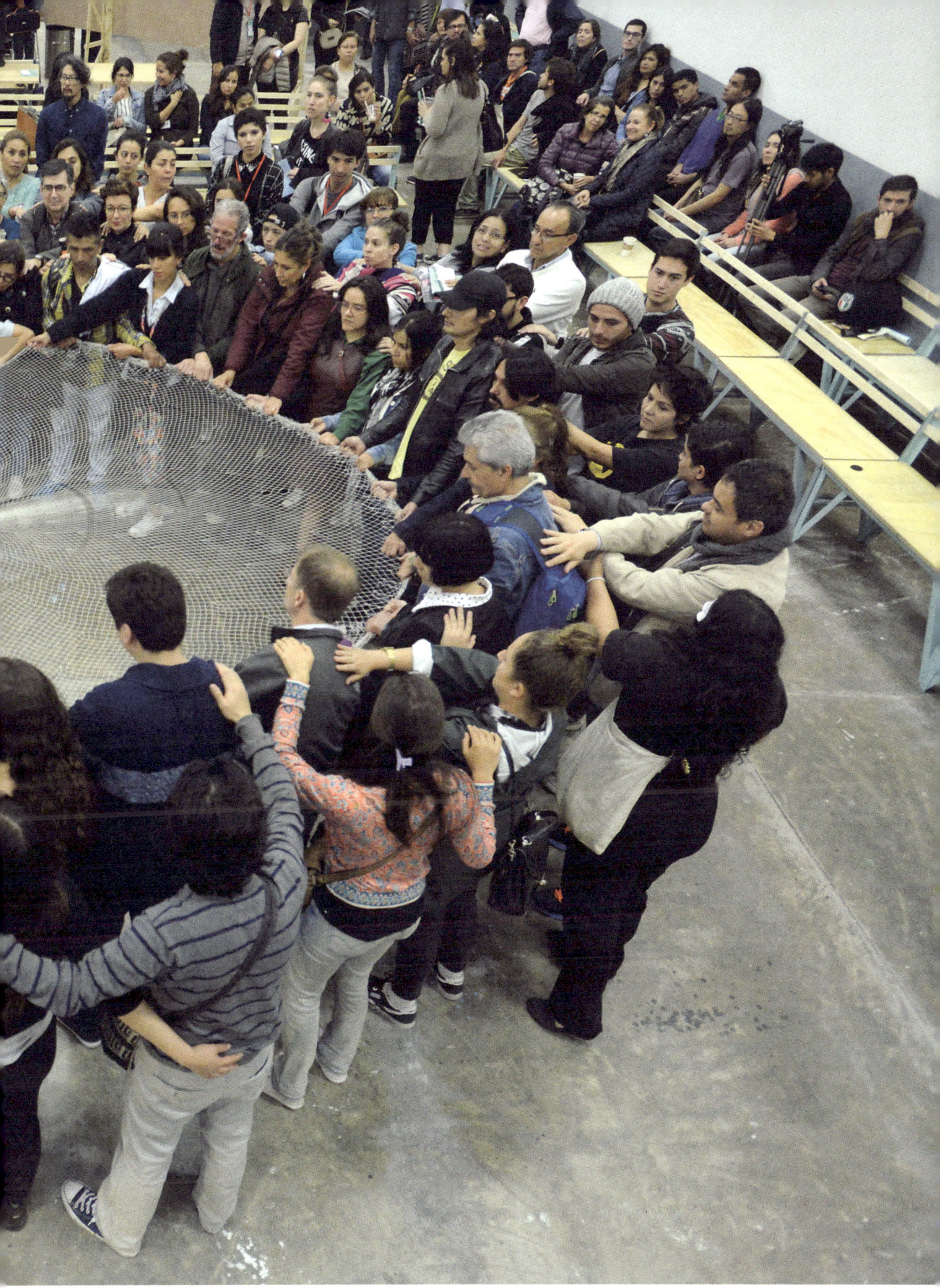

Atarraya (Fishing Net), 2016. Performance for ARTBO 2016.

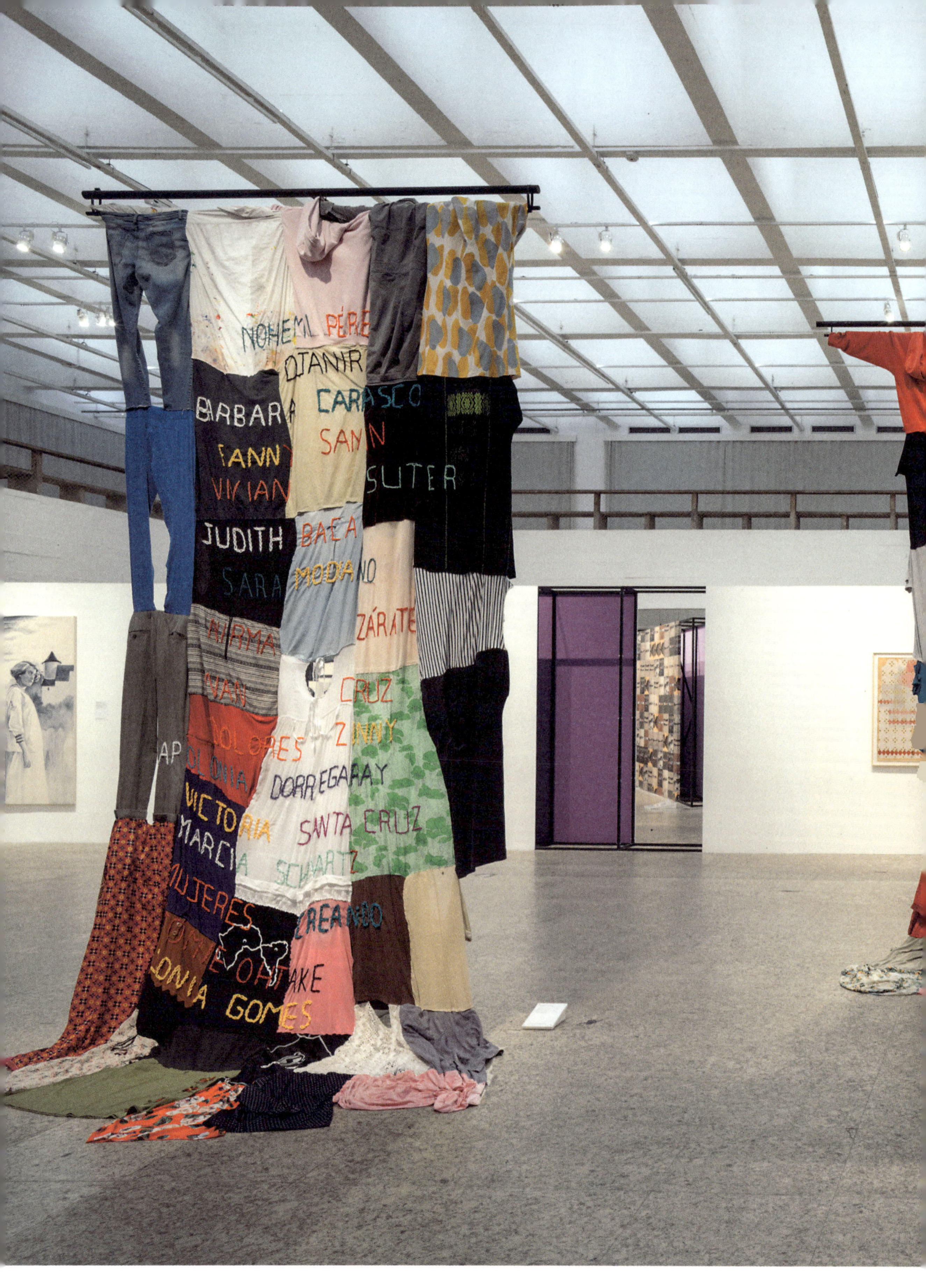
DJANIRA
CARRASCO
FANNY
VIVIAN
SUTER
JUDITH
SARA
BACA
MODIANO
ZÁRATE
CRUZ
DOLORES
DORREGARAY
VICTORIA
SANTA CRUZ
MUJERES
GOMES

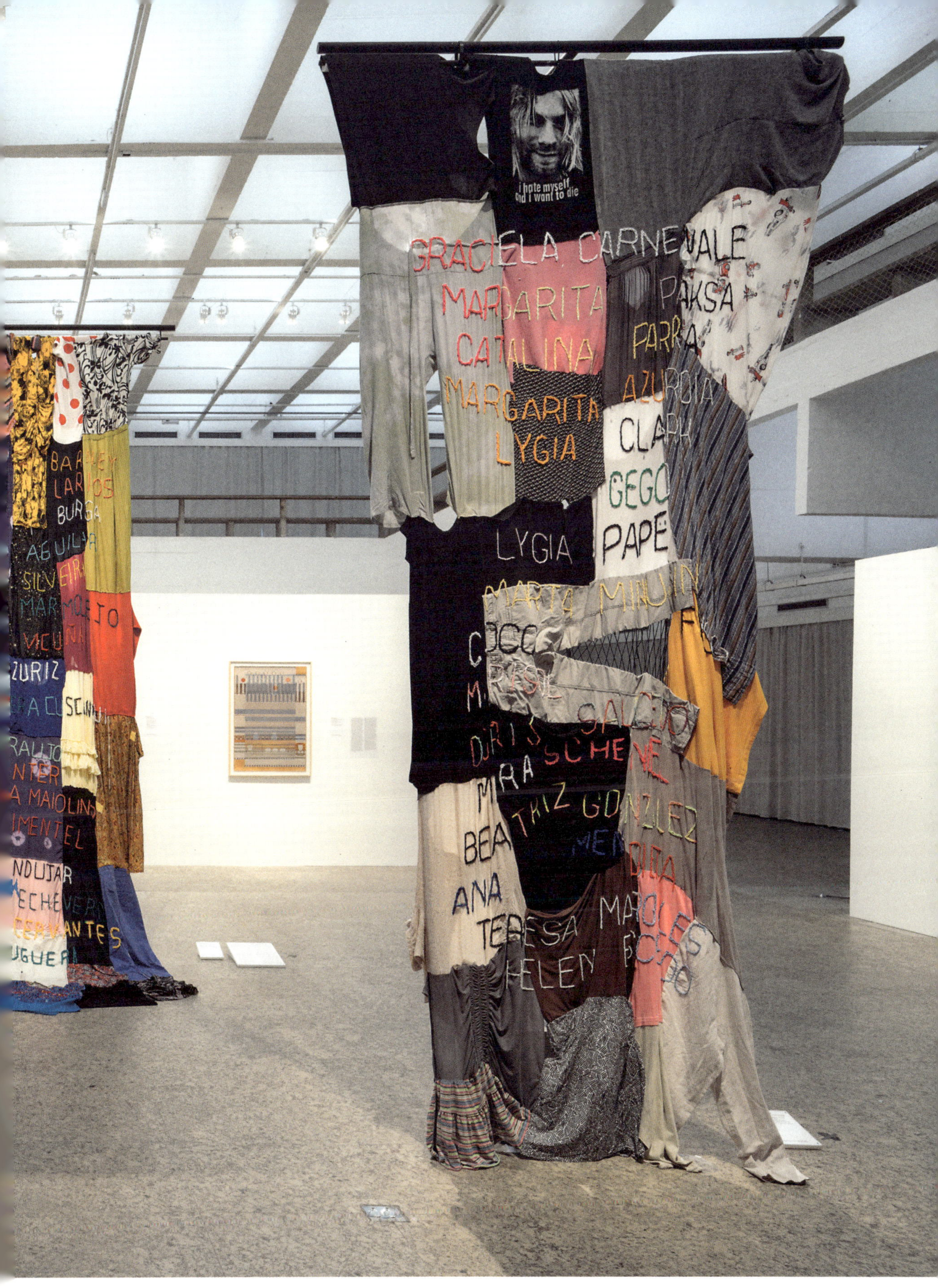

Installation view of *Historias feministas: artistas depois de 2000 (Feminist Histories: Artists After 2000)*, Museo de Arte São Paulo, São Paulo, Brazil, 2019. Work shown from the *Mujeres en Mi* series (2010–). Embroidery on clothing, synthetic yarn, and thread; 3 panels, each 12 × 6 ft. (3.66 × 1.83 m).

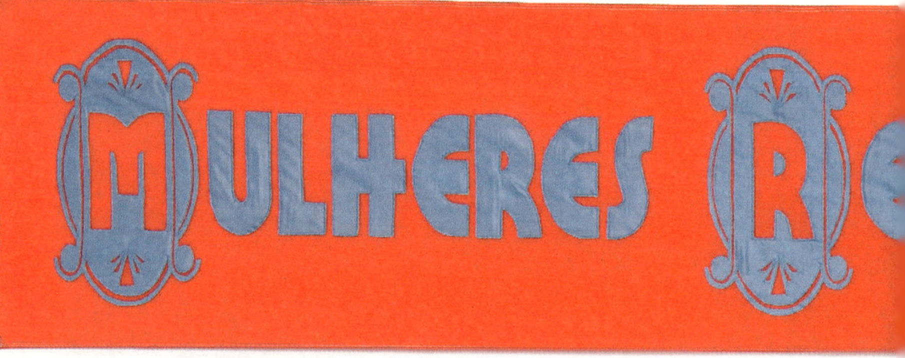
CRISIS IS A
MULHERES
DON'T
NI DIOS, NI
TRUST

Installation view of *CGEM: apuntes sobre la emancipación (CGEM: Notes About Emancipation)*, Museo de Arte Contemporáneo de Castilla y León (MUSAC), León, Spain, 2010. Works from the *Banners* series (2007–). Nylon banners; 3 × 18 ft. (0.91 × 5.49 m).

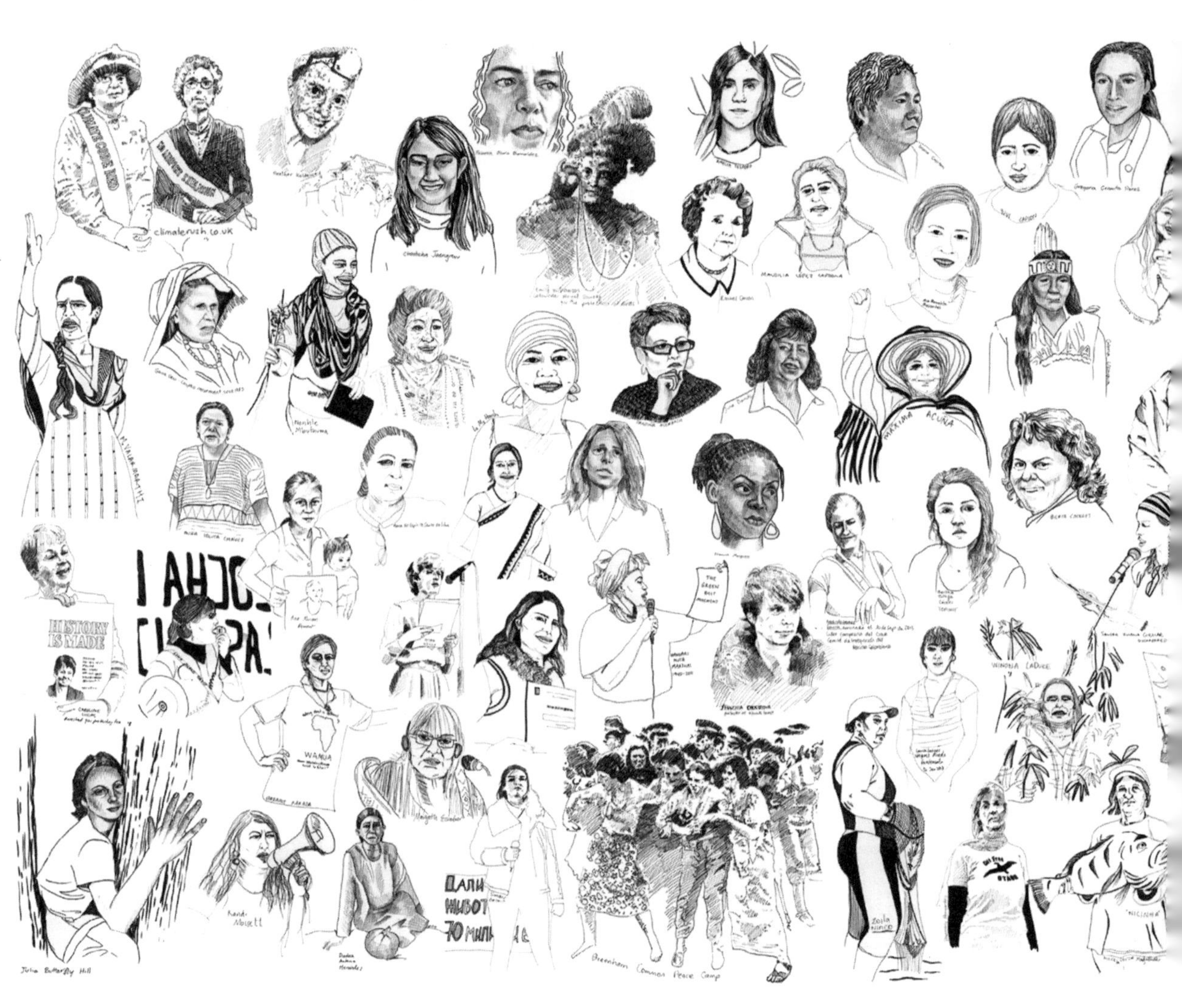

climaterush.co.uk
HISTORY IS MADE
MAXIMA ACUÑA
WINONA LADUKE
Julia Butterfly Hill
Greenham Common Peace Camp

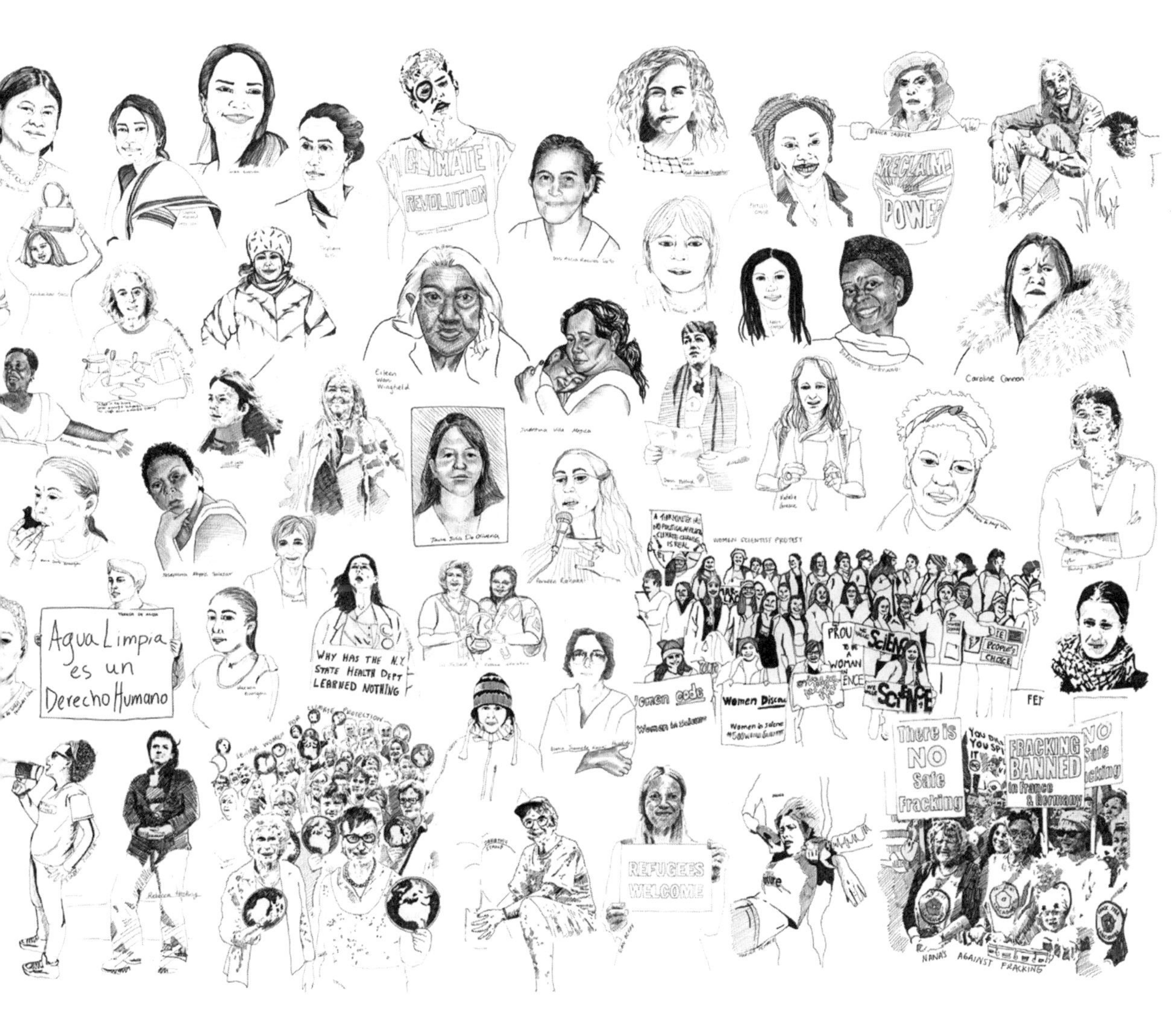

My Feminine Lineage of Environmental Struggle, 2019.
Printed canvas banner; 65 × 250 in. (165 × 635 cm).

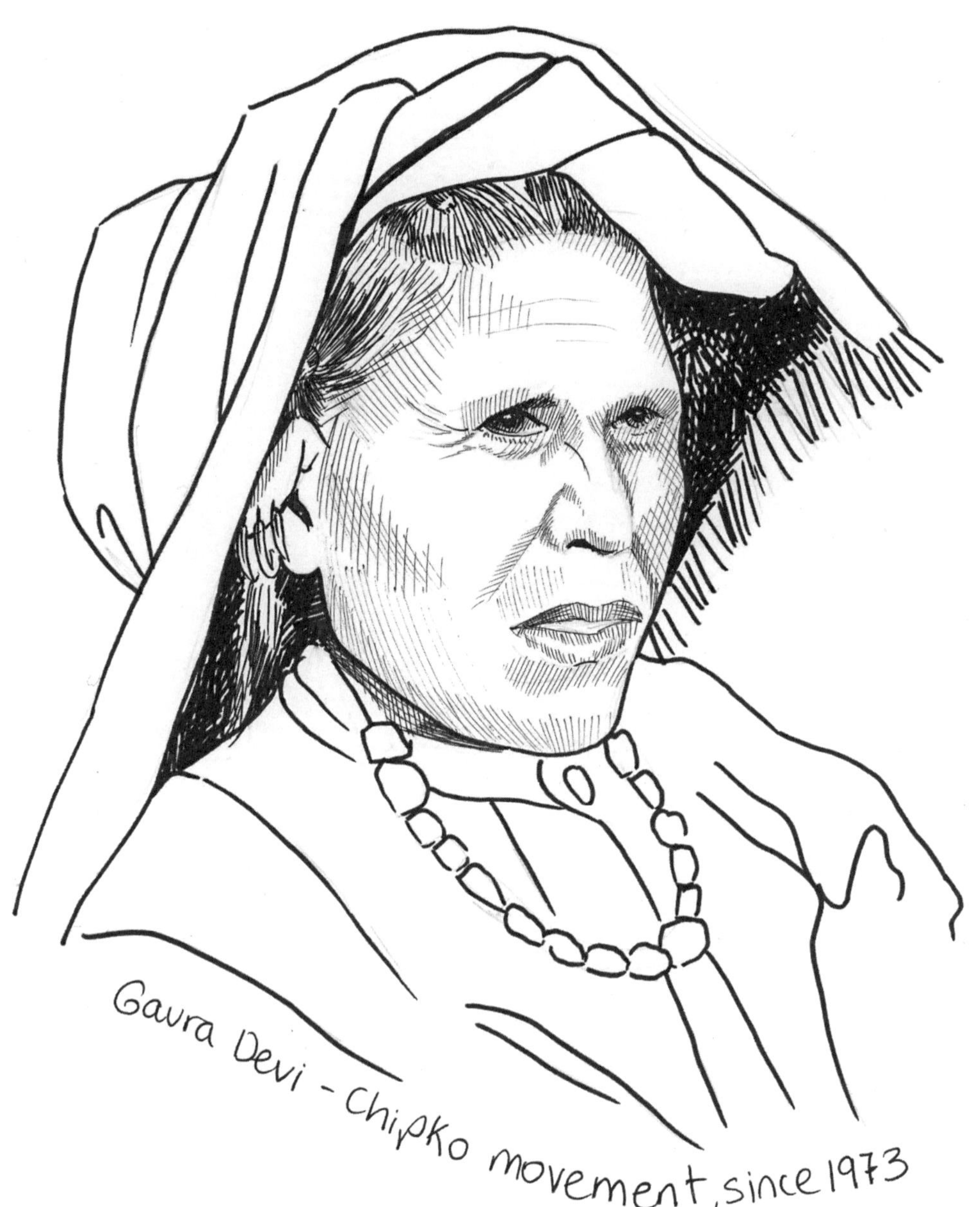
Gaura Devi - Chipko movement, since 1973

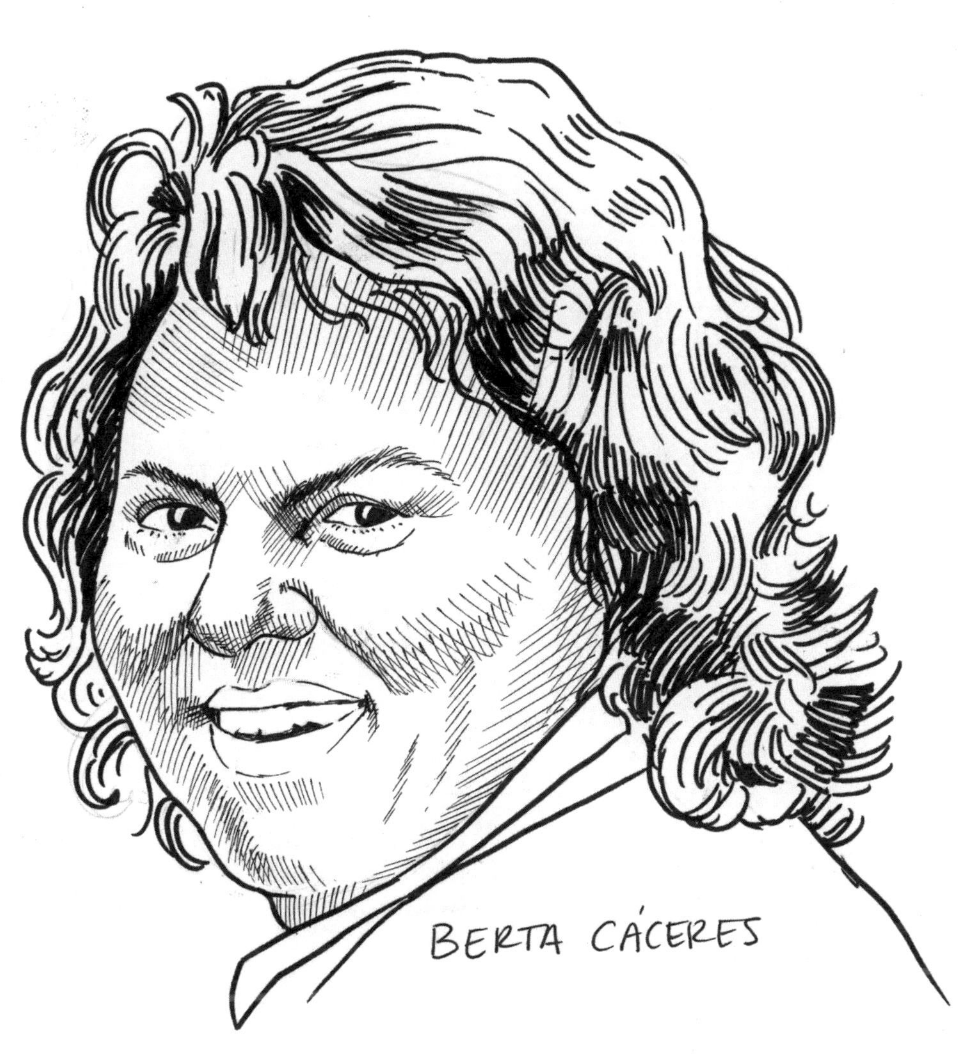

My Feminine Lineage of Environmental Struggle (details), 2019.
Left: Gaura Devi; above: Berta Cáceres.

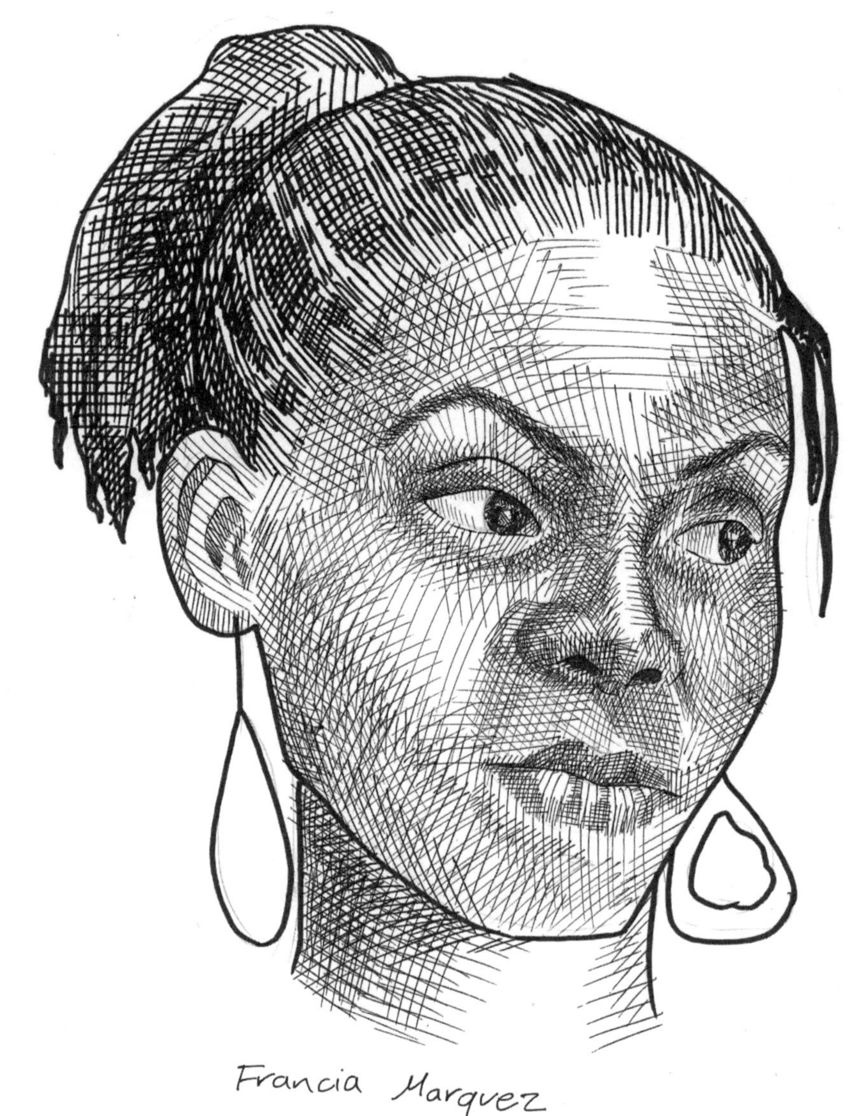
Francia Marquez

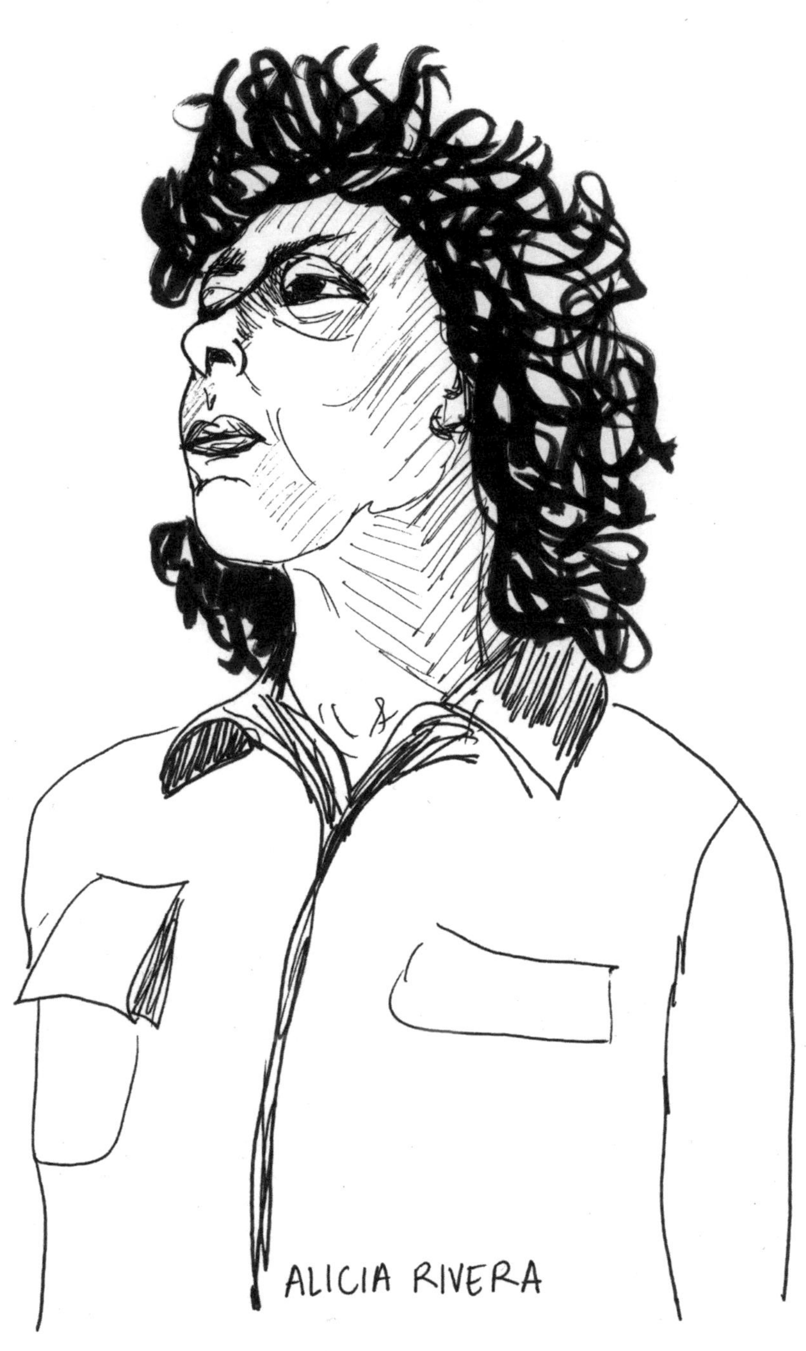

My Feminine Lineage of Environmental Struggle (details), 2019.
Left: Francia Marquez; above: Alicia Rivera.

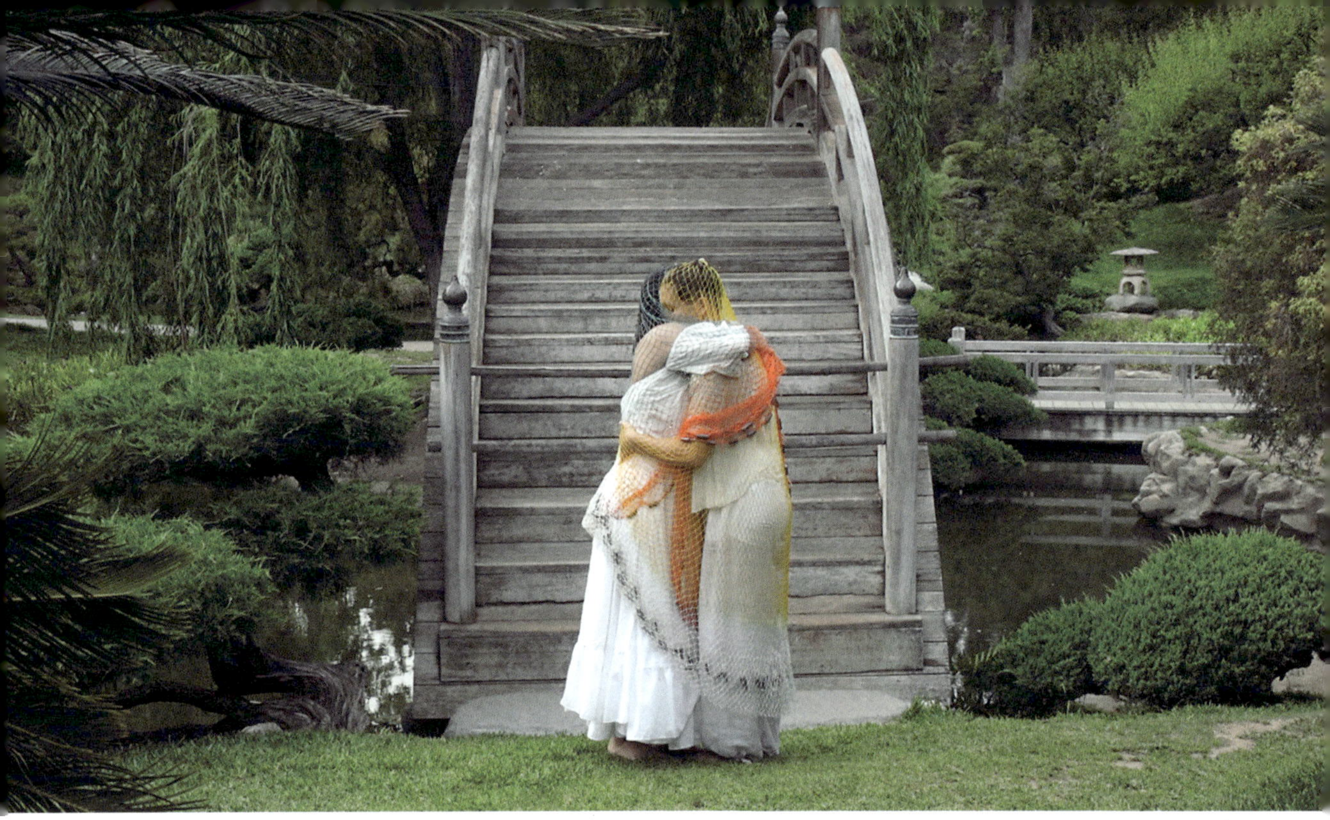

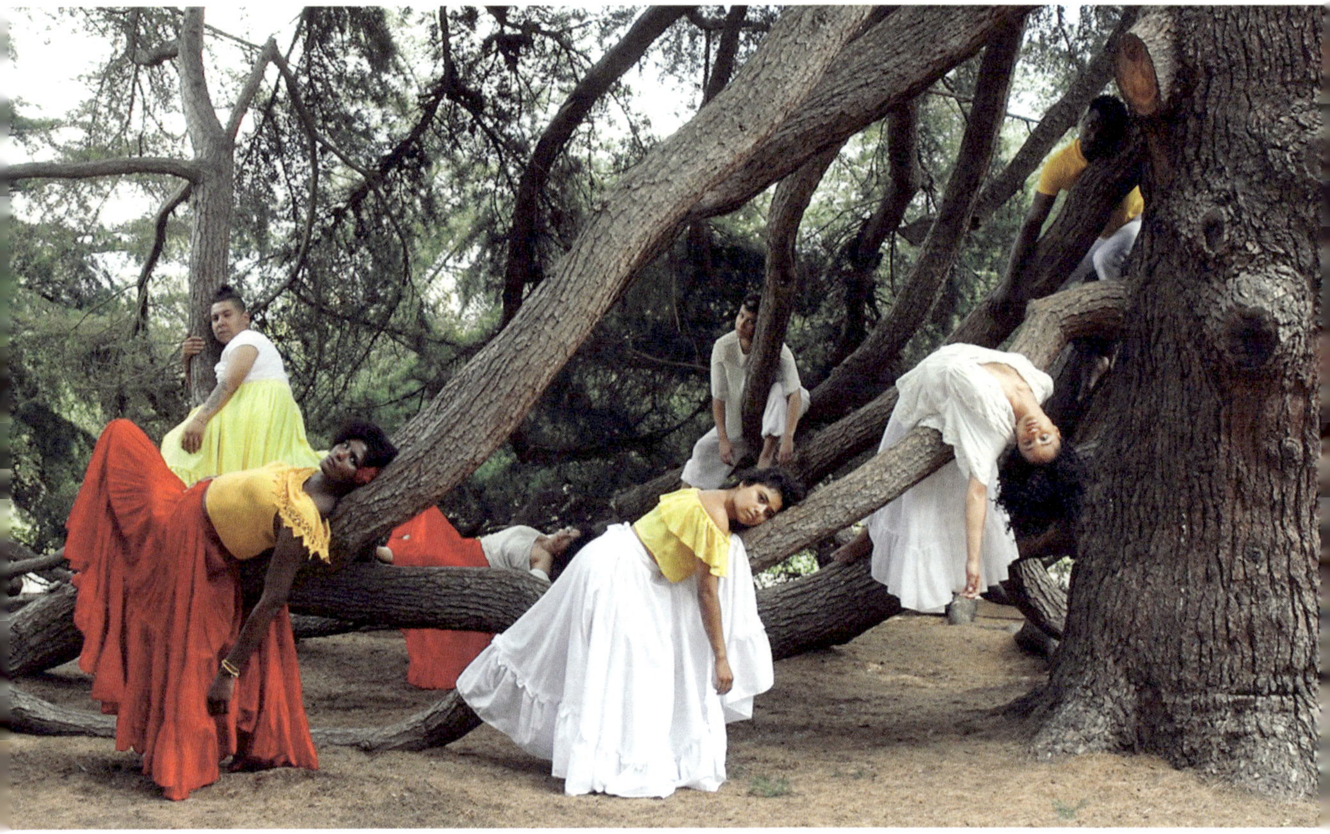

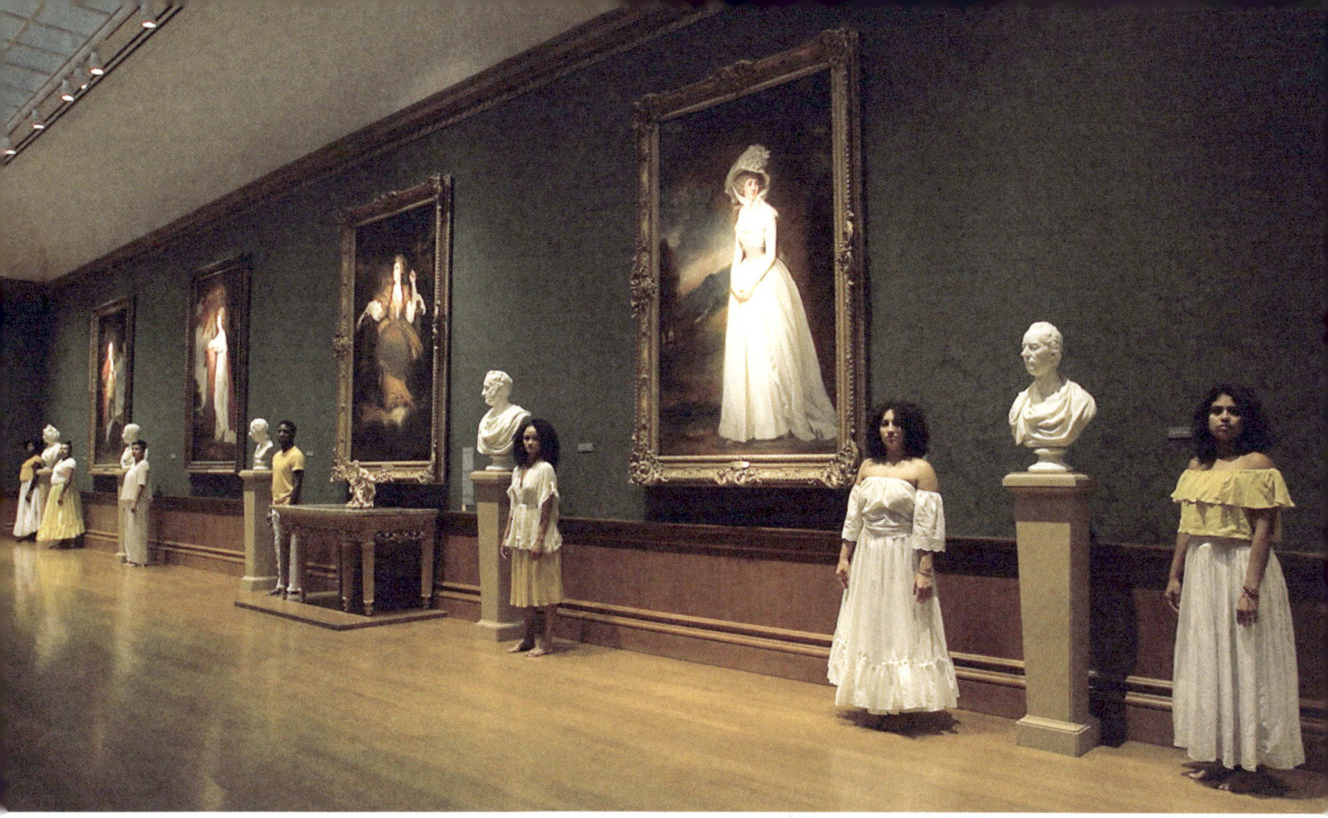

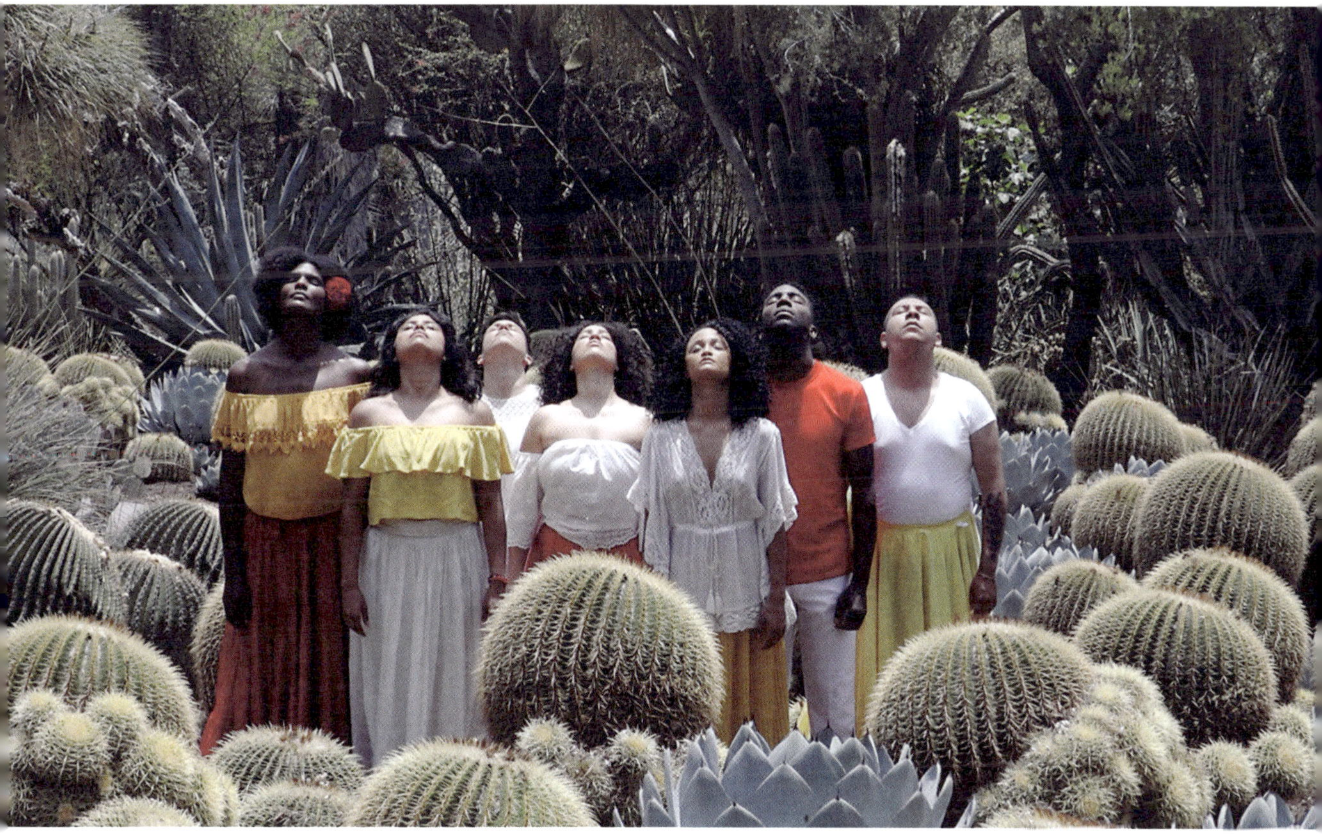

Stills from *Apariciones / Apparitions*, 2018. With: Marina Magalhães (Choreography), Isis Avalos, Samad Guerra, Celeste Tavares, Bianca Medina, Jose Aviles, and Natali Miciche. Cinematography: David de Rozas. Sound Mix: Simon Guzmán.

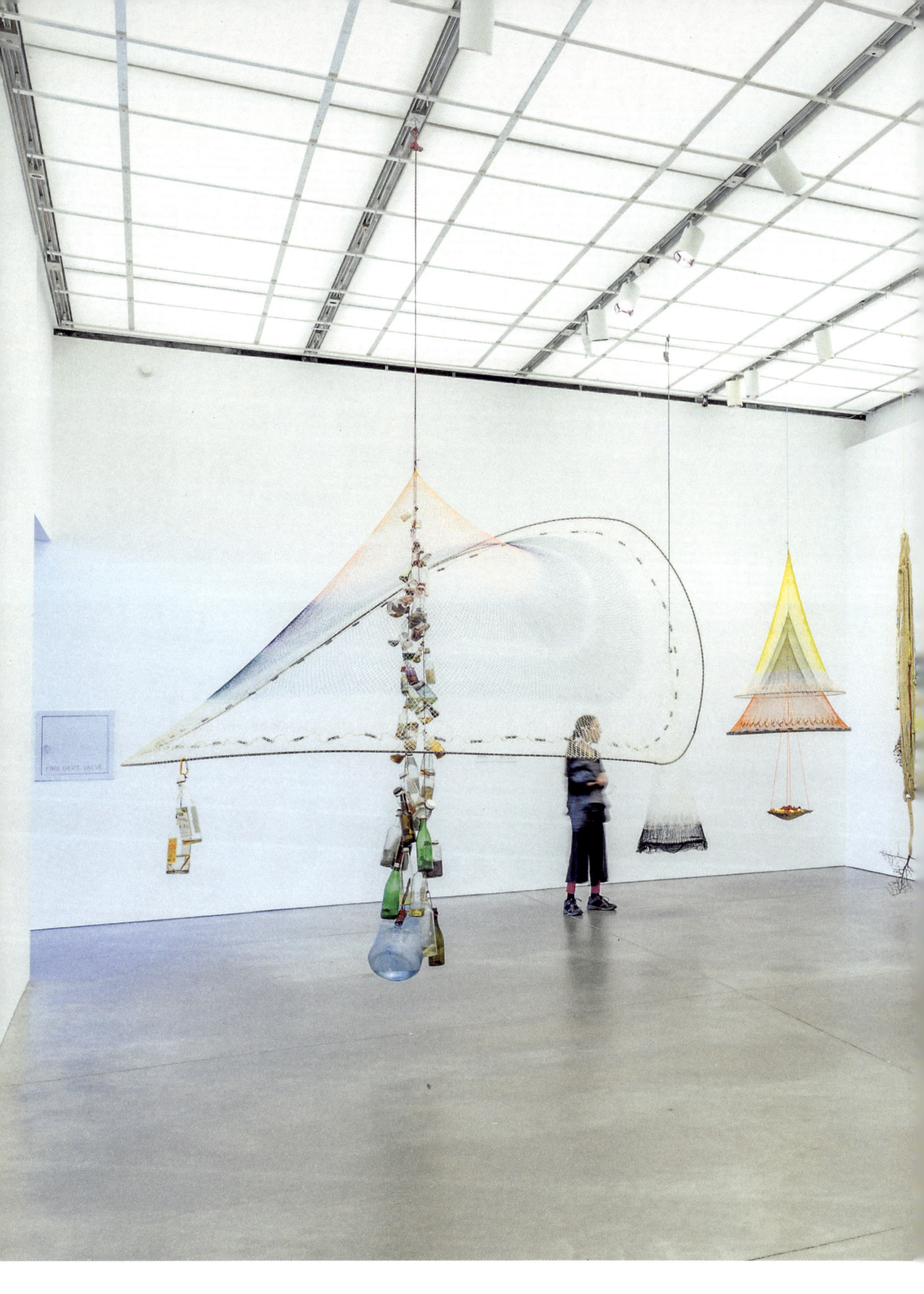
FIRE DEPT. VALVE

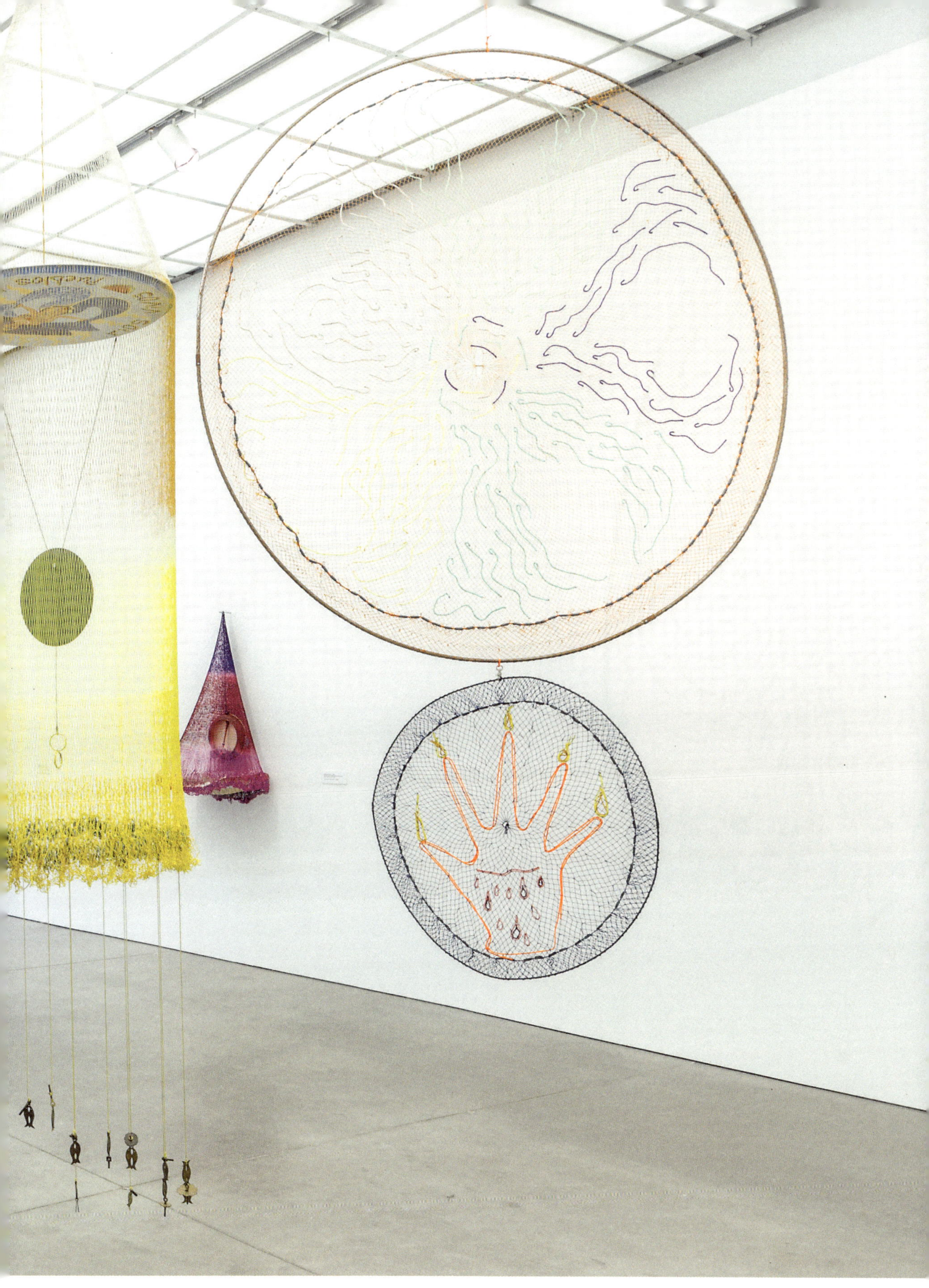

Installation view of *Carolina Caycedo: Cosmotarrayas*,
the Institute of Contemporary Art / Boston, 2020.

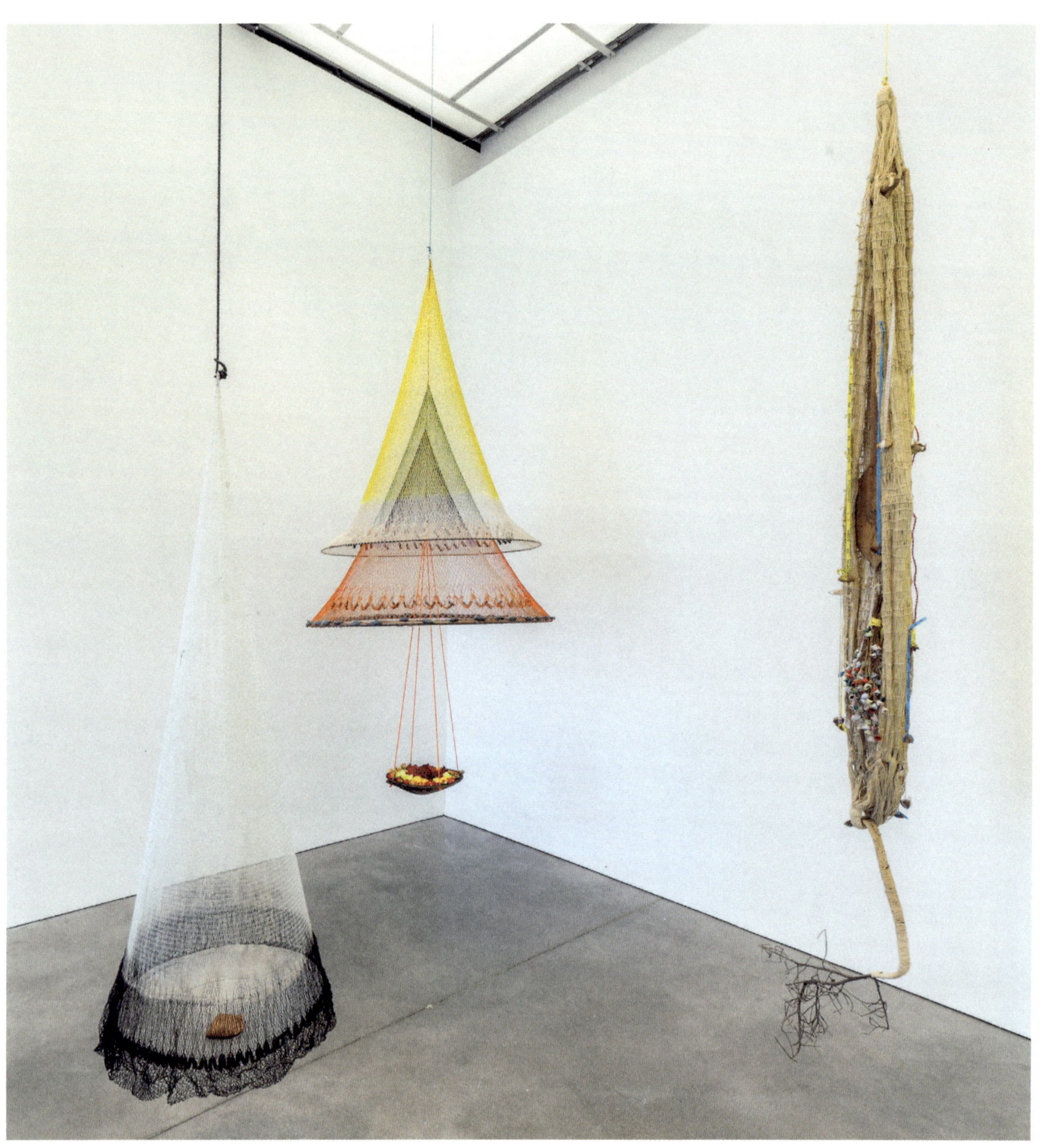

↑ Installation view of *Carolina Caycedo: Cosmotarrayas*, the Institute of Contemporary Art / Boston, 2020.

→ Installation view of *I've known rivers: I've known rivers ancient as the world and older than the flow of human blood in human veins*, Disjecta Contemporary Art Center, 2018. Curated by Suzy Halajian. Work shown: *Ósun* (detail), 2018.

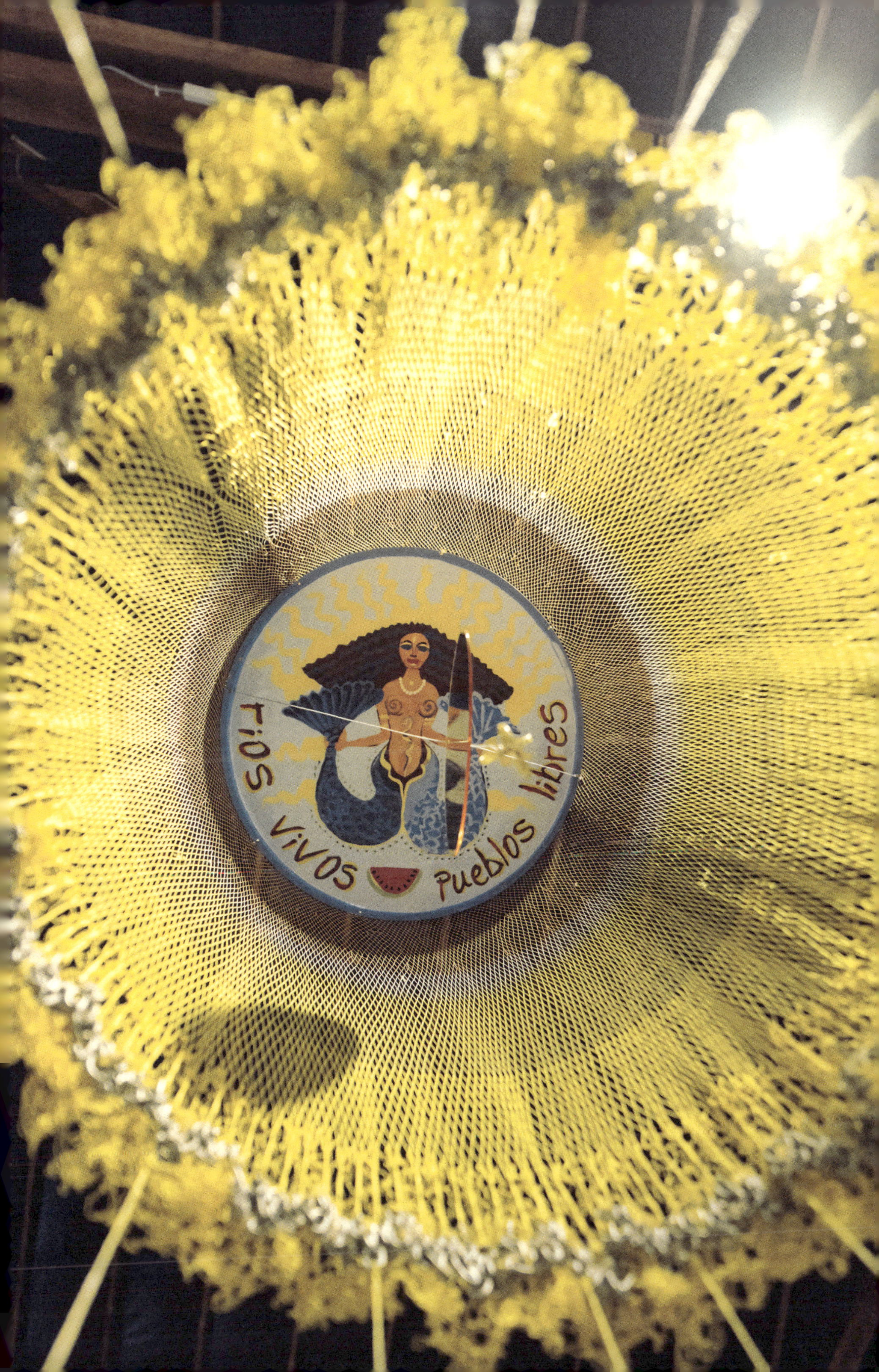
rios vivos pueblos libres

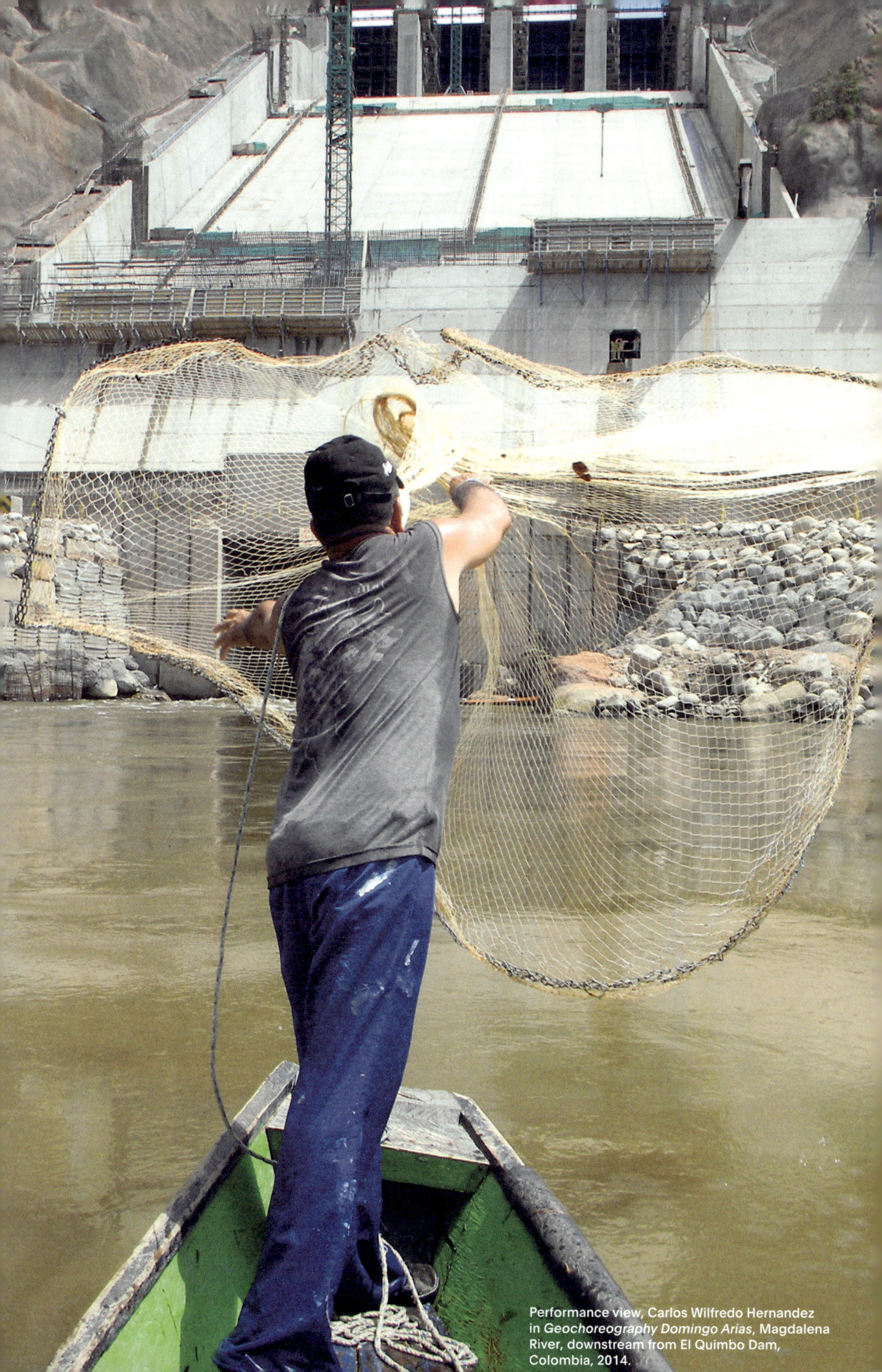

Performance view, Carlos Wilfredo Hernandez in *Geochoreography Domingo Arias*, Magdalena River, downstream from El Quimbo Dam, Colombia, 2014.

When Territory and Geography Reside Within Each Individual

Cuando el territorio y la geografía quedan dentro de cada uno

David Hernández Palmar

> To all the people who have forged their way down difficult paths, crossed borders, navigated labyrinths without walls, jumped over gates...
>
> We, the Wayuu, are an Indigenous people living in northern Colombia and Venezuela. In the Wayuunaiki language, the name of this territory is *Wounmainkat*, which means "Our Land."

Today, for many Venezuelan Wayuus traveling to Colombia, and many Colombian Wayuus traveling to Venezuela, the journey entails reflecting on our identity through the lens of migration, and reflecting on whether there really is such a thing as being "Colombian Wayuu" or "Venezuelan Wayuu." Especially considering that these paths were first forged by our ancestors, long before it ever occurred to any state to draw imaginary lines that would divide an ancestral land.

In early 2019, I decided to settle in Colombia, in a lovely town known as La Jagua, a community at the confluence of the Yuma (Magdalena) and the Cuacua (Suaza) Rivers, in the municipality of Garzón, Huila. This decision wasn't about leaving Venezuela or getting away from the crisis there. Rather, it was about making a home with my life partner, Entre Aguas, so that we could work together on a business venture and launch several cultural and artistic initiatives, such as our cinema exhibitions and workshops on communication, muralism, and food sovereignty. But most of all, my decision was about strengthening and contributing to *Jaguos Por El Territorio* (Jaguans for the Territory), a collective that offers alternative cultural and communicative projects as a means of defending the territory in the population center of La Jagua and other regions along the Upper Yuma and Colombian Massif. Beginning with the question "What belongs to us?" this organization considers alternative aspects of territorial defense, with the goal of making the territorial struggle within these same communities more inclusive. Jaguos Por El Territorio teaches and disseminates everyday environmental practices, the use of art as a strategy for raising awareness and furthering our struggle, and processes that drive the restoration of local ecosystems and our own identity.

Given its location, and based on archaeological discoveries in the area, La Jagua was an important ancestral site for meeting and exchange between several Indigenous people (the Andaqui, Tama, Yalcón, Timaná, Pijao, and Nasa). Today, it is known as "The Village of the Sorcerers," and it is famous for its handcrafts made from the maguey plant. Every November, it celebrates the "Festival of Sorcerers" with parades, plays, distinctive dances, traditional Huilan music, bands, and craft and food fairs. Garzón, La Jagua's larger municipality, was one of the six municipalities directly affected by the construction of El Quimbo Dam.

La Jagua has also been the site of significant community organizing efforts, like Jaguos Por El Territorio, which has carried out acts of resistance through direct action, including the 2013 seizure of three properties that had been purchased and abandoned by Emgesa (the electric utility company behind El Quimbo Dam, a hydroelectric project that has had deep repercussions on the community) so that they could again be used to grow beans and corn. However, in late September of that same year, the Escuadrón Móvil Antidisturbios (ESMAN, Mobile Riot Squad) violently evicted the families that had reclaimed the land.

It was during that time of resistance that I met and became friends with the artist Carolina Caycedo and her daughter. In November and December of 2014, nine cultural direct actions (performances) were conducted in defense of the territory: five in rural spaces and four in urban spaces. This initiative was carried out by Jaguos Por El Territorio together with Carolina Caycedo, who undertook a process involving both research and bodily and audiovisual training called *Geocoreografías (Geochoreographies)*, in which everyday bodily gestures and movements such as those involved in fishing, planting, and artisanal mining served as starting points for feeling, considering, and strengthening the body as a tool for the defense of our territory and of the Magdalena River. Along with two other friends,

1 David Hernández Palmar (left) and Jonathan Luna (right) with a sculpture of El Poira, a mythical figure that inhabits the eponymous cascade and pond in the town of El Agrado, Huila, 2014.

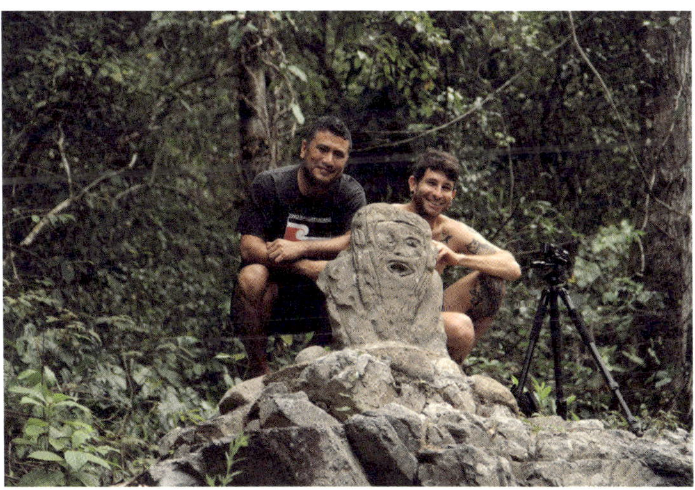

Sabine Sinigui (Embera) and Juan Jamioy (Kamëntsá), I participated in this audiovisual training process as a facilitator in the introduction of one of the audiovisual modules. We helped participants create the short film *Una nutria en La Jagua* (An Otter in La Jagua), in which a little girl's drawing inspires her grandfather to take her to the river and tell her about his encounter with an otter on the Cuacua (Suaza) River.[1]

That same year, at the Casa Museo de La Jagua, I witnessed one of the most beautiful and striking performances of *Geochoreographies*: more people than I had ever seen in one place in La Jagua, of all different ages, gathered to perform a dance that involved throwing a casting net, a gesture that I knew was going to vanish. It was very hard to remain silent as I watched them perform these bodily movements, so closely linked to a territory that is going to vanish, like a language that is going to disappear, because of the new hydroelectric dam's interference with the river's contours.

Many of those who joined in the performance also felt an imminent sadness, despite the strength they drew from the struggle. Since then, the artistic undertaking known as *Geochoreographies* has only strengthened my astonishment before such generous everyday gestures, and strengthened my drive to carry the spirit of these gestures—which are now invisible—within me. I bear them like a message of hope, a strength that the peoples of the world need.

The universe that Carolina Caycedo sees in the casting nets of La Jagua occupies the same mental spaces as José Barros's cumbia, which

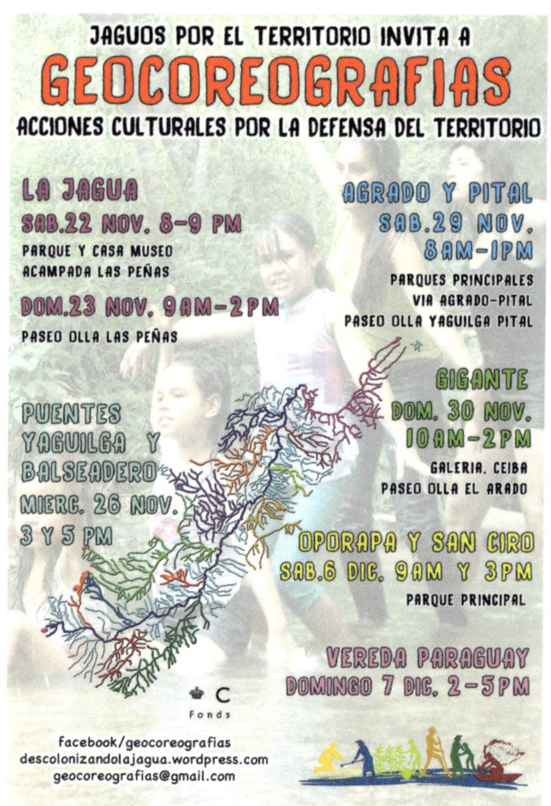

2 Poster for *Geocoreografías (Geochoreographies)* with Jaguos Por El Territorio, 2014.

describes the conversation between a fisherman and the moon and the seashore. For Carolina, casting the net, despite the injustices and systematic murder of Colombia's social leaders, is an act of campesino resistance, and with her words she underscores that not all things can be bought or sold, and that the river cannot be privatized: "It isn't a stubborn gesture. It's a practice that talks about the continuity of a way of life and about a culture that has been passed down through the generations." As she further states: "A casting net represents the food sovereignty of river communities, of the campesinos and the fisherfolk. A casting net is weaved through with wisdom, and it is through the casting net that fisherwomen and fishermen embody the knowledge of the river's cycles, of its ebbs and its flows."[2]

In addition to facilitating mass participation in performances and direct actions, Carolina Caycedo's work also has a political dimension. In fact, her work encourages the building of a historical/environmental memory of our territories, recognizing that the body is native to one and all, and that we can defend the body through the connection it has with water. For us—as communities, collectives, women, young people, campesinos, Indigenous and Afro-descendant peoples, among many others—historical/environmental memory consists not only of remembering and assuming a responsibility for our ancestral heritage, but also of taking political control of our own survival, with the participation of others.

The allusions to the historical/environmental memory that Carolina Caycedo shares have been a recurrent feature in my own cinematic work, in which I utilize those gestures that say so much more than words, and which are important characteristics in various peoples' own narratives. Carolina invites us to consider how fish gaze at the world, how other living creatures gaze at the world. In my work, this makes me foreground our stories' right to be told.

Carolina Caycedo's work links abundance with hope, and that is the strength that all living things hold. Entre Aguas offers a compelling summary of this line of thought through the Huilan spirit, with these words:

> The blood runs through our veins with the same pulse as the river's yearning to flow and the cosmos that surrounds our island sphere, floating in space, and at some point those waters, which are slowly rising, will slowly return from whence they came. The walls of the dams will collapse and the river will run once again. The pataló, the dorada and the bocachico (native fish of the Magdalena River) will return and the water, the water they tried to repress, will sing once again, as if it had never missed a note.

Undoubtedly, territory and geography reside within each individual, and they will remain alive so long as the casting net is thrown, so long as we know that within it there is a world that contains multitudes of worlds. We remain united in hope, defending and caring for the blood of the earth, and of the spirits.

A todos los pueblos que han forjado vericuetos, cruzado fronteras, laberintos sin paredes y han saltado muros...

El Pueblo Wayuu somos indígenas que vivimos en el norte de Colombia y Venezuela, y el nombre del territorio en idioma Wayuunaiki es Wounmainkat que significa "Nuestra Tierra".

En la actualidad, venir a Colombia para muchos wayuu venezolanos y viajar a Venezuela para muchos wayuu colombianos, ha significado reflexionar sobre nuestra identidad ante los conceptos de migración, y si realmente existe eso de ser wayuu colombiano o venezolano. Sobre todo, sabiendo que los caminos que labraron nuestros ancestros, se hicieron mucho antes de que se les ocurriera a los Estados trazar las líneas imaginarias que dividen parte de un territorio ancestral.

A principios de 2019, decidí establecer mi domicilio en Colombia, en un hermoso pueblo llamado La Jagua, comunidad asentada en el cruce de las aguas del río Yuma (Magdalena) y el río Cuacua (Suaza), ubicada en el municipio de Garzón, Huila. Esta decisión no obedeció a un tema de irme de Venezuela por la crisis que estamos viviendo. Más bien, obedeció a la tarea de hacer hogar como compañero de vida junto a mi pareja, Entre Aguas, para trabajar juntos en un emprendimiento comercial y crear varias iniciativas culturales y artísticas, tales como muestras de cine, talleres de comunicación, muralismo y soberanía alimentaria. Pero ante todo, mi decisión era fortalecer y aportar a "Jaguos Por El Territorio", un colectivo de personas que crean propuestas alternativas desde la cultura y la comunicación en pro de la defensa del territorio en el centro poblado de La Jagua y otras regiones del Alto Yuma y el Macizo colombiano. Partiendo de la pregunta "¿Qué es lo propio?" la organización busca darle otras dimensiones al tema de la defensa territorial con la intención de hacer más inclusiva la necesidad de la lucha territorial desde las mismas comunidades. Jaguos Por El Territorio trabaja el aprendizaje y la divulgación de prácticas cotidianas ecológicas, el uso del arte como estrategia de concientización y lucha, y procesos que impulsen la recuperación de los ecosistemas locales y una identidad propia.

Por su ubicación y los hallazgos arqueológicos, La Jagua fue un importante sitio ancestral de encuentro e intercambio entre varios pueblos indígenas (Andaquí, Tama, Yalcón, Timaná, Pijao, Nasa). Actualmente este lugar es conocido como "El pueblo de las brujas", y por su prominente trabajo de artesanías de fique. Cada año, en el mes de noviembre, celebran el "Festival de las brujas" con comparsas, representaciones teatrales, danzas típicas, música tradicional huilense, orquestas y muestras artesanales y gastronómicas. Garzón, municipio en donde se encuentra La Jagua, fue uno de los seis municipios afectados directamente por la construcción de la represa El Quimbo.

Allí, se emprendieron fuertes procesos de organización de base comunitaria, como Jaguos Por El Territorio, que han llevado a cabo resistencias con acciones directas como la toma de tres fincas en abril de 2013, compradas y abandonadas por Emgesa (empresa de energía eléctrica responsable de El Quimbo, el proyecto hidroeléctrico que afectó a las comunidades), para volver a cultivar fríjol y maíz, hasta que a finales de septiembre del mismo año el Escuadrón Móvil Antidisturbios (ESMAD) desalojó violentamente a las familias que habían recuperado las tierras.

Fue en esa época de resistencia cuando conocí y me hice amigo de la artista Carolina Caycedo y de su hija. Durante los meses de noviembre y diciembre del año 2014 se realizaron nueve acciones directas culturales (performances) por la defensa del territorio: cinco en espacios rurales y cuatro en espacios urbanos. Esta iniciativa fue llevada a cabo por Jaguos Por El Territorio junto a Carolina Caycedo, quienes hicieron un proceso de investigación y de formación corporal y audiovisual llamado

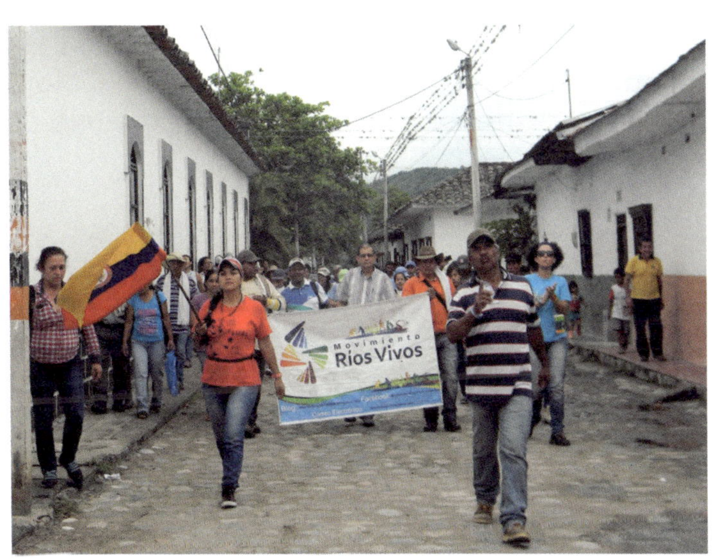

3 Members of Asoquimbo, Jaguos Por El Territorio, and Ríos Vivos Colombia march through the village of La Jagua in opposition to the construction of the Quimbo Hydroelectric Project. La Jagua, Huila, October 2014.

Geocoreografías, en donde los gestos y movimientos corporales cotidianos tales como la pesca, la siembra y la minería artesanal fueron puntos de partida para sentir, pensar y reforzar el cuerpo como herramienta para la defensa de nuestro territorio y del río Magdalena. Dentro del marco del proceso de formación audiovisual, participé como facilitador en la parte introductoria de uno de los módulos audiovisuales junto a otros dos amigos, Sabine Sinigui (embera) y Juan Jamioy (kamëntsá). Logramos que los participantes hicieran el cortometraje "Una nutria en La Jagua", en el que un dibujo hecho por una niña, inspira a su abuelo a llevarla al río para contarle a su nieta cómo fue su encuentro con una nutria en el río Cuacua (Suaza).[1]

En la Casa Museo de La Jagua presencié, por ese mismo año, una de las performances más hermosas y emotivas de las *Geocoreografías*.

Nunca había visto tanta gente de distintas edades en un solo sitio de La Jagua, todos haciendo la coreografía de lanzar una atarraya, sabiendo que este mismo gesto iba a desaparecer. Fue muy difícil ver en silencio los movimientos corporales conectados con un territorio que va a desaparecer, sus grafías, las líneas de los ríos afectados por la construcción de una represa hidroeléctrica.

Muchas personas que participaban de la performance sintieron también una inminente tristeza, a pesar de la fortaleza que genera la lucha. Desde entonces, la iniciativa artística llamada *Geocoreografías* me reforzó el estupor por los gestos generosos de la cotidianidad y por llevar en el espíritu aquellos gestos que ahora son invisibles y que asumo como un mensaje de esperanza, una fuerza que necesitamos los pueblos del mundo.

Así como tiene eco la letra de la cumbia de José Barros, que cuenta esa conversación que tiene el pescador con la luna y la playa, así queda también en la mente el universo que ve Carolina Caycedo en las atarrayas de La Jagua. Para ella, lanzar la atarraya, a pesar de las injusticias y el asesinato sistemático de líderes sociales en Colombia, es un acto de resistencia campesina, y con sus palabras reitera que no todo se compra

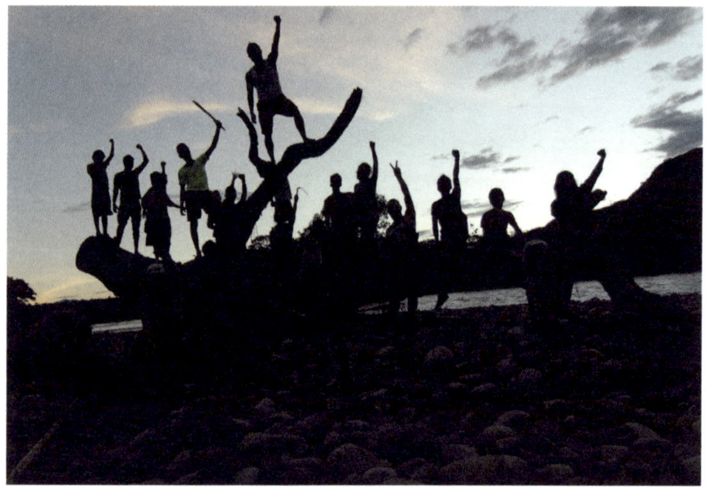

4 Members of Jaguos Por El Territorio participating in a Performance Techniques workshop with instructor Fernando Pertuz at "Las Penas" of the Magdalena River in La Jagua as part of *Geocoreografías (Geochoreographies)*, August 2014.

ni se vende, y que el río no puede ser privatizado: "No es un gesto terco. Es una práctica que habla de la continuidad de una forma de vida y de una cultura que ha sido transmitida por generaciones". Y reafirma: "Una atarraya equivale a la soberanía alimentaria de las comunidades ribereñas, de campesinos y pescadores. Una atarraya contiene la sabiduría del tejido y a través de la atarraya las pescadoras y los pescadores encarnan el conocimiento de los tiempos del río, de sus corrientes y de sus crecientes".[2]

El trabajo de Carolina Caycedo no solo hace que las personas participen masivamente de las puestas en escena o acciones directas, también tiene una dimensión política. De hecho, su trabajo invita a la construcción de la memoria histórica ambiental de nuestros territorios, reconociendo que el cuerpo es originario de una y de varias partes, y que podemos defender el cuerpo a través de la conexión que tiene con el agua. Para nosotros, como comunidades, colectivos, mujeres, jóvenes, campesinos, pueblos indígenas y afrodescendientes, entre otros, la memoria histórica ambiental no consiste solo en recordar y asumir una responsabilidad respecto a nuestra ancestralidad, sino en apropiarnos políticamente de nuestra pervivencia con la participación de otros.

La referencia de la memoria histórica ambiental compartida por Carolina Caycedo ha sido recurrente en mi trabajo en el cine, al plantearme esas gestualidades que dicen más que las palabras, y que son importantes rasgos para las narrativas propias de los pueblos. Carolina invita a plantearnos cómo miran los peces, como miran los demás seres vivos, y esto en mi trabajo me hace tener presente el derecho a que nuestras historias sean contadas.

El trabajo de Carolina Caycedo enlaza la abundancia con la esperanza y esta es la fuerza que todo ser vivo tiene. Entre Aguas resume bien este pensamiento desde su espíritu huilense, con estas palabras:

> En nuestras venas la sangre corre con el mismo latido que el río anhela fluir y con la que los cosmos rodean a nuestra isla esfera, flotando en el espacio, y en algún momento esas aguas que lentamente van subiendo, lentamente retornarán de donde vienen. Los muros de las represas se fragmentarán y el río correrá de nuevo. El pataló, la dorada y el bocachico (peces nativos del río Magdalena) volverán, y el agua, el agua que intentaron ahogar, volverá a cantar como si nunca se le hubiese escapado una nota.

En efecto, el territorio y la geografía quedan dentro de cada uno, y seguirán vivos mientras se tire la atarraya y se sepa que dentro de ella hay un mundo donde caben muchos mundos. Sigamos juntos con esperanza defendiendo y cuidando la sangre de la tierra y los espíritus.

1 To watch the short film *Una nutria en La Jagua*, visit https://vimeo.com/149880645.
2 Carolina Caycedo, "Atarraya," [n.d.], Museo de Memoria de Colombia, http://museodememoria.gov.co/arte-y-cultura/atarraya/.

1 Para ver el cortometraje "Una nutria en La Jagua," favor de acceder al siguiente enlace: https://vimeo.com/149880645.
2 Carolina Caycedo, "Atarraya," [n.d.], Museo de Memoria de Colombia, http://museodememoria.gov.co/arte-y-cultura/atarraya/.

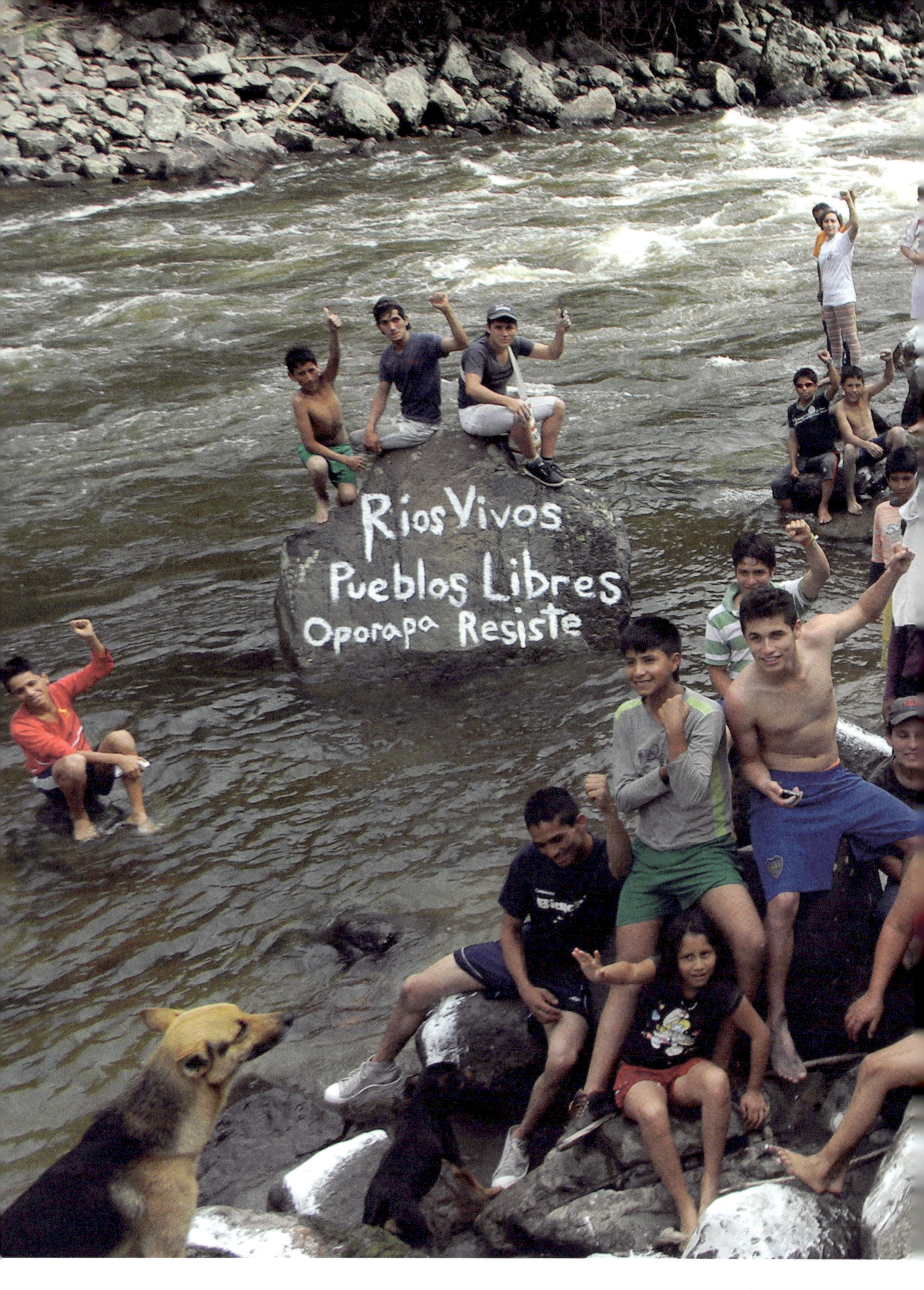
Rios Vivos
Pueblos Libres
Oporapa Resiste

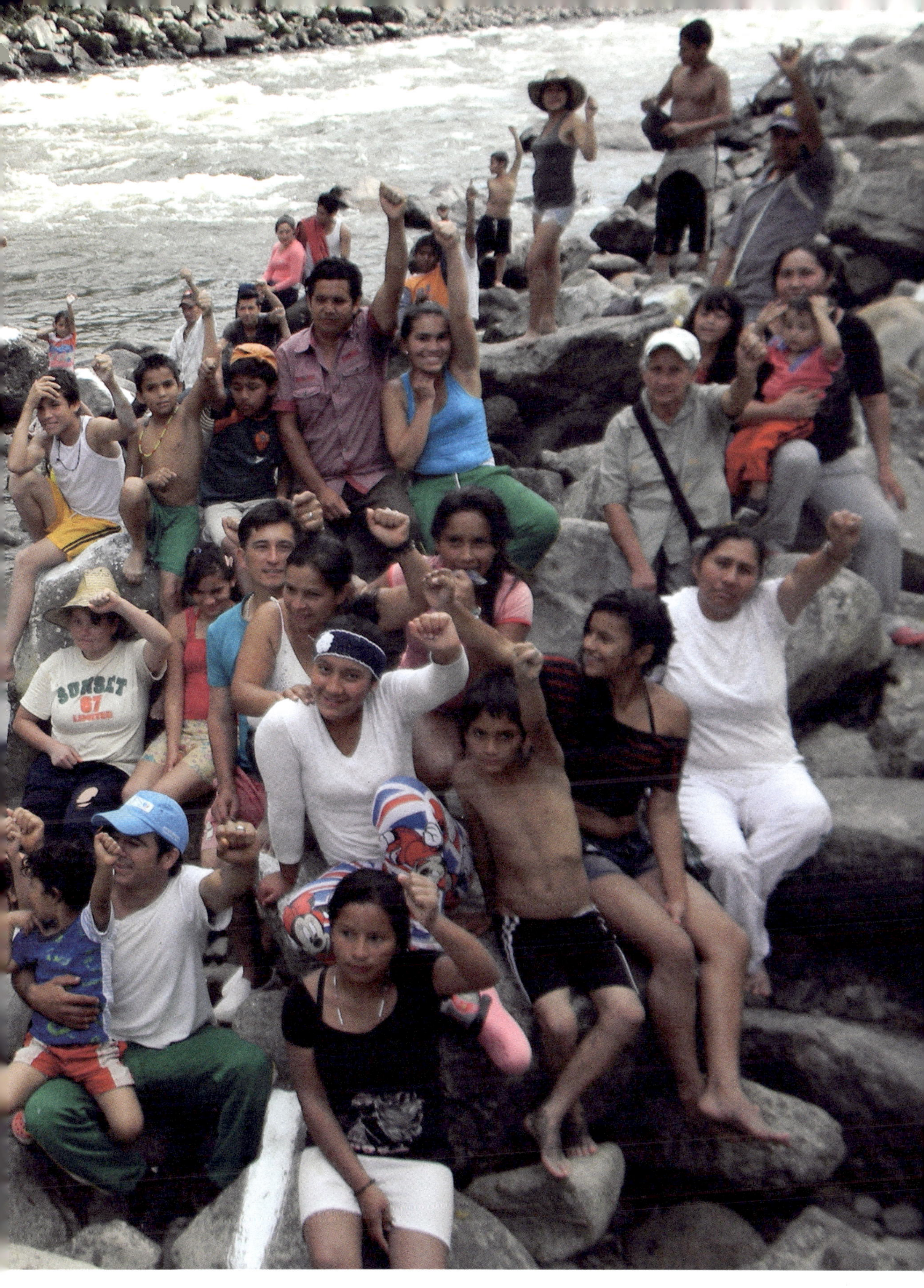

Members of Asonaret from the community of Paraguay, Municipality of Oporapa, during a *Geochoreogaphies* performance action at the Magdalena River, August 2014.

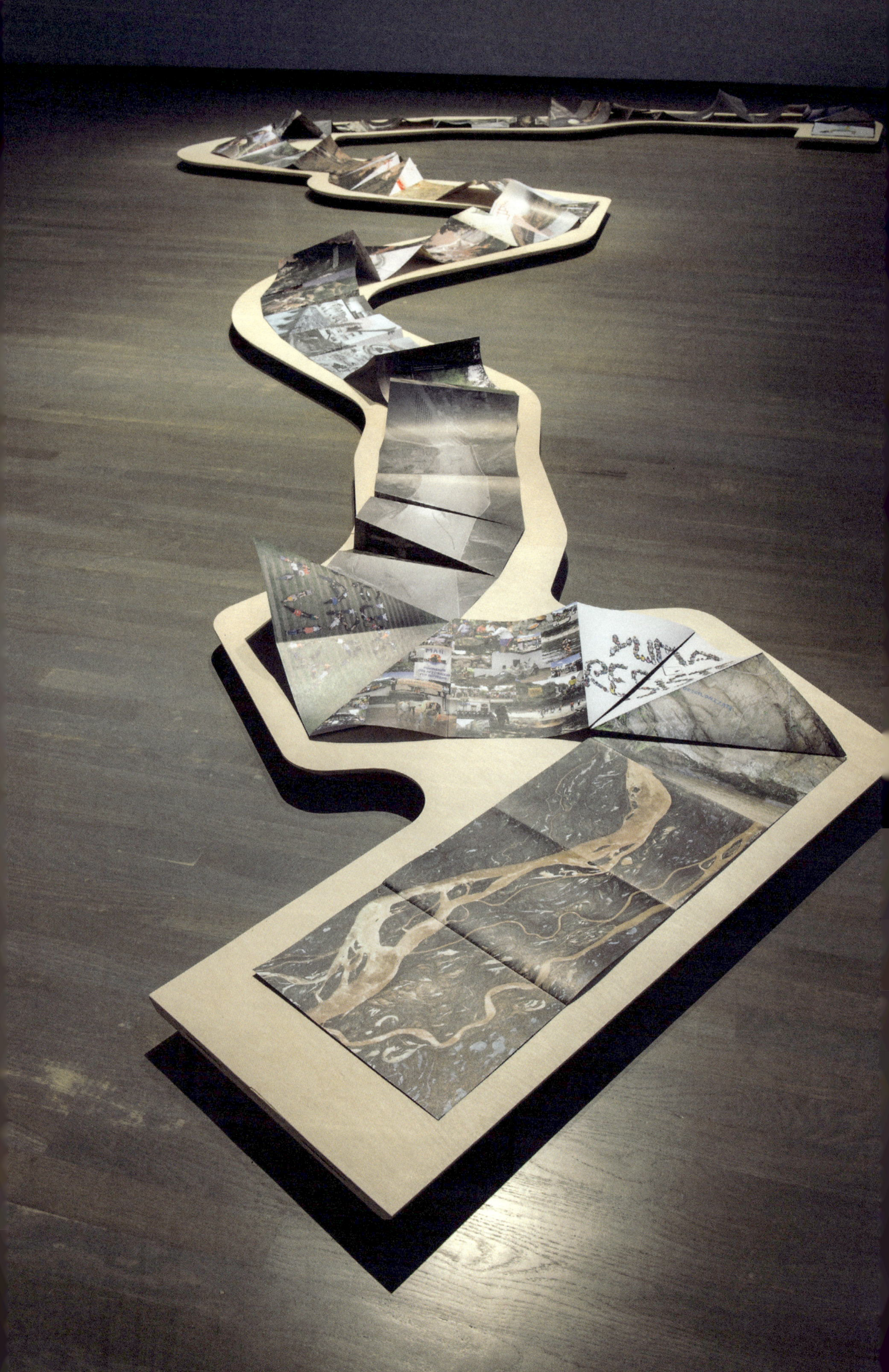

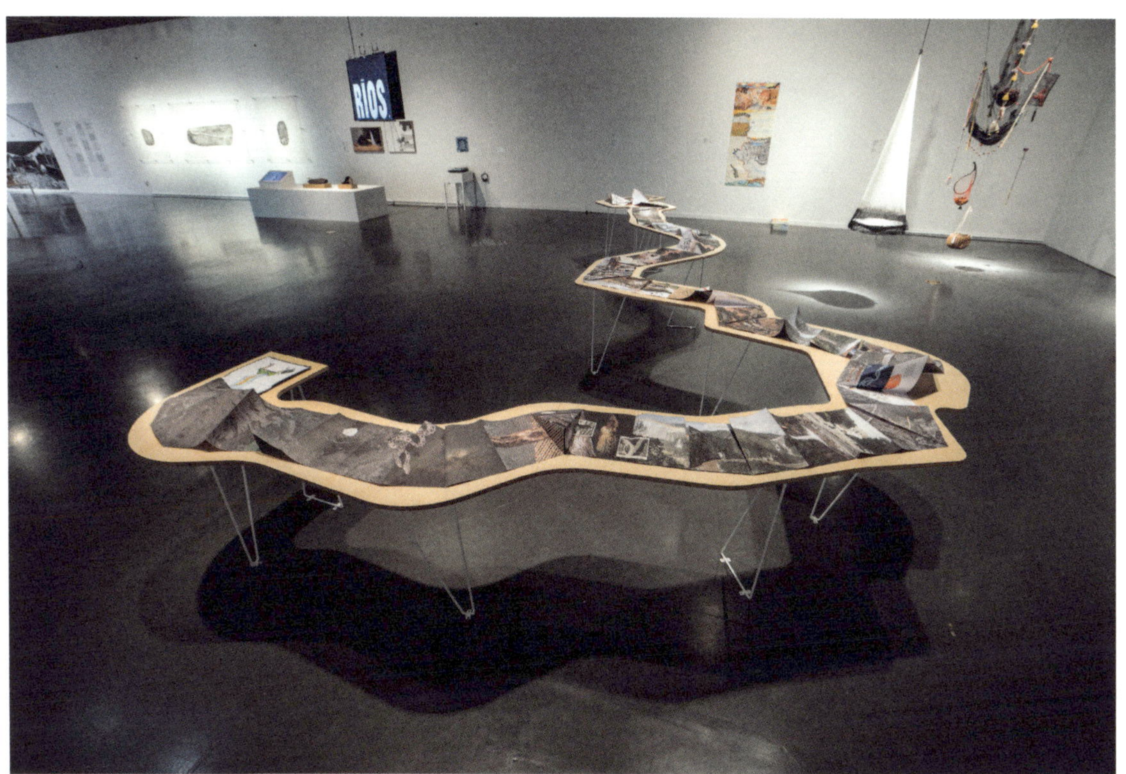

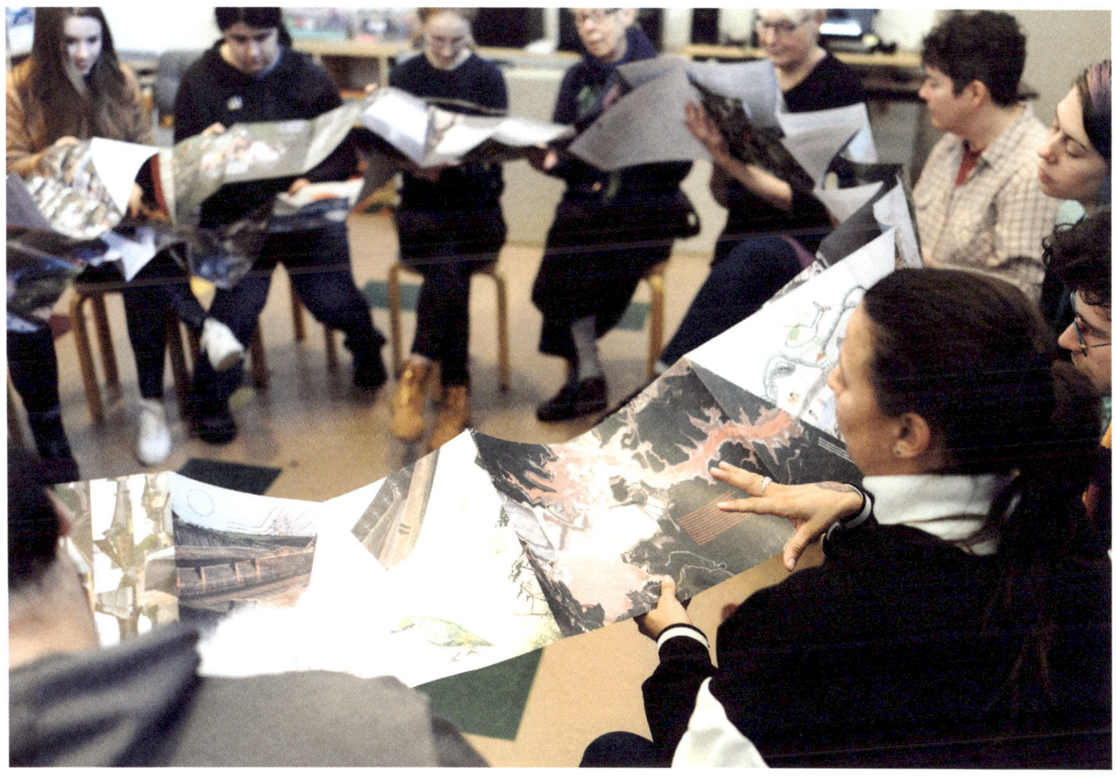

← Installation view of *If the river ran upwards*, Walter Phillips Gallery, Banff Centre for Arts and Creativity, 2018. Work shown: *Serpent River Book*, 2017.

↑ Installation view of *Working for the Future Past*, Seoul Museum of Art, Seoul, South Korea, 2017–18.

↑ Documentation of *Serpent River Book* Workshop with Carolina Caycedo, February 21, 2019. Henry Art Gallery, University of Washington, Seattle.

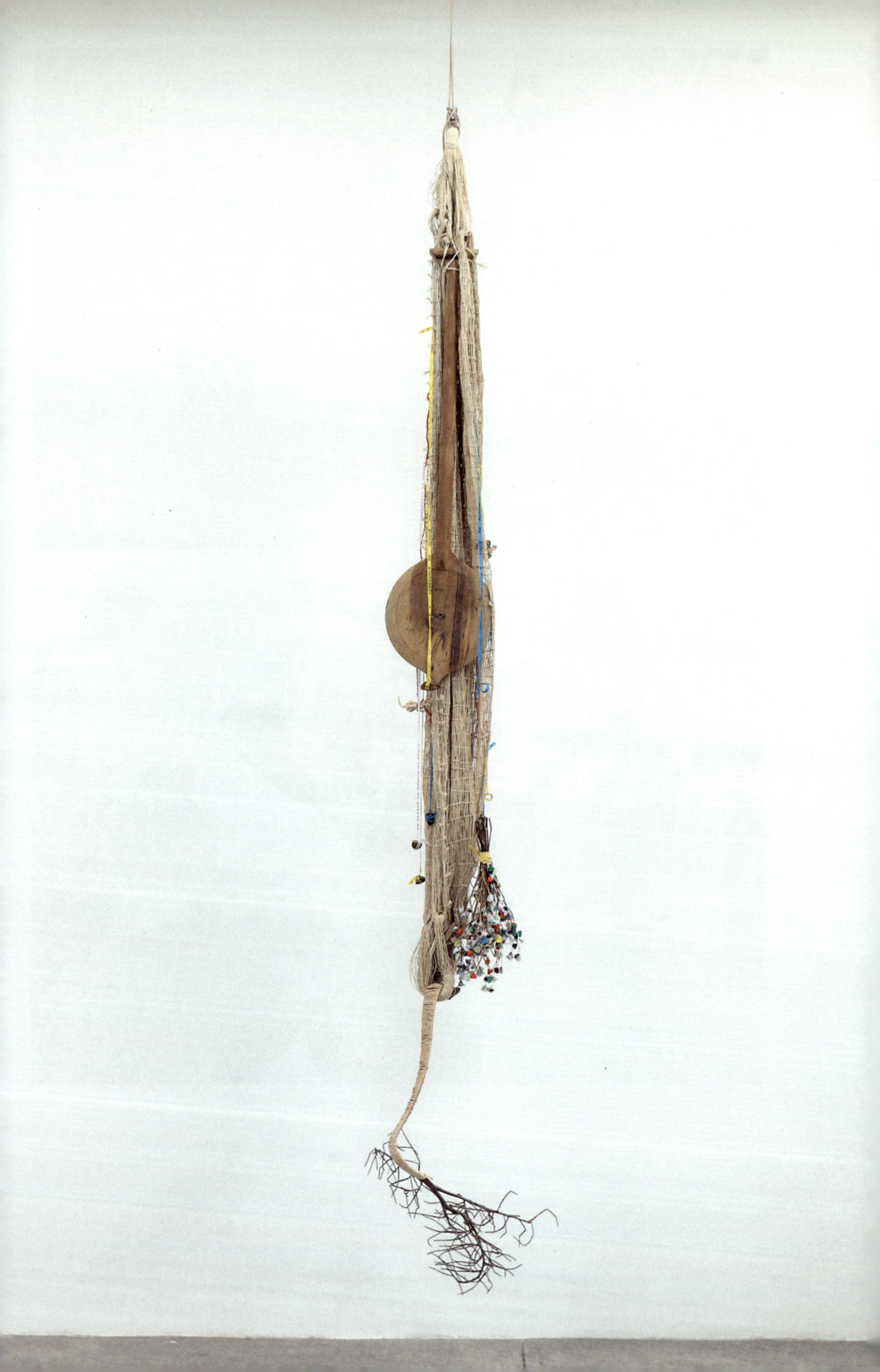

Cosmotarrafa Hamaca, 2016.

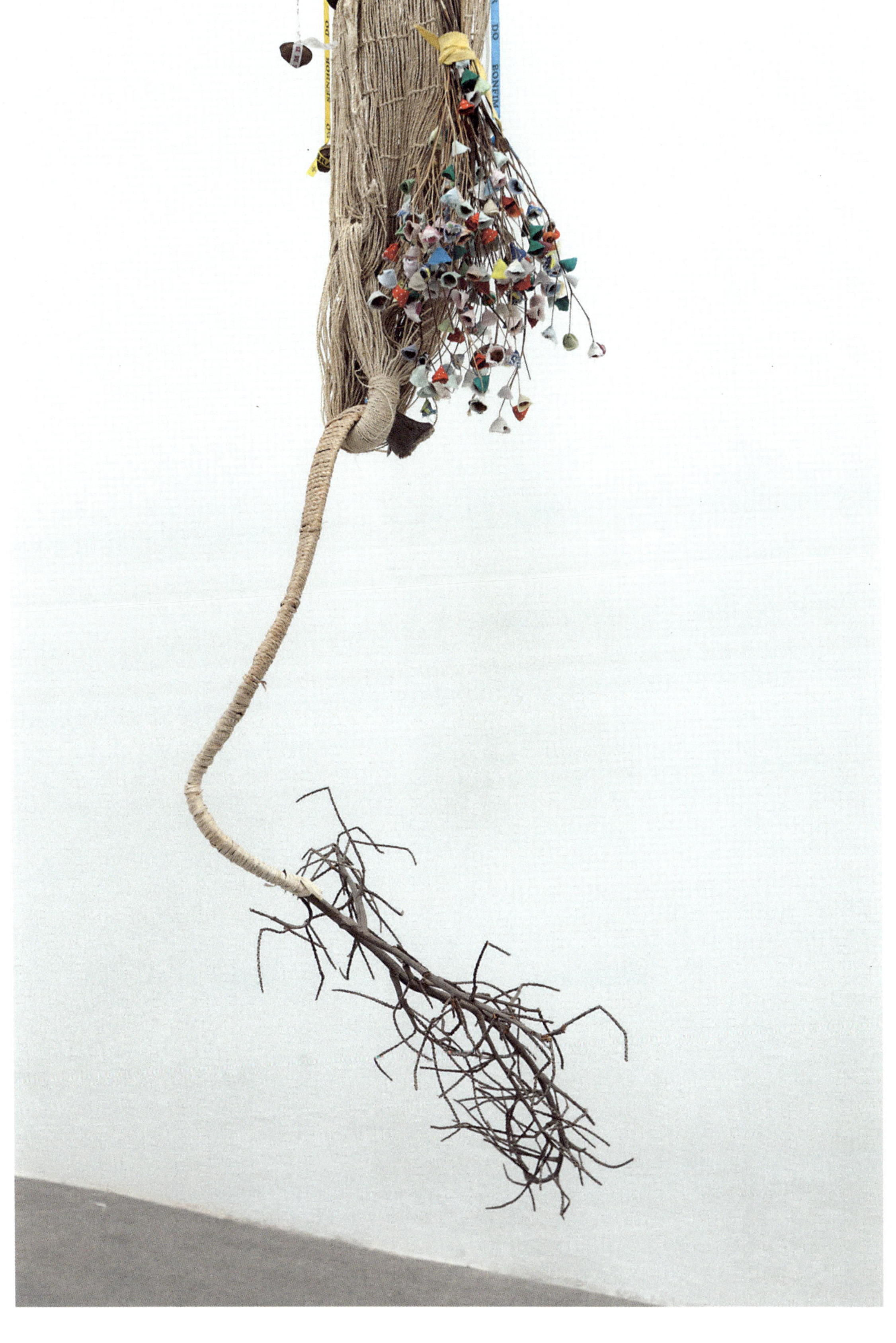

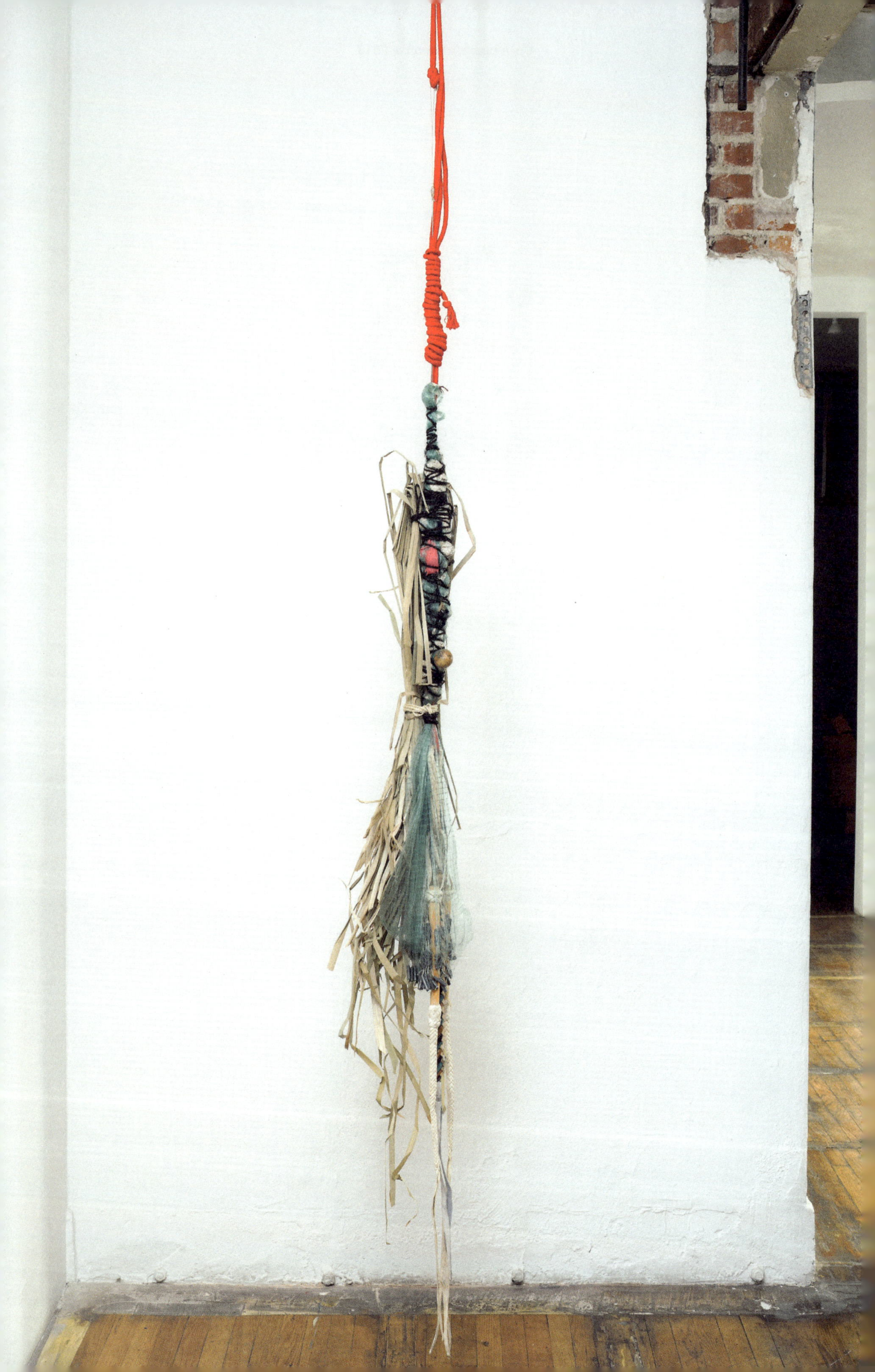

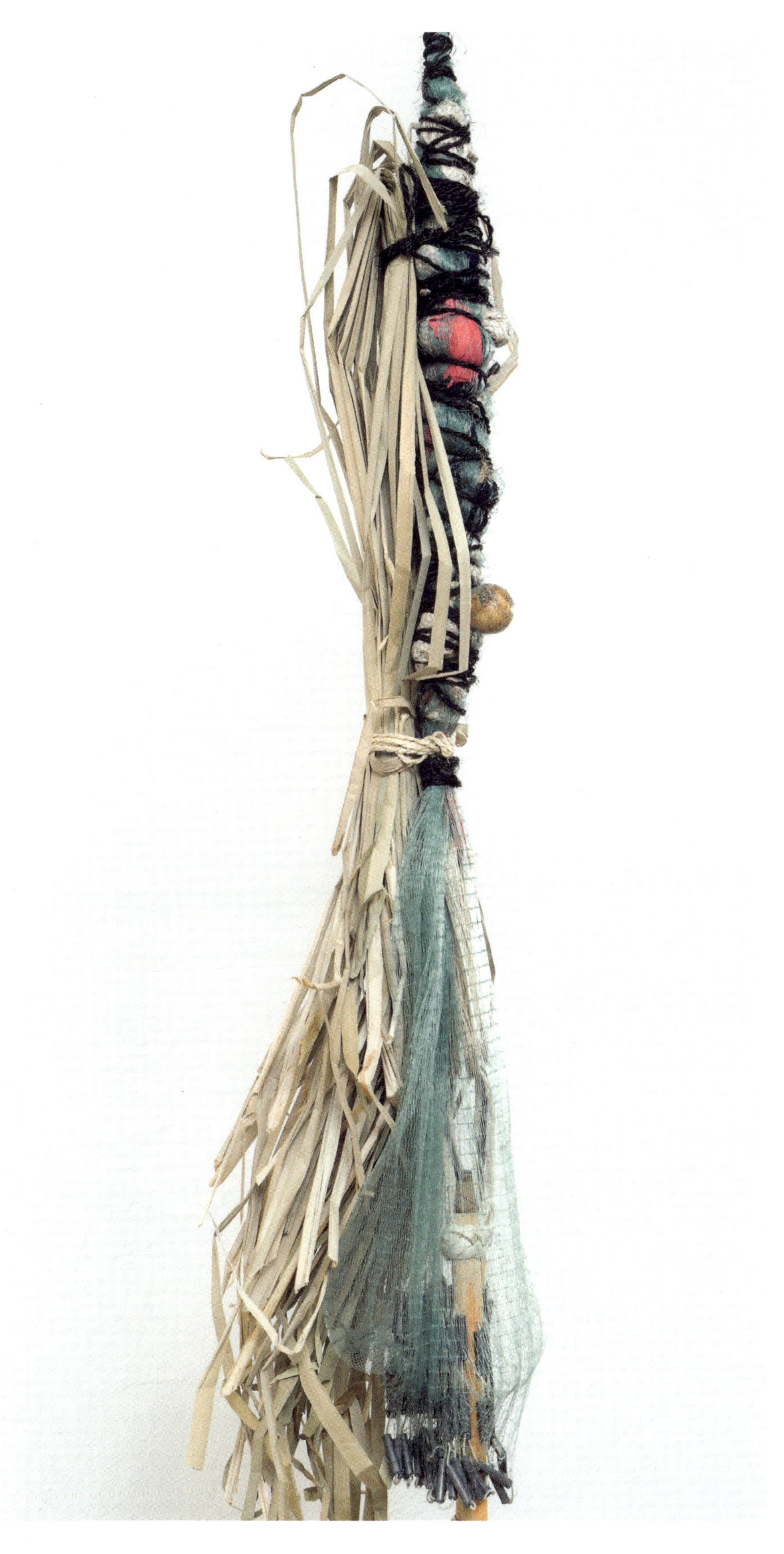

Installation views of *Carolina Caycedo: Hunger as Teacher / El Hambre Como Maestra*, Commonwealth and Council, Los Angeles, 2017. Work shown: *The Binding / El amarre*, 2017.

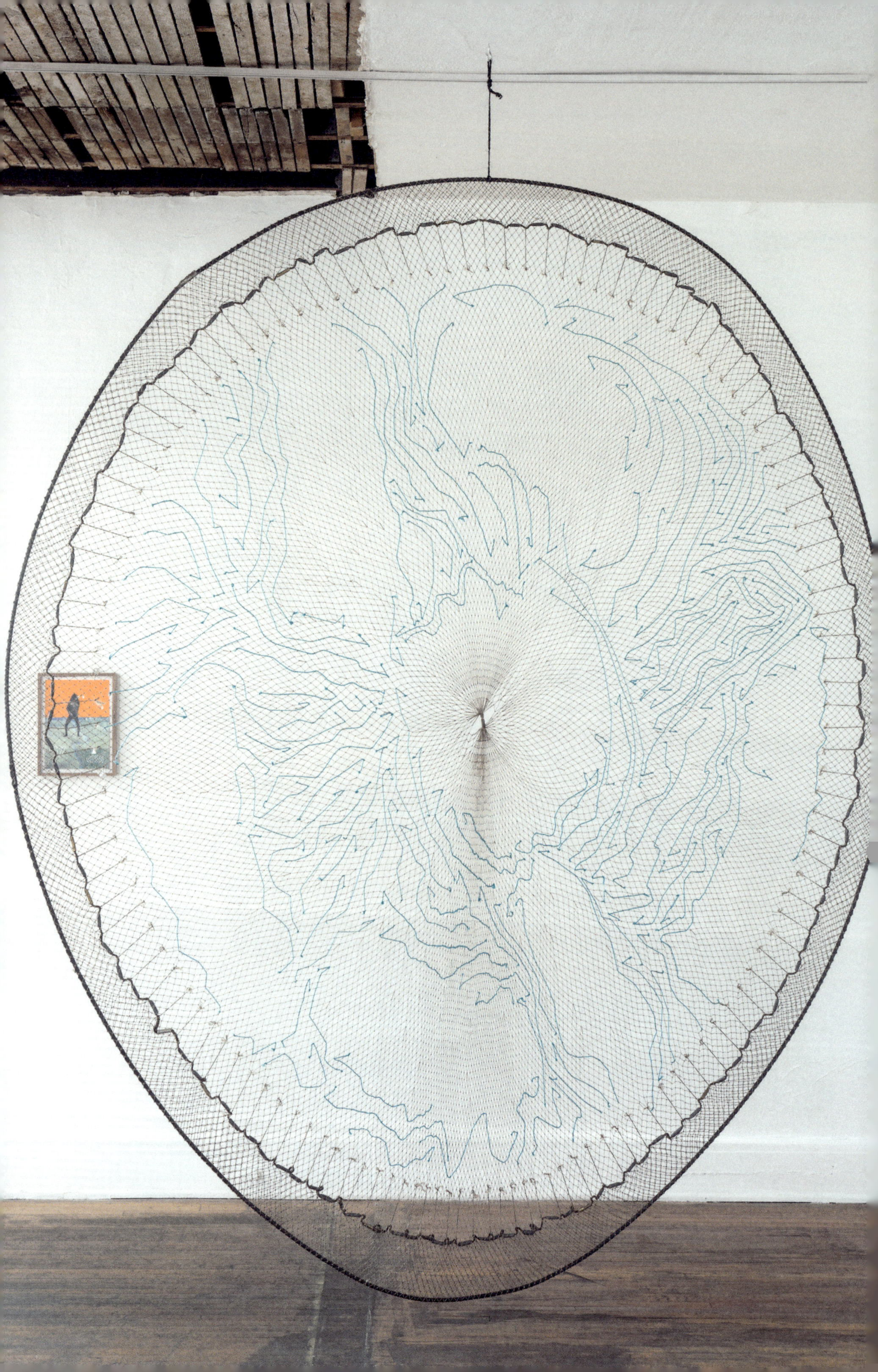

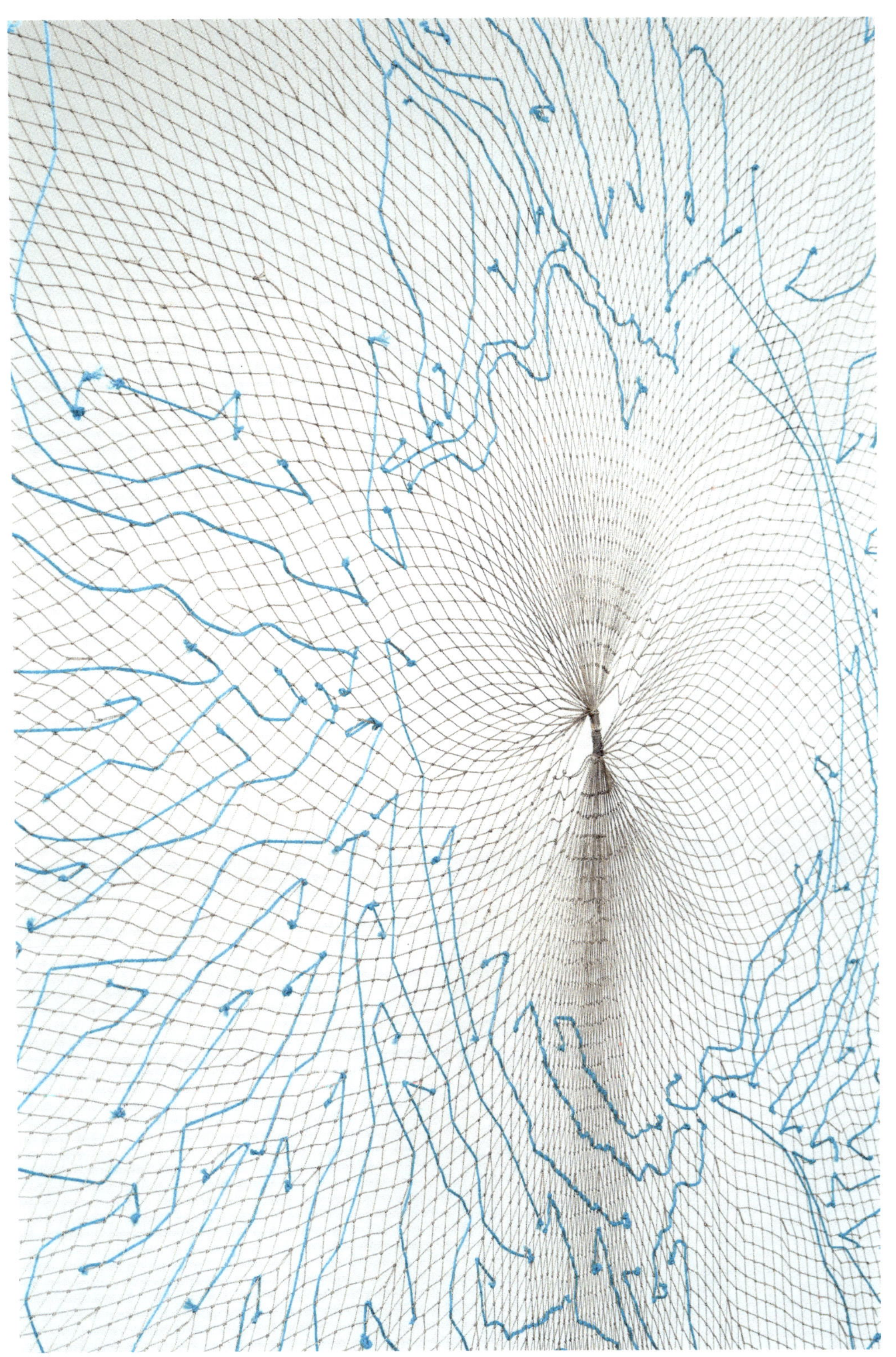

Installation views of *Carolina Caycedo: Hunger as Teacher / El Hambre Como Maestra*, Commonwealth and Council, Los Angeles, 2017.
Work shown: *Just Energy Transition / Trancisión energética justa*, 2017.

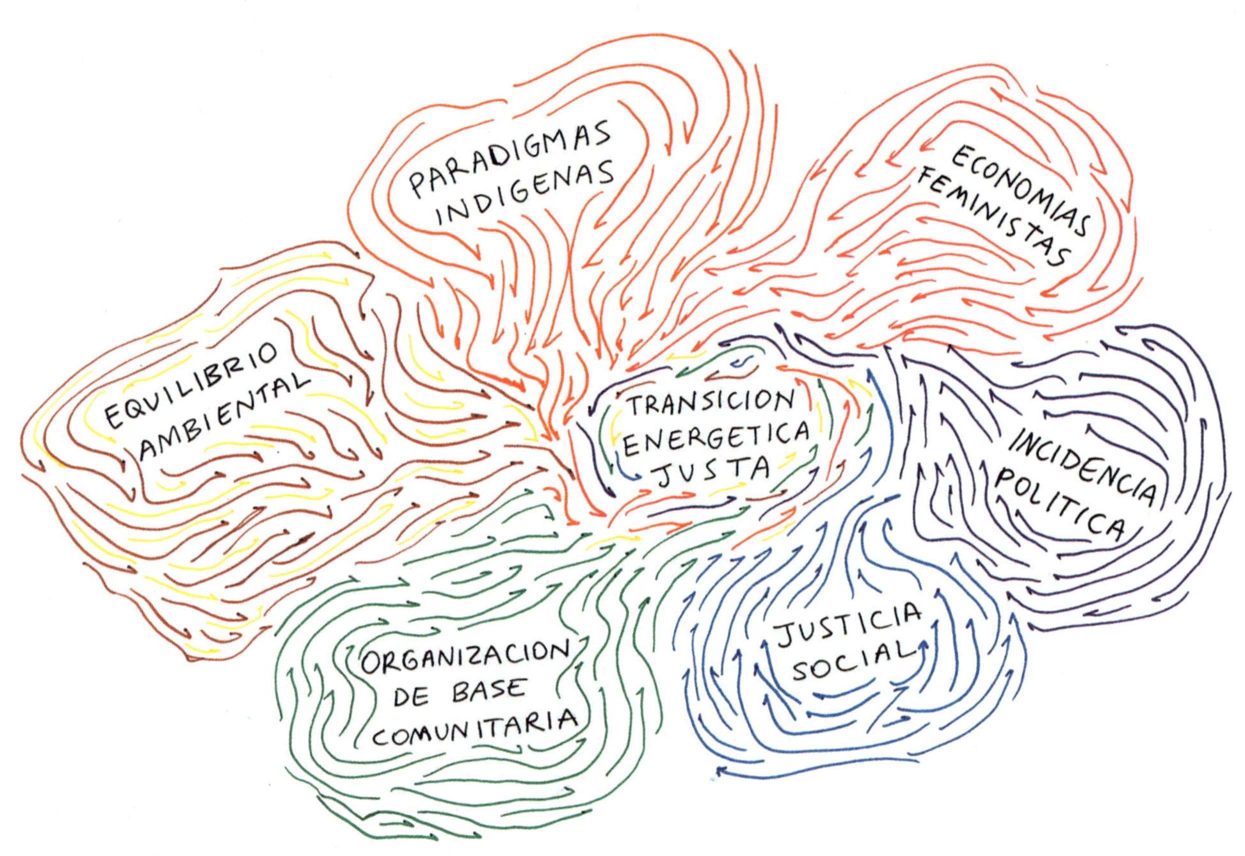

↑ *Just Energy Transition / Transición energética justa*, 2020. Color markers on paper.

→ Installation view of *Carolina Caycedo: Hunger as Teacher / El Hambre Como Maestra*, Commonwealth and Council, Los Angeles, 2017. Work shown: *Sustainable My Ass / A la mierda la sustentabilidad*, 2017. Collage; 12 1/2 × 10 × 1 1/2 in. (31.75 × 25.4 × 3.81 cm).

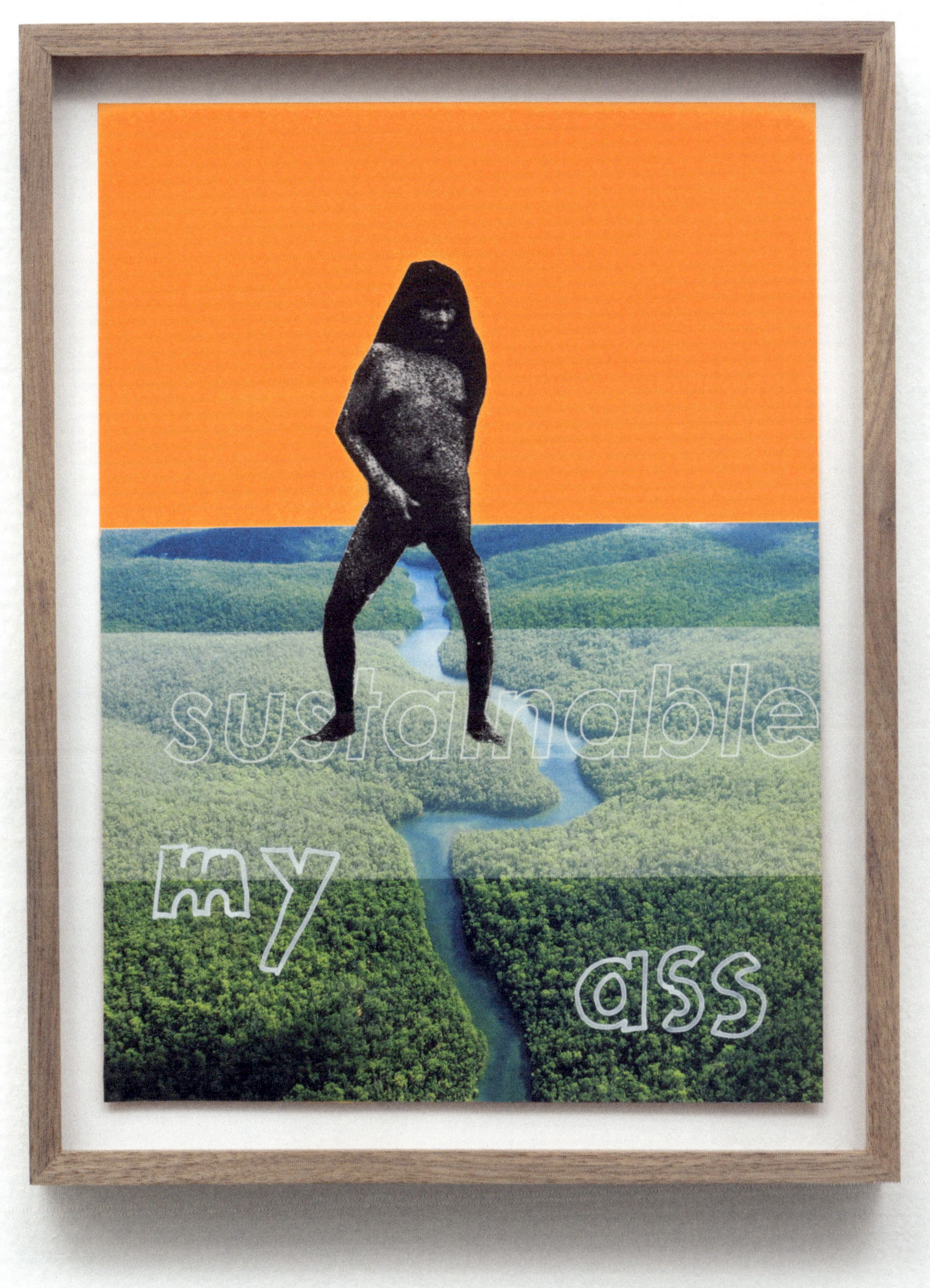
sustainable
my
ass

↓ *Lolita Lebron* from *Criminal Women* drawing series (2012–).

→ *Bree Newsome* from *Criminal Women* drawing series (2012–).

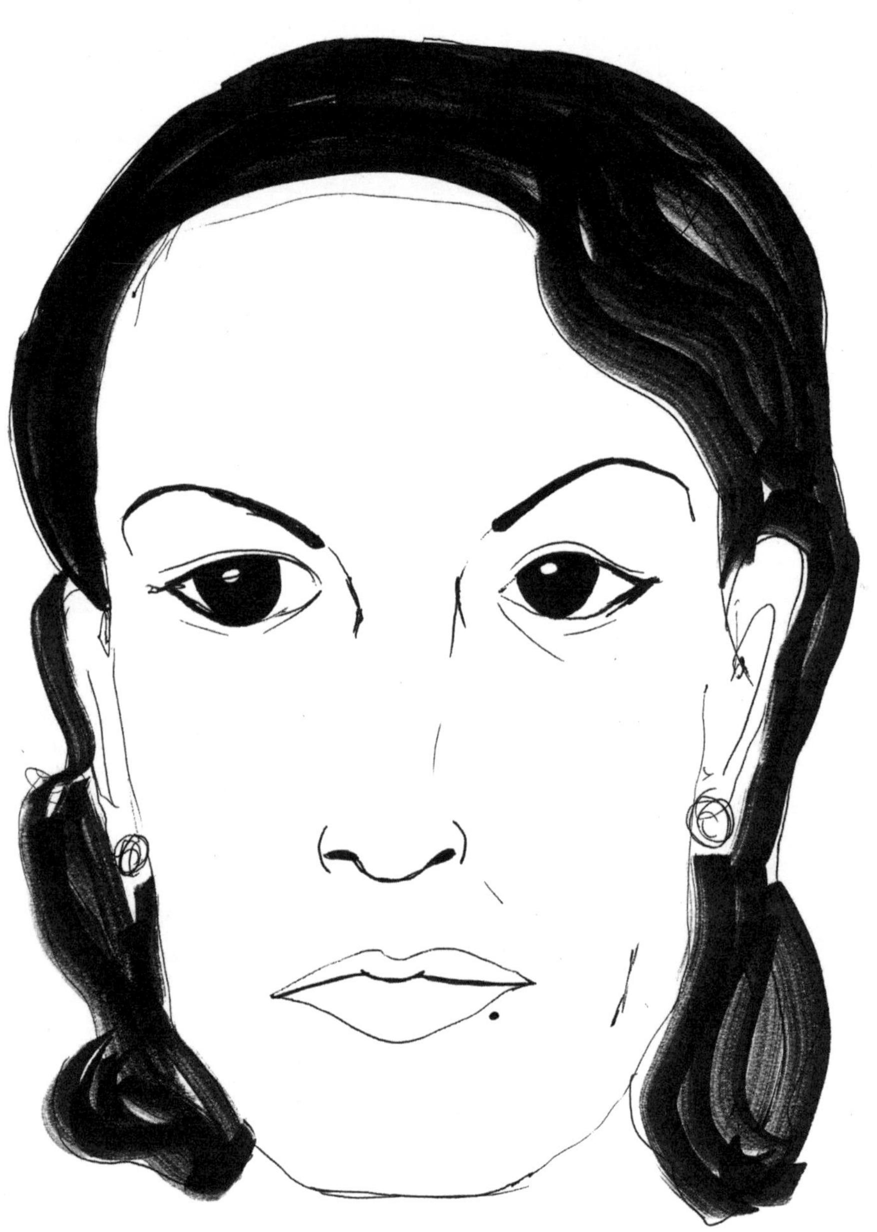

·BREE NEWSOME·
Arrested for taking down the Confederate Flag from a pole at a Statehouse in Columbia, USA

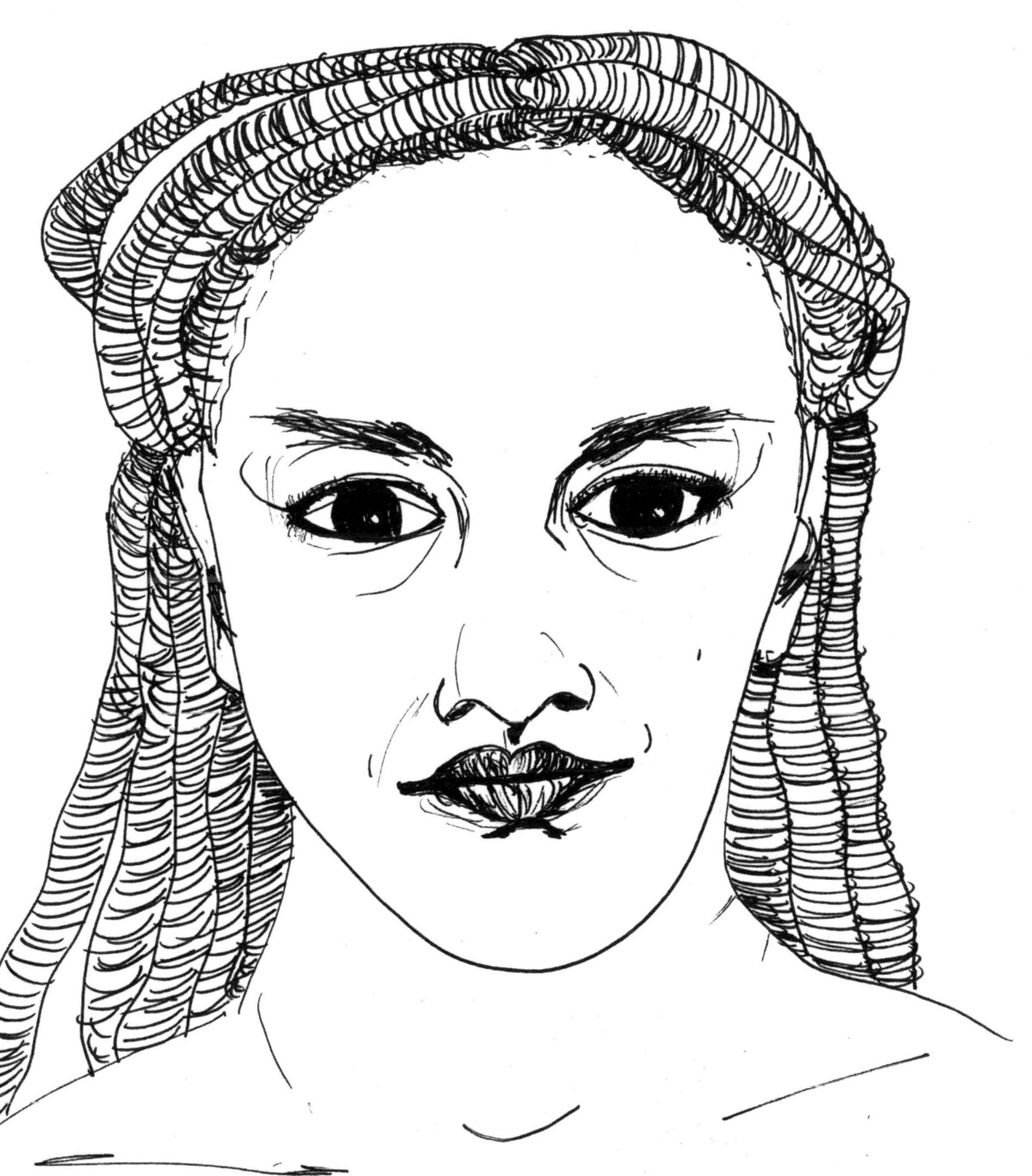

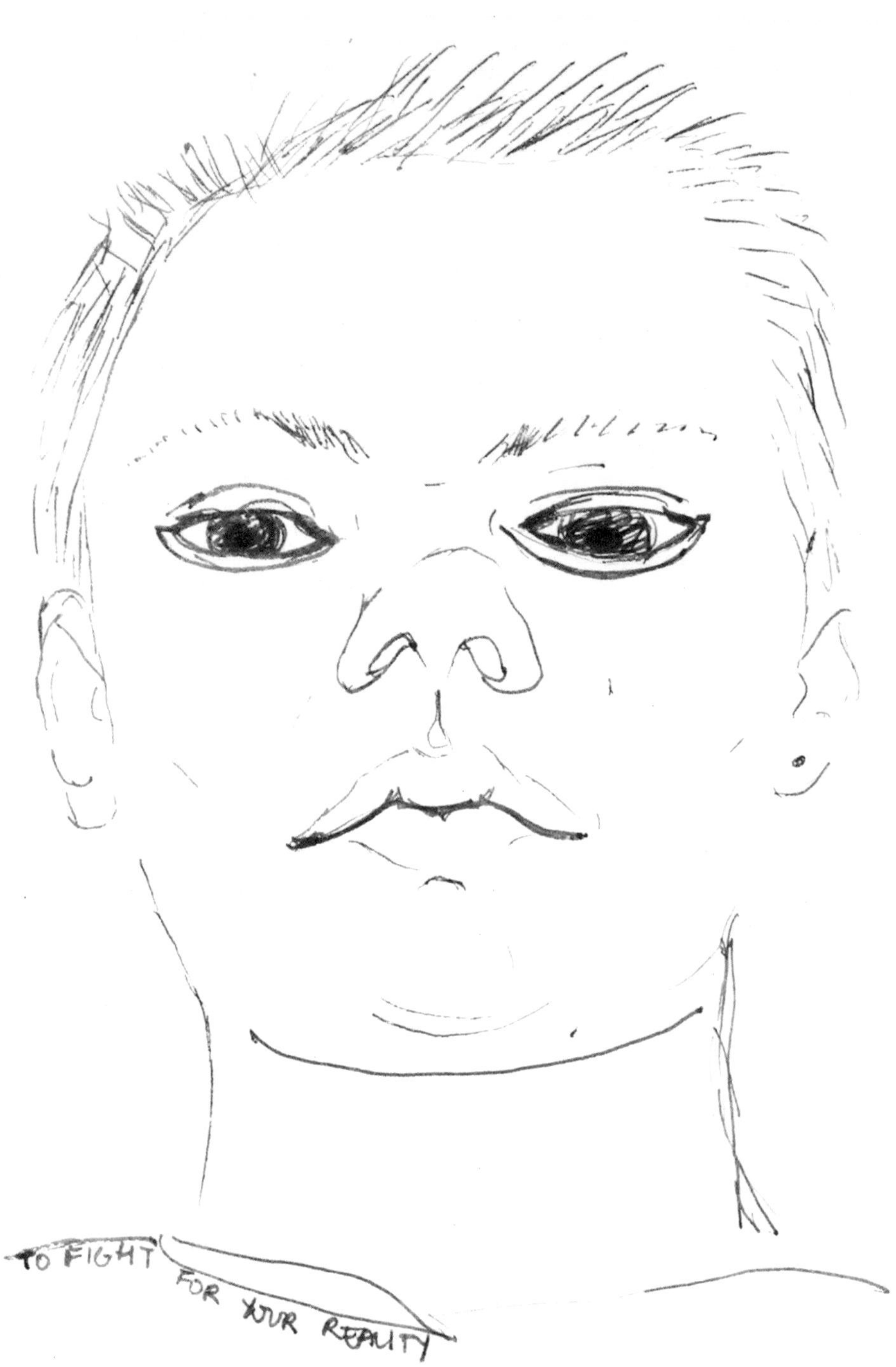

↑ *Self-Portrait*, 2002.

→ *Self-Portrait* (verso), 2002.

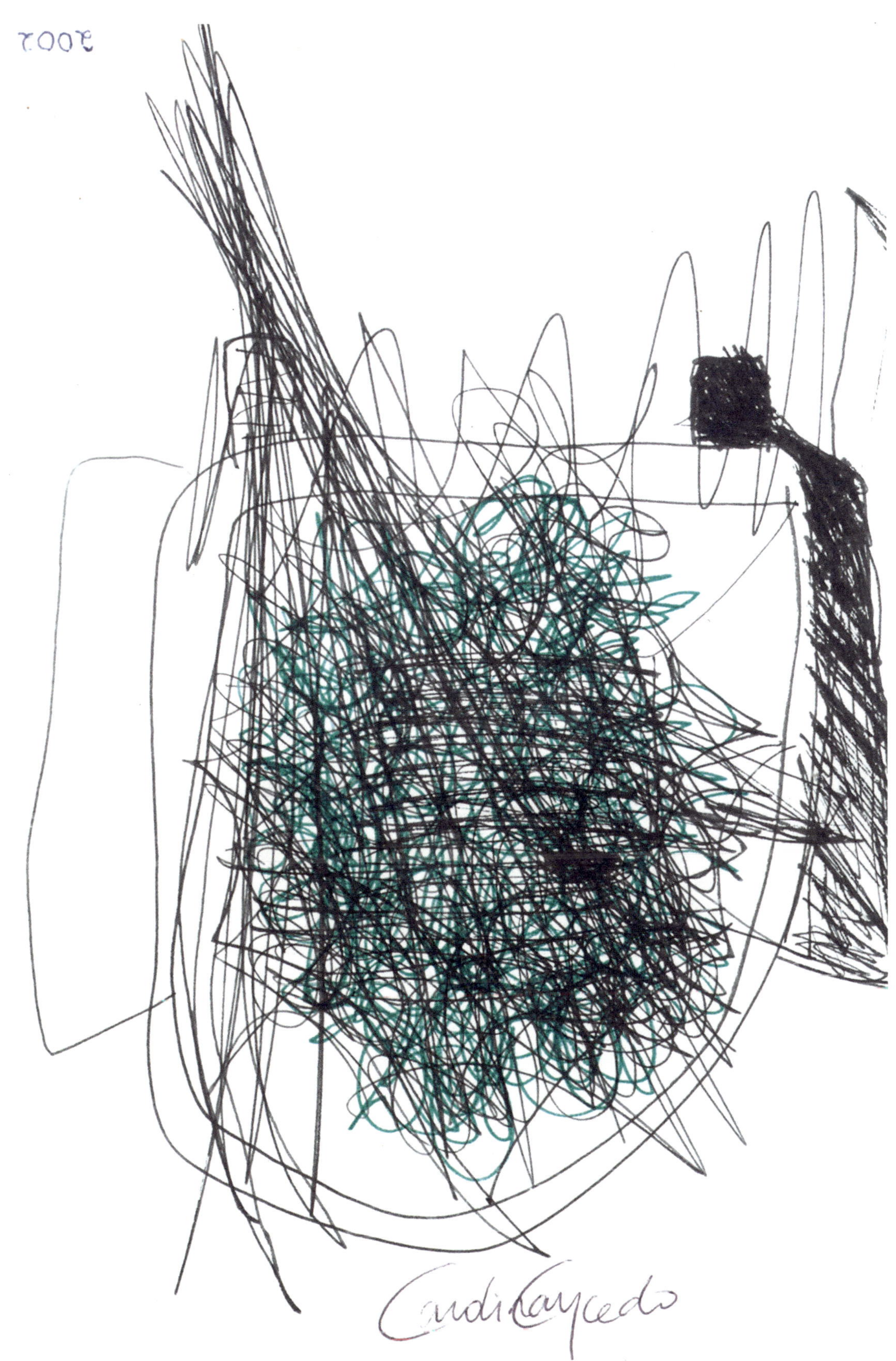

Born in London, England, in 1978
Lives and works in Los Angeles, California

EDUCATION

2012 MFA, Roski School of Fine Arts, University of Southern California, Los Angeles

1999 BFA, Los Andes University, Bogotá, Colombia

SELECTED SOLO EXHIBITIONS AND PROJECTS

2020 *From the Bottom of the River*, Museum of Contemporary Art Chicago, Chicago

When Walls Become Rivers, Art Exchange, University of Essex, United Kingdom

Cosmotarrayas, Institute of Contemporary Art, Boston

2019 *The Care Report,* Muzeum Sztuki, Łódź, Poland

Wanaawna, Rio Hondo and Other Spirits, Orange County Museum of Art, Santa Ana, California

Apariciones / Apparitions, Vincent Price Art Museum, East Los Angeles College, Los Angeles

2018 *Let Our Souls Grow Deep Like Rivers*, la_cápsula, Zürich

Those at the Great River-Mouth, Blackwood Gallery, University of Toronto Mississauga, Mississauga, Ontario

When The Land Speaks: Land of Friends, Projection Gallery, MSU Broad, Michigan State University, East Lansing, Michigan

2017 *El Hambre Como Maestra / Hunger as a Teacher,* Commonwealth and Council, Los Angeles

Conjuro de la Locura / Spell of Madness, Nuevo Museo de Arte Contemporáneo, Guatemala City

2015 *One Body of Water*, The Bowtie Project, Clockshop, Los Angeles

2014 *Tierra de los Amigos*, Instituto de Visión, Bogotá

Land of Friends, Gayle & Ed Roski Master of Fine Arts Gallery, University of Southern California, Los Angeles

2013 *The Headlong Stream is Termed Violent...*, DAAD Gallery, Berlin

Be Dammed, 18th Street Arts Center, Santa Monica, California

Humane Materiale II, Dispari & Dispari, Reggio Emilia, Italy

Criminal Women, Galerie du Jour, agnès b., Paris

2012 *Humane Materiale*, Hordaland Kunstsenter, Bergen, Norway

Criminal Women, Frieze Frame, London

Costo Sentimental, Galería La Central, Bogotá

2010 *La Stargate*, Intermediae, Matadero Madrid, Madrid

Mujeres en Mi, Solo Projects ARCO, Madrid

2009 *DAYTODAY Closure*, Impossible Exchange, Frieze Projects, Frieze Art Fair, London

DAYTODAY in L.A., g727, Los Angeles

2002 *DAYTODAY*, Secession, Vienna, Austria

SELECTED GROUP EXHIBITIONS AND PROJECTS

2020 *Potential Worlds 1: Planetary Memories*, Migros Museum für Gegenwartskunst, Zürich, Switzerland, and YARAT Contemporary Art Space, Baku, Azerbaijan

The Willow Sees the Heron's Image Upside Down, Tenerife Espacio de las Artes, Santa Cruz, Tenerife, Spain

Sacrifice, Röda Sten Konsthall, Göteburg, Sweden

Commonwealth, Institute for Contemporary Art at Virginia Commonwealth University, Richmond, Virginia, in partnership with Beta-Local, San Juan, and Philadelphia Contemporary, Philadelphia

Lange Filmnacht, Internationales Frauen Film Festival, Dortmund, Germany

2019 *...and other such stories*, Chicago Architecture Biennial, Chicago

Cosmopolis 2: Rethinking the Human, Centre Pompidou, Paris

Feminist Histories: Artists After 2000, Museo de Arte de São Paulo, São Paulo

Spill, Morris and Helen Belkin Art Gallery, University of British Columbia, Vancouver

Eco-Visionaries, Royal Academy of Arts, London

Universos Desdoblados, 45 Salón Nacional de Artistas, Museo de Arte Moderno de Bogotá, Bogotá

El Arbol de la Vida y la Abundancia, Instituto de Visión, Bogotá

The Green Goddess, Eldorado, lille3000, Lille, France

Pangea United, Muzeum Sztuki, Łódź, Poland

Unravelling Collective Forms, Los Angeles Contemporary Exhibitions, Los Angeles

PASADO TIEMPO FUTURO: Arte en Colombia en el siglo XXI, Museo de Arte Moderno, Medellín, Colombia

2018 *How to talk with birds, trees, fish, shells, snakes, lions and bulls*, Hamburger Bahnhof, Museum für Gegenwart, Berlin

Submerged, Contemporary Image Collective, Cairo, Egypt

Rituals of Labor and Engagement, The Huntington Library, Art Museum, and Botanical Gardens, San Marino, California

Made in L.A. 2018, Hammer Museum, Los Angeles

If the river ran upwards, Banff Centre for Arts and Creativity, Banff, Canada

Eco-Visionaries, Bildmuseet, Umea, Sweden, MAAT, Lisbon, Portugal, and LABoral, Gijón, Spain

Between the Waters, Whitney Museum of American Art, New York

Conjuro de Ríos, Museo de Arte, Universidad Nacional de Colombia, Bogotá

there will come soft rains, basis, Frankfurt, Germany

Between Bodies, Henry Art Gallery, University of Washington, Seattle

Still I Rise: Feminisms, Gender, Resistance, Act 1, Nottingham Contemporary, United Kingdom

Fields of Invisibility, Sesc Belenzinho, São Paulo

2017 *Working for the Future Past*, Seoul Museum of Art, Korea

ARTifariti, International Art and Human Rights Meeting in Western Sahara

La Nariz del Diablo, Espacio Odeón, Bogotá

A Universal History of Infamy, Los Angeles County Museum of Art, Los Angeles

La Vuelta, Les Rencontres d'Arles, Chapelle Saint-Martin du Méjan, Arles, France

A Decolonial Atlas: Strategies in Contemporary Art of the Americas, Vincent Price Art Museum, East Los Angeles College, Los Angeles

Almost There, Vargas Museum, University of the Philippines Diliman, Quezon City, Philippines

2016 *Incerteza Viva*, 32nd Bienal de São Paulo, São Paulo

AÚN, 44 Salón Nacional de Artistas, Museo de Arte de Pereira, Colombia

O Que Vem Com a Aurora, Casa Triângulo, São Paulo

El Origen de la Noche, Museo de Arte de la Universidad Nacional de Colombia, Bogotá

The Distance Plan: Climate and Infrastructure, Human Resources, Los Angeles

Beyond 2º, Museum of Contemporary Art Santa Barbara, California

2015 *Something Else*, Off Biennale Cairo, Egypt

HTUOS/HTRON: The New Coordinates of the Americas, Nuit Blanche Toronto, Toronto

En y entre geografías, Museo de Arte Moderno, Medellín, Colombia

Bring in the Reality, No Longer Empty, Nathan Cummings Foundation, New York

2014 *Acciones Territoriales*, Ex Teresa Arte Actual, Mexico City

Compassion Fatigue, New Wight Biennial, University of California Los Angeles, Los Angeles

8th Berlin Biennale, KW Institute for Contemporary Art, Berlin

2013 *The Phylogenesis of Generosity*, The First Prinzessinnengarten Outdoor Sculpture Triennial, Berlin

The Past is Present, Museum of Contemporary Art Detroit, Michigan

2012 *Here, There and Elsewhere: Assembling Communities,* San Francisco Museum of Modern Art, San Francisco

Agency of Unrealized Projects, DAAD Gallery, Berlin

Intense Proximity, La Triennale d'art contemporain, Palais de Tokyo, Paris

2011 *Living as Form*, Creative Time, New York

2009 2nd San Juan Poly/Graphic Triennial, San Juan, Puerto Rico

Younger Than Jesus, New Museum, New York

10th Havana Biennial, Cuba

2007 *New York States of Mind*, Queens Museum, New York

Displaced: Contemporary Art from Colombia, Glynn Vivian Art Gallery, Swansea, Wales

2006 *Day for Night*, Whitney Biennial, Whitney Museum, New York

Estrecho Dudoso, TEOR/éTica. San José, Costa Rica

2005 *J'en rêve*, Cartier Foundation for Contemporary Art, Paris

Transurbancia, La Casa Encendida, Madrid

2003 *The Structure of Survival*, 50th Biennale di Venezia, Italy

To Be Political It Has To Look Nice, apexart, New York

2002 *Enactments of the Self*, Steirischer Herbst / Styrian Festival, Graz, Austria

Big Social Game, International Biennal of Young Art, Torino, Italy

2001 *Egofugal—Fugue from Ego for the Next Emergence*, 7th International Istanbul Biennial, Istanbul, Turkey

Da Adversidade Vivemos, Musèe d'Art Moderne de la Ville de Paris, Paris

SELECTED GRANTS, RESIDENCIES, AND AWARDS

2020 Borderlands Fellowship, Vera List Center for Art and Politics at The New School, New York, and Center for Imagination in the Borderlands at Arizona State University, Tempe, Arizona

Wanlass Artist in Residence, Oxy Arts, Occidental College, Los Angeles

2019 Visiting Artist, International Studio Program, Office for Contemporary Art Norway

2018 Artist in Residence, /five Initiative, The Huntington Library, Art Museum, and Botanical Gardens, San Marino, California

2017 The Fellowship for Visual Arts, California Community Foundation, Los Angeles

2016 Artist in Residence, Fundação Armando Alvares Penteado (FAAP), São Paulo

2015 Creative Capital Visual Arts Award

Harpo Foundation Visual Artist Grant

2014 Art Matters Foundation Grant

2013 Rethinking Public Space, Grant Collaboration, Prince Claus Fund, Amsterdam

2012 Artists-in-Berlin Residency Program, DAAD Gallery, Berlin

2010 Artist in Residence, El Ranchito, Matadero Madrid

2009 International Cultural Exchange Grant, Department of Cultural Affairs, Los Angeles

2020 Durón, Maximilíano. "Best Practices: Each one of Carolina Caycedo's 'Cosmotarrayas' Is a Universe Unto Itself." Art News, February 27, 2020.

Hanna, Maeve. "Citizenship Through Art: A Conversation with Carolina Caycedo." *Sculpture Magazine,* February 17, 2020.

Miranda, Carolina. "Ghosts in the Water: Carolina Caycedo's River Portraits and Video Apparitions Tell Difficult Stories." *Los Angeles Times,* January 7, 2020.

2019 Allen, Lila. "Chicago Architecture Biennial: Rights to Resources." *Metropolis Magazine,* September 13, 2019.

Arora, Ankush. "Chicago Architecture Biennial interrogates historical narratives of built environments." *Architectural Digest India,* October 11, 2019.

Clemans, Gayle. "'Between Bodies' at Henry Art Gallery asks us to consider the natural world through different lenses." *The Seattle Times,* January 1, 2019.

Nguyen, Minh. "In this Mess Together: Interspecies Entanglements at Henry Art Gallery." *Art in America,* 11 March 11, 2019.

Thackara, Tess. "Colombian Artist Seeks Justice for the Natural World." *New York Times,* October 23, 2019.

2018 Abramovitch, Ingrid. "Haunting Views of a Planet Declining Faster for Some Communities Than for Others." *onEarth,* March 12, 2018.

Caycedo, Carolina. "Hunger as a Teacher." *Social Text Dossier,* Periscope, June 7, 2018.

Elkamel, Sara. "Submerged: The first exhibition in CIC's new space skims the surface of water as a subject." Mada Masr, 8 December 8, 2018.

Furman, Anna. "How virtual art appearing along the LA River tackles Gentrification, Immigration, and Environmental Issues." *Los Angeles Times,* November 8, 2018.

Gadanho, Pedro, ed. *Eco-Visionaries: Art, Architecture, and New Media After the Anthropocene.* Published by Hatje Cantz, Berlin.

Guzmán, Joaquín. "Arte colombiano y realidad aumentada en el espacio público de Los Angeles." *Arcadia,* November 28, 2018.

Harris, Gareth. "Feminisms, Gender, Resistance: Three Curators Choose Their Favourite Works From Politically Charged Show." *The Art Newspaper,* November 19, 2018.

Lin, Candice. "Licking the Wound: Three Works from Pacific Standard: LA/LA." *X-TRA Contemporary Art Quarterly* Vol. 20, No. 4, Summer 2018.

Lozano, Catalina and Carolina Caycedo. "We Were Never Modern." *Terremoto* Issue 12, September 3, 2018.

Murray, Yxta Maya. "Two Artists of Color Boldly Provoke a Conservative Museum Locked in the Past." Artsy, December 31, 2018.

Stromberg, Matt. "Resolutely Political LA Artists Focus on the Body in the City's Latest Biennial." Hyperallergic, June 4, 2018.

Wagley, Catherine. "The Hammer's 'Made in LA' Avoids Common Biennial Pitfalls to Paint a Compelling Portrait of a Vibrant Art Community." artnet news, June 11, 2018.

"We Are the River." emisférica (Expulsion), Vol. 14, Issue1. Published by the Hemispheric Institute.

Wiesner, Christoph. "Serpent River Book." *The Photobook Review* Issue 14, Spring 2018.

2017 Fragoza, Carribean. "What is Latin American Art? Finding Answers at Pacific Standard Time: LA/LA." *LA Weekly*, September 12, 2017.

Gómez-Barris, Macarena. *The Extractive Zone: Social Ecologies and Decolonial Perspectives*. Published by Duke University Press, Durham, North Carolina.

Miranda, Carolina. "From Donald Duck to Donald Trump, an unprecedented look at Latin American art holds up a mirror to the U.S." *Los Angeles Times*, September 6, 2017.

Mizota, Sharon. "Our Rivers, Ourselves: One Artist's Very Personal Take on the Impact of Dams." *Los Angeles Times*, September 18, 2017.

"Vigilia en Manila recuerda la muerte de activistas medioambientales." EFE/EPA, March 4, 2017.

2016

Amirsadeghi, Hossein and Catherine Petitgas, eds. *Contemporary Art Colombia*. Published by Thames & Hudson, London.

Gómez-Barris, Macarena. "Inverted Visuality: Against the Flow of Extractivism." *Journal of Visual Culture* Vol. 15, Issue 1, 2016.

Halart, Sophie and Mara Polgovsky Ezcurra. *Sabotage Art: Politics and Iconoclasm in Contemporary Latin America*. Published by I.B. Tauris, London.

Jaggi, Maya. "São Paulo Biennial: A Leap Into the Unknown." *Financial Times*, September 16, 2016.

Molina, Camila. "A ecologia aparece em diferentes níveis na 32ª Bienal de São Paulo." *Estadão*, June 15, 2016.

Schwendener, Martha. "Uncertainty in Brazil, Vitality in Its Arts." *New York Times*, October 12, 2016.

Strecker, Márion. "Nenhum homem é uma ilha." *Revista SeLecT*, September 1, 2016.

Suazo, Félix. "Después de la identidad: cuerpo e in-disciplina." Tráfico Visual, November 10, 2016.

2015

Caycedo, Carolina. "One Body of Water." Published by Clockshop in collaboration with California State Parks.

Caycedo, Carolina and Entre Aguas. "'We Need the River to be Free': Activists Fight the Privatization of Colombia's Longest River." Creative Time Reports, March 17, 2015.

Garcia, Ángeles. "Seis Nuevas Caras Colombianas en Arco." *Babelia El País*, February 20, 2015.

2014

Albarracín, Victor. "Carolina Caycedo: Be Dammed." Artishock, March 8, 2014.

Crow, Kelly. "Colombia's Art Scene Heats Up." *The Wall Street Journal*, June 26, 2014.

Malvern, Sue and Gabriel Koureas, eds. *Terrorists Transgressions: Gender and the Visual Culture of the Terrorist*. Published by I.B. Tauris, London.

2013

Rivas, Pilar Tompkins. "Geochoreographies: Carolina Caycedo Versus Social and Natural Erasure." Artbound, KCET, December 9, 2013.

2012

Roca, José and Sylvia Suarez, eds. *Transpolítico: Art in Colombia, 1992–2012*. Published by Lunwerg Editores, Barcelona, Spain.

Thompson, Nato, ed. *Living as Form: Socially Engaged Art from 1991–2011*. Published by MIT Press, Cambridge, Massachussetts.

2011

Bernal, María Clara. "Raíces, rutas y otros radicalismos: el desplazamiento más allá del trauma." *Revista ERRATA #5*, August 2011.

Rehberg, Vivian Sky. "CGEM: Notes About Emancipation." *Frieze Magazine*, Issue 137, March 1, 2011.

2010

Guaza, Luisa Fuentes. *#USTEDES NOSOTROS*. Published by Index Book, Madrid, Spain.

Self-Portrait, 2002
Ink on paper
10 1/4 × 7 3/4 in. (26.04 × 19.69 cm)
Collection of Mima and César Reyes, Puerto Rico

TRUST EACH OTHER, 2007, from the *Banners* series (2004–)
Embroidered nylon banner
3 × 18 ft. (0.91 × 5.49 m)
Courtesy of the artist and Instituto de Visión, Bogotá

NI DIOS, NI PATRÓN, NI MARIDO, 2009, from the *Banners* series (2004–)
Embroidered nylon banner
3 × 18 ft. (0.91 × 5.49 m)
Courtesy of the artist and Instituto de Visión, Bogotá

LA CRISIS ES UNA MANEA DE GOBERNAR, 2010, from the *Banners* series (2004–)
Embroidered nylon banner
3 × 18 ft. (0.91 × 5.49 m)
Courtesy of the artist and Instituto de Visión, Bogotá

Mujeres en Mi / Women in Me (1 of 4), 2010, from the *Mujeres en Mi* series (2010–)
Embroidery on clothing, synthetic yarn, and thread
12 × 6 ft. (3.66 × 1.83 m)
Elisa Estrada F-S

Spaniards Named Her Magdalena, But Natives Call Her Yuma, 2013
Two-channel video installation, HD video (color, sound), concrete, metal, and water
26 minutes, 6 seconds
Dimensions variable
Courtesy of the artist, Instituto de Visión, Bogotá, and Commonwealth and Council, Los Angeles

Yuma, or the Land of Friends II, 2013–20
Print on vinyl
20 × 50 ft. (6.09 × 15.24 m)
Courtesy of the artist

Cosmotarraya Elwha, 2016–20
Hand-dyed artisanal fishing net with lead weights, wood panel, hand-dyed jute cord, Bonfim ribbon, sage bundle, cord, wood stick, metal bells, drumstick, leather sandals, Mizac sheep's wool *ruana, Abrus herba* bundles, with herbs including chili pepper, sage, and copal (replaceable by any medicinal herb)
66 × 39 × 14 in. (421 × 99.1 × 35.56 cm)
Courtesy of the artist and Instituto de Visión, Bogotá

Cosmotarrafa Hamaca, 2016
Artisanal Kayapo hammock, dry palm branch wrapped with reed cord, wooden paddle, Bonfim ribbon, and Brazil nuts
118 1/8 × 11 3/4 × 7 7/8 in. (300 × 30 × 20 cm)
Collection of Benedicta M. Badia de Nordenstahl

Cosmotarrafa Ver-o-Peso, 2016
Hand-dyed funnel fishing nets with iron ring, embroidery on cotton fabric, dyed cotton rope, and a wooden stick
102 3/8 × 23 5/8 × 23 5/8 in. (260 × 60 × 60 cm)
Collection of Tracy O'Brien and Thaddeus Stauber

Elwha, 2016, from the *River Books* series (2016–)
Marker on Canson paper
70 × 17 3/4 in. (170 × 45 cm)
Collection of Mima and César Reyes, Puerto Rico

Yaqui, 2016, from the *River Books* series (2016–)
Marker on Canson paper
70 × 17 3/4 in. (170 × 45 cm)
Collection of Mima and César Reyes, Puerto Rico

Yuma, 2016, from the *River Books* series (2016–)
Marker on Canson paper
70 × 17 3/4 in. (170 × 45 cm)
Collection of Mima and César Reyes, Puerto Rico

The Binding / El amarre, 2017
Nylon fishing net, lead weights, hand-dyed cotton cord, hand-dyed jute cord, leather whips, jute thread, dried cattails, seeds, and plastic sack
117 × 11 1/4 × 11 1/4 in. (297.2 × 28.6 × 28.6 cm)
Whitney Museum of American Art, New York
Purchase, with funds from the Painting and Sculpture Committee
2018.182

Just Energy Transition / Transición energética justa, 2017
Tar-dipped fishing net, lead weights, iron rod, wool, and rope
Approx. 104 × 91 in. (264 × 231 cm)
Collection of Kristin Rey and Michael Rubel, Los Angeles

Pisisbaiya, 2017, from the *River Books* series (2016–)
Marker on Canson paper
70 × 31 1/2 in. (170 × 80 cm)
Courtesy of the artist and Commonwealth and Council, Los Angeles

Serpent River Book & Serpent Table, 2017
Installation
Artist book, wooden table, and metal table legs
Dimensions variable
Edition 1 of 10 aside from 2 artist proofs
Courtesy of the artist, Commonwealth and Council, Los Angeles, and Instituto de Visión, Bogotá

Undammed / Desbloqueada, 2017
Hand-dyed fishing net, lead weights, metal gold pan, Navajo sandstone, copper intrauterine device (IUD), thread, and rope
64 × 19 × 19 in. (162.5 × 48 × 48 cm)
Collection of Ann Soh Woods

Apariciones / Apparitions, 2018
Single-channel HD video installation (color, sound)
9 minutes, 30 seconds
Courtesy of the artist, Instituto de Visíon, Bogotá, and Commonwealth and Council, Los Angeles

My Feminine Lineage of Environmental Struggle II, 2018–19
Printed canvas banner
65 × 250 in. (165 × 635 cm)
Courtesy of the artist, Commonwealth and Council, Los Angeles, and Instituto de Visión, Bogotá

Ósun, 2018
Hand-dyed fishing net, steel chain, steel pot lid, mirror, enamel, spray paint, hoop earrings, paracord, string, and brass handles
120 × 48 × 48 in. (304.8 × 121.92 × 121.92 cm)
From the collection of Vibiana Molina

Sap, 2018
Artisanal fishing net, paracord, plastic rope, metal chain, and carabiner
132 × 132 × 2 in. (335.28 × 335.28 × 5 cm)
Courtesy of the artist and Instituto de Visión, Bogotá

Ume Vindel, 2018, from the *River Books* series (2016–)
Marker on Canson paper
Diptych, each: 70 × 22 in. (170 × 56 cm)
Courtesy of the artist and Commonwealth and Council, Los Angeles

Limen, 2019
Three hand-dyed artisanal fishing nets, lead weights, metal rings, paracord, batea (carved wooded gold pan), and fresh flowers
80 × 46 × 46 in. (203.2 × 116.8 × 116.8 cm)
Collection of Maria and Harry Hopper

Muxeres en Mi / Womyn in Me (1 of 2), 2019, from the *Mujeres en Mi* series (2010–)
Embroidery on clothing, synthetic yarn, and thread
12 × 6 ft. (3.66 × 1.83 m)
Courtesy of the artist and Commonwealth and Council, Los Angeles

Muxeres en Mi / Womyn in Me (2 of 2), 2019, from the *Mujeres en Mi* series (2010–)
Embroidery on clothing, synthetic yarn, and thread
12 × 6 ft. (3.66 × 1.83 m)
Courtesy of the artist and Instituto de Visión, Bogotá

San Gabriel, 2019
Photograph printed on cotton canvas (double-sided)
63 × 670 in. (160 × 1701.8 cm)
Courtesy of the artist and Commonwealth and Council, Los Angeles

From the Bottom of the River / Desde el fondo del río III 2020, 2020
Hand-painted blown glass, artisanal fishing net, and lead weights
Diptych, overall: 24 4/5 × 77 1/5 × 5 9/10 in. (63 × 196 × 15 cm)
Collection of Nada and Michael Gray

Benedicta M. Badia de Nordenstahl
Carolina Caycedo
Commonwealth and Council, Los Angeles
Elisa Estrada
Nada and Michael Gray
Maria and Harry Hopper
Instituto de Visión, Bogotá
Vibiana Molina
Tracy O'Brien and Thaddeus Stauber
Kristin Rey and Michael Rubel, Los Angeles
Mima and César Reyes, Puerto Rico
Ann Soh Woods
Whitney Museum of American Art, New York

Lead support is provided by the Harris Family Foundation in memory of Bette and Neison Harris: Caryn and King Harris, Katherine Harris, Toni and Ron Paul, Pam Szokol, Linda and Bill Friend, and Stephanie and John Harris; the Margot and W. George Greig Ascendant Artist Fund; R. H. Defares; Zell Family Foundation; Julie and Larry Bernstein; Cari and Michael Sacks; and Anonymous.

Major support is provided by Estrellita and Daniel Brodsky; and Charlotte Cramer Wagner and Herbert S. Wagner III of the Wagner Foundation.

Generous support is provided by Anonymous; Commonwealth and Council; Marisa Murillo; and David Walega.

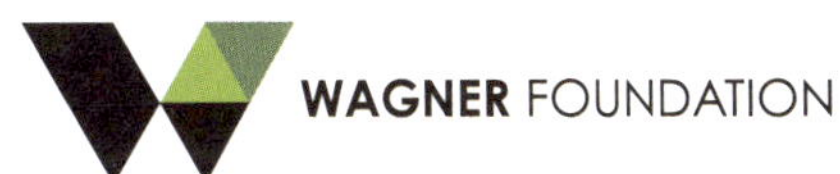

CARLA ACEVEDO-YATES

Carla Acevedo-Yates was born in San Juan, Puerto Rico, and has worked as a curator, researcher, and art critic across Latin America, the Caribbean, and the United States. She is the Marilyn and Larry Fields Curator at the Museum of Contemporary Art Chicago. Previously, she was the associate curator at the Eli and Edythe Broad Art Museum at Michigan State University, where she organized solo exhibitions of new work by Johanna Unzueta, Claudia Peña Salinas, Jesús "Bubu" Negrón, Duane Linklater, and Scott Hocking. She recently organized *Fiction of a Production*, a major exhibition of work by Argentinian conceptual art pioneer David Lamelas, and cocurated *Michigan Stories: Mike Kelley and Jim Shaw*. She earned an MA in curatorial studies and contemporary art from the Center for Curatorial Studies at Bard College, where she was awarded the Ramapo Curatorial Prize, and a BA in Spanish and Latin American Cultures from Barnard College, where she received the Clara Schifrin Memorial Spanish Prize in Poetry. In 2015 she was awarded a Creative Capital | Andy Warhol Foundation Arts Writers Grant for an article on Cuban painter Zilia Sánchez.

DAVID HERNÁNDEZ PALMAR

David Hernández Palmar is a photographer, videographer, program organizer, and journalist. He has produced documentaries for Deutsche Welle and Canal Arte and has worked collaboratively on documentaries on the Wayuu such as *Dalia se va de Jepira* (2006). He has participated twice in the National Museum of the American Indian's Native American Film + Video Festival, both as a co-director of the documentary *Owners of the Water* (2009) and as a discussant in the roundtable "Mother Earth in Crisis." Hernández Palmar has also independently curated Indigenous film programs in Venezuela and abroad. In 2007 he received the Premio Sebastián Garrido Award for Photography at the III Bienal Nacional de Artes Plásticas of Puerto La Cruz, Venezuela, for his series *Iconocomunicantes*, and in 2010 he was distinguished with an Honorable Mention for his photo essay "Wayuu Life: a View From Within" by National Geographic's All Roads Photography Awards. He studied journalism at the Universidad Rafael Belloso Chacín and photography at Escuela Julio Vengoechea in Maracaibo, Venezuela. Hernández Palmar lives in Maracaibo, where he works as an independent reporter for several publications, including the Wayuu journal *Wayuunaiki*.

PILAR TOMPKINS RIVAS

Pilar Tompkins Rivas is the Chief Curator and Deputy Director of Curatorial and Collections at the The Lucas Museum of Narrative Art. Previously she was the director of the Vincent Price Art Museum (VPAM) at East Los Angeles College. Specializing in US Latinx and Latin American contemporary art, she has organized dozens of exhibitions throughout the United States, Colombia, Egypt, France, and Mexico. At VPAM she spearheaded partnerships between the museum and the Smithsonian, the Los Angeles County Museum of Art (LACMA), and the Huntington Library, Art Collections, and Botanical Gardens. Prior to her appointment as director, she served as the coordinator of curatorial initiatives at LACMA, where she helped launch and co-direct two Mellon-funded programs for the museum: the UCLA-LACMA Art History Practicum Initiative and the Andrew W. Mellon Undergraduate Curatorial Fellowship Program. Tompkins Rivas is currently pursuing a PhD in Cultural Studies at Claremont Graduate University (CGU). She holds a Master of Arts in Cultural Studies from CGU, a Bachelor of Arts in Latin American Studies, and a Bachelor of Fine Arts from the University of Texas at Austin.

CHAIR
Michael O'Grady

VICE CHAIRS
Leslie Bluhm
King Harris*
Anne L. Kaplan*
Cari B. Sacks

SECRETARY
Nickol Hackett

TREASURER
Marquis D. Miller

TRUSTEES
Sara Albrecht
Michael Alper
Peter Barack
Rob Bellick
Julie Bernstein
Gerhard Bette
Marlene Breslow-Blitstein
Marc Brooks
Michael Canmann
Ellen-Blair Chube
Carol Cohen
Nancy Crown
Dimitris Daskalopoulos
Robert H. Defares
Cheryl S. Durst
Stefan Edlis+
Lois Eisen
Dr. Julius Few
Larry Fields
Nicholas Giampietro
James A. Gordon
Kenneth C. Griffin
Madeleine Grynsztejn**
Jack Guthman
John B. Harris
Cynthia Hunt
Liz Lefkofsky
Jonathan Levin
Ron Levin
James H. Litinsky
Laura Keidan Martin
Carrie Reyes Murphy
Sylvia Neil
Kate Neisser
Martin Nesbitt
Ashley Hemphill Netzky
Jay Owen, Jr.
Carol Prins
Eve Rogers
Joshua Rogers
Ilan Shalit
William Silverstein
Sara Szold
Nigel F. Telman
Ellen B. Wallace**
Dia S. Weil
Pedro Weiss
Ben Weprin
Helen Zell*

LIFE TRUSTEES
Marilynn B. Alsdorf+
John D. Cartland*
Marshall Front
Helyn D. Goldenberg*
William Hood
Mary Ittelson*
Don Kaul
Sally Meyers Kovler*
Gael Neeson
Penny Pritzker*
Dorie Sternberg
Daryl Gerber Stokols
Donna A. Stone
Marjorie Susman
Allen M. Turner*

ARTIST TRUSTEE
Lorna Simpson

EMERITUS TRUSTEE
Jennifer Aubrey
Donald J. Edwards

*PAST CHAIR
**EX-OFFICIO
+ In Memoriam

As of February 24, 2020

DIRECTOR'S OFFICE
Brad Cape
Madeleine Grynsztejn
Rebecca Holbrook-Erhart
Lisa Key
Stephanie Morgan
Janet Wolski

OPERATIONS DIVISION
Amy Buczko

COLLECTIONS AND EXHIBITIONS
Matt Byler
Joseph Church
Michael Collyer
Erica Erdmann
Kayla Foster
Colette Lehman
Amy Louvier
Brad Martin
Angie Morrow
Emilie Puttrich
Claire Ritchie
Liz Rudnick
Leah Singsank

FACILITIES AND OPERATIONS
Duncan Anderson
David Badesch
Paul Deuth
Dennis O'Shea
Eddie Ramos
Medina Robinson
Mario Salgado
Matthew Test
Jameson Zaerr

HUMAN RESOURCES
Margaret Barnard
Yolanda Davis
Josh Mann
Adrienne Quint

INFORMATION TECHNOLOGY
Radu David
Wail Hussein
John Koper
Lorenza Stephens

AUDIENCE DIVISION

AUDIENCE ENGAGEMENT
Matti Allison
Gina Crowley
Cagla Gillis
Charlotte Gruman
Kristen Kaniewski
Julia Kriegel
Molly Laemle
Peyton Lynch
Phongtorn Phongluantum
Clinton Shepherd
Arissé Stephens
Casey VanWormer
Lacey Whittaker

DEVELOPMENT
Grace Brandt
Steven Cianciarulo
Antonia Constantine
Hillary Hanas
Marian Hillebrand
Rachel Hite
Gwendolyn Perry Davis
Vanessa Roman
Claire Serpi
Kristen Taylor
Monserrat Wisdom
Nina Yung

RETAIL EXPERIENCE
Patrese DeJulio-Smith
John Gustafson
Katrina Lake
Dakota Lecos
Laura Ralston
Brooke Riewer
Kevin Slattery
Michael Thomas
Keidra Turner Jeffries
Carl Wiggins
Stephen Zirbel

STRATEGIC COMMUNICATIONS
Paul Knipper
Karla Loring
Brontë Marsteller
Greta McGuire
Georgie Morvis
Katy O'Malley
Jill Perez
Abraham Ritchie
Melissa Roels
Alexander Shoup
Michelle Silverblatt
Lauren Smallwood
Camille Smith
Anne Walaszek
Christine Zavesky

ARTISTIC DIVISION
Michael Darling
Aya Nimer
Claire Ruud

CONTENT STRATEGY
Leah Froats
Nora James
Tyler Laminack
Elyssa Lange
Erin Matson
Bridget O'Carroll
Mary Richardson
Bonnie Rosenberg

LEARNING
Sarah Adler
Meagan Burger
Emily Gallaugher
Jeremy Kreusch
Billy McGuinness
Grace Needlman

PERFORMANCE AND PUBLIC PRACTICE
Kendall Karg
Laura Paige Kyber
Cameron McEwen
Rich Norwood
January Parkos Arnall
Matthew Sharp
J. Gibran Villalobos
Anthony Williams
Tara Willis
Marguerite Wynter

VISUAL ARTS
Carla Acevedo-Yates
Line Ajan
Naomi Beckwith
Harry C. H. Choi
Iris Colburn
Jack Schneider

FINANCE AND ACCOUNTING DIVISION
Janelle Brooks
Angela Burke
Anthony Chan
Joan Cesario
Anne-Marie Eischen
Lindsy Lee
Lee Warzecka

Every reasonable attempt has been made to locate the owners of copyrights in the book and to ensure the credit information supplied is accurately listed. Errors or omissions will be corrected in future editions.

All artworks by Carolina Caycedo are reproduced courtesy of the artist; Commonwealth and Council, Los Angeles; and Instituto de Visión, Bogotá.

Credits are listed by page number. Every reasonable attempt has been made to locate the owners of copyrights in the book and to ensure the credit information supplied is accurately listed. Errors or omissions will be corrected in future editions.

12: Photo: Alonso Parra; 20, 100–102: Courtesy of the Institute of Contemporary Art/Boston. Photo: Mel Taing; 22, 118–119: Courtesy of the artist and Instituto de Visión. Photo: Santiago Pinyol; 25: Photo: Jorge Caycedo; 26, 28, 32, 36, 39, 52–54, 92–97, 107, 124, 126–127: Courtesy of the artist; 29, 74, 104, 111–112, 114–115: Courtesy of Jaguos Por El Territorio. Photo: Jonathan Luna; 33: Courtesy of the Henry Art Gallery. Photo: Mark Woods; 40, 108: Courtesy of the artist and Jaguos Por El Territorio; 42: Courtesy of the artist and Instituto de Visión. Photo: Sebastian Cruz Roldán; 45, 66–67: Courtesy of the artist and Instituto de Visión. Photo: Sofia Toscano; 50–51: Courtesy of the artist and Commonwealth and Council, Los Angeles. Photo: Krzysztof Zielinski; 55: Photo © Ilana Bar/Estúdio Garagem/Fundação Bienal de São Paulo; 56–57: Courtesy of Clockshop. Photo: Gina Clyne; 58: Courtesy of Instituto de Visión, Bogotá. Photo: Craig Kirk; 59, 68, 90–91: Courtesy of the artist and Instituto de Visión, Bogotá; 60–61, 120–123, 125: Courtesy of the artist and Commonwealth and Council, Los Angeles. Photo: Ruben Diaz; 62–63: Photo: Lauren Hillary; 64–65: Photo: Juliana Paciulli; 71, 84–85: Courtesy of the artist. Photo: Medellín Museum of Modern Art; 77: Courtesy of Jaguos Por El Territorio, Ríos Vivos Colombia, and Más Arte Más Acción; 78: Courtesy of the artist and The Main Museum, Los Angeles; 81: Photo: Sergio Zalis; 82: © Projeto Lygia Pape. Photo: Paula Pape; 86–87: Photo: ARTBO | International Art Fair of Bogotá 2016, a program of The Chamber of Commerce of Bogotá; 88–89: Photo: Eduardo Ortega–MASP Research Center; 98–99, 117 (top): Courtesy of the artist and Commonwealth and Council, Los Angeles; 103: Photo: Mario Gallucci; 116: Courtesy of Walter Phillips Gallery, Banff Centre for Arts and Creativity. Photo: Jessica Wittman; 117 (bottom): Courtesy of the Henry Art Gallery. Photo: Jonathan Vanderweit; 128–129: Photo: Raquel Pérez Puig.

Fair Use Statement

The MCA asserts its Fair Use rights in the reproduction of comparative illustrations in its exhibition catalogues. Essays, timelines, interviews, and other scholarly texts are often accompanied by images to help clarify concepts and enhance readers' overall understanding of the subject matter. According to the Association of Art Museum Directors' Guidelines for the Use of Copyrighted Materials and Works of Art by Art Museum, these uses should be "confined, in the extent of copyrighted materials and in the size and quality of images of works of art, to that necessary to illustrate the educational, scholarly or critical text and no more." We adhere to these standards and make every reasonable attempt to ensure the accuracy of credit and caption information for each image. We welcome any uncredited creators to come forward so that we may acknowledge them and correct any errors or omissions in future editions.

Cover and back cover: Documentation from the filming of *Apariciones / Apparitions*, 2018. Commissioned by The Huntington Library, Art Museum, and Botanical Gardens, and the Vincent Price Art Museum. Photo: Kate Lain. Courtesy of The Huntington Library, Art Museum, and Botanical Gardens. Pictured: Samad Guerra.

Opening pages: Excerpts from the *Serpent River Book*, 2017. Artist book, 72 pages, concertina fold, hardcover in printed canvas, elastic band, and custom table; closed: 8 2/3 × 12 1/5 × 13 4/5 in. (22 × 31 × 3.5 cm). Numbered edition of 250. Courtesy of the artist.

This book is published on the occasion of the exhibition *Carolina Caycedo: From the Bottom of the River*, organized by the Museum of Contemporary Art Chicago, curated by Carla Acevedo-Yates, Marilyn and Larry Fields Curator, and presented in the Bergman Family Gallery at the Museum of Contemporary Art Chicago, December 5, 2020–March 21, 2021.

View the exhibition video and installation shots online at mcachicago.org/Exhibitions/2020/Carolina-Caycedo.

Published as part of the Ascendant Artist series by the Museum of Contemporary Art Chicago and DelMonico Books•D.A.P.

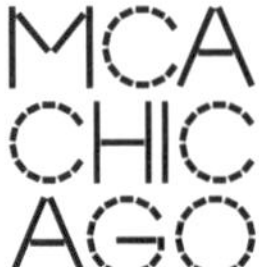

Museum of Contemporary Art Chicago
220 E Chicago Ave
Chicago, IL 60611
312-280-2660

DelMonico Books
Available through ARTBOOK | D.A.P.
75 Broad Street, Suite 630
New York, NY 10004
artbook.com
delmonicobooks.com

For Museum of Contemporary Art Chicago
Director of Content Strategy: Kelsey Campbell-Dollaghan
Senior Designer: Christine Zavesky
Editor: Tyler Laminack
Manager of Rights and Images: Bonnie Rosenberg
Rights and Images Assistant: Elyssa Lange

For DelMonico Books
Publisher: Mary DelMonico
Production Director: Karen Farquhar

Designed by: Pouya Ahmadi

Translated by: Eriksen Translations Inc.

All rights reserved. No part of this book may be reproduced or transmitted in any form or by any means, electronic or mechanical, including photocopy, recording, or any other information storage and retrieval system, or otherwise without written permission from the publisher.

Printed and bound in Slovakia

Library of Congress Control Number: 2020914085

ISBN 978-1-942884-73-6

Copyright © 2020 by the Museum of Contemporary Art Chicago and DelMonico Books · New York